Yo Soy Negro

New World Diasporas

UNIVERSITY PRESS OF FLORIDA

Florida A&M University, Tallahassee
Florida Atlantic University, Boca Raton
Florida Gulf Coast University, Ft. Myers
Florida International University, Miami
Florida State University, Tallahassee
New College of Florida, Sarasota
University of Central Florida, Orlando
University of Florida, Gainesville
University of North Florida, Jacksonville
University of South Florida, Tampa
University of West Florida, Pensacola

Tanya Maria Golash-Boza

University Press of Florida

Gainesville

Tallahassee

Tampa

Boca Raton

Pensacola

Orlando

Miami

Jacksonville

Ft. Myers

Sarasota

Yo Soy Negro

Blackness in Peru

Copyright 2011 by Tanya Maria Golash-Boza

Printed in the United States of America. This book is printed on Glatfelter Natures Book, a paper certified under the standards of the Forestry Steward-ship Council (FSC). It is a recycled stock that contains 30 percent post-consumer waste and is acid-free.

16 15 14 13 12 11   6 5 4 3 2 1

LIBRARY OF CONGRESS CATALOGING-IN-PUBLICATION DATA

Golash-Boza, Tanya Maria.

Yo soy negro : blackness in Peru / Tanya Maria Golash-Boza.

p. cm.—(New world diasporas)

Includes bibliographical references and index.

ISBN 978-0-8130-3574-1 (alk. paper)

1. Blacks—Race identity—Peru—Piura (Dept.) 2. Blacks—Peru—Piura (Dept.)— Social conditions. 3. Piura (Peru : Dept.)—Race relations.

4. Slavery—Peru—History. I. Title.

F3451.P5G65 2011

305.800985—dc22   2010042234

The University Press of Florida is the scholarly publishing agency for the State University System of Florida, comprising Florida A&M University, Florida Atlantic University, Florida Gulf Coast University, Florida International University, Florida State University, New College of Florida, University of Central Florida, University of Florida, University of North Florida, University of South Florida, and University of West Florida.

University Press of Florida

15 Northwest 15th Street

Gainesville, FL 32611-2079

http://www.upf.com

Contents

Acknowledgments

This book has benefited immensely from conversations, writing groups, social media, class discussions, seminars, workshops, online communities, and the goodwill of many people. I feel inclined to thank everyone I have met in the past few years. Alas, I cannot do that individually, but will do so en masse: thank you! In addition, I will take the time to thank, in chronological order, some of the people who have contributed in significant ways to this book.

Sequential order means starting with my parents. Thank you for raising me to believe that I can do whatever I want in life, and that I should do it with passion and with an eye for social justice. Thank you to my brothers and sisters who, each in their own way, have helped me along the way. Thank you to my husband, Fernando, for accompanying me on all of my trips to Peru, and for providing nothing but unconditional support for my research and writing. Thank you to my children, Soraya, Tatiana, and Raymi, for helping me tremendously with my research and writing by being there and by reminding me that life is to be lived, valued, and enjoyed.

Thank you to Marisol de la Cadena for suggesting that I write about Afro-Peruvians, and for encouraging me to chart new academic territory. Thank you to other people at the University of North Carolina and Duke: Judith Blau for your visionary leadership and support, Ted Mouw for believing in me, Charles Kurzman for talking to me about anything, Sandy Darity for your encouragement, John French for your important critiques, and Karolyn Tyson for pushing me to clarify my own ideas. I also thank

Catherine Harnois and Krista McQueeny for pushing me to think more carefully about gender.

In Peru, I thank the people of Ingenio for welcoming me into their village and allowing me to ask all sorts of questions especially Don Laureano, Señora Juana, Don Raúl, Señora Emperatriz, Naila, and Milene. I also thank the generous and high-spirited staff of Centro de Desarrollo Étnico (CEDET) for their unflagging support, especially Lilia Mayorga, Oswaldo Bilbao, Newton Mori, Adriana Mandrós, Zoraida Santé, Carlos Velarde, Carlos López, and Sofía Arizaga. A very special thank you to Humberto Rodríguez Pastor for your generosity during my time in Lima. I also would like to thank profoundly the late Octavio Céspedes.

At the University of Kansas, I can't find enough words to thank Joane Nagel for being a fantastic mentor and role model. I also greatly appreciate the support and valuable feedback from all of my colleagues at KU. My wonderful colleagues at Kansas who have contributed to this manuscript include Bob Antonio, Meredith Kleykamp, Michelle McKinley, Sherrie Tucker, Jessica Vasquez, Ayu Saraswati, Christina Lux, Jake Dorman, Ruben Flores, Tanya Hart, Elif Andac, Ebenezer Obadare, Yajaira Padilla, Jorge Pérez, Anne Choi, Crystal Anderson, Bill Staples, Marta Caminero-Santangelo, Ben Chappell, Charles Stansifer, Betsy Kuznesof, Melissa Birch, Greg Cushman, Akiko Takeyama, Holly Goerdel, and Kelly Chong. A special thanks to Kathy Porsch at the Hall Center for her assistance in garnering outside support for this project.

At the University of Illinois at Chicago, I was extraordinarily lucky to find yet another fabulous mentor, Kerry Ann Rockquemore. I also benefited greatly from the feedback and encouragement of many others at UIC, including Paul Zeleza, Amalia Pallares, Maria Krysan, Amanda Lewis, and Tyrone Forman. While in Chicago, I was fortunate to be part of a great community of writers that included Marisha Humphries, Dave Stovall, Angela Black, David Embrick, and Cherise Harris. I also have to thank my fantastic BAC online community, especially Eileen Diaz-McConnell for your consistent virtual support, Jafari Sinclaire-Allen for your incisive feedback, and Jemima Pierre for your extremely helpful critiques on the final version of the manuscript.

I have benefited immensely from the support of many colleagues who have read my work and provided great insights. These colleagues include Peter Wade, Kevin Yelvington, Izu Ahaghotu, Rachel O'Toole, Rogelio Saenz, April Mayes, and Christina Sue. I am also very appreciative of the comments provided by the two readers for the University Press of Florida: Stanley Bailey and Leo Garofalo.

This work would not have been possible without the generous financial support of the College of Liberal Arts and Sciences at the University of Illinois at Chicago; a Junior Scholars of Democracy in Latin America Fellowship from the Woodrow Wilson Center; two Ford Foundation Fellowships from UNC; a Fellowship from UNC–Chapel Hill; a Foreign Language and Areas Studies Fellowship; the General Research Fund of the University of Kansas, the Office of International Programs at the University of Kansas; the University of Kansas/Universidad de San Marcos Faculty Exchange Program; the Sociology Department, the American Studies Program, the College of Liberal Arts and Sciences at the University of Kansas; and a National Science Foundation Grant.

Finally, I thank Amy Gorelick at the University Press of Florida for her interest in my work and for her support along the way, and Kirsteen Anderson for her skillful copyedits.

Introduction

It was a typically hot September afternoon in Ingenio de Buenos Aires, a small village in northern Peru. The Ingenio soccer team had won a match with the neighboring village. The losing team had gone back to their village, and a few men from Ingenio gathered around in a circle, passing a pitcher of *chicha* (corn beer) and a *poto* (gourd) from one person to the next. Sitting on a bench near them, I saw one of the men pour the dregs from his gourd, wipe his mouth with his sleeve, and declare loudly "yo soy negro" (I am black).[1] This caught my attention, and when the men invited me to sit with them, I joined them. When I introduced myself, I told them I was visiting from the United States and was conducting research on the people and history of Ingenio. They offered suggestions of people I should talk to who would be able to tell me more about the history of the town.

Don Esteban, the man who had declared "yo soy negro," asked me if there was racism in the United States, and if it was true that, in the United States, blacks lived separately from whites. I started explaining segregation patterns in U.S. cities when another man, Don Isaac, interrupted me to tell me about racism in Peru. He said that, in his country, whites regard blacks as lesser and undesirable, and that racism is a problem.

Our conversation turned quickly to romance and to the fact that, although racism exists, people often marry across color lines in Peru. Don Esteban said that, when he was younger, he wondered how anyone would want to be with him, a black man. He and Don Isaac agreed that they both had desired white partners. Don Isaac said he wanted a white partner so that his children wouldn't be as dark as him. Don Esteban also pointed out that "opposites attract." They concurred that it was better for darker-skinned people to seek out lighter partners.

This conversation about race, color, and racism was one of many such discussions I would have in Ingenio while conducting ethnographic research there between 2002 and 2007. The preference for lighter-skinned partners in intimate relationships was a common theme in these exchanges. Despite this preference, people in Ingenio did not hesitate to call themselves or others black. I often heard people claim the label *negro* (black), as Don Esteban did. I also heard people use the label as an insult in some situations, as for instance, when one woman called another a "filthy black" in a heated discussion over who had the right to build a house in the center of town. On other occasions, people used *black* in a teasing fashion, as when a brother called his sister an "ugly black." And, sometimes men used *black* while flirting, such as when several young men called out "hola, negrita" (hey, black girl) to a woman passing by in the town square. Other times *black* was simply a neutral descriptor, as when people referred to Señora Negra, the nickname of a woman who lived on the edge of town.

When I first arrived in Ingenio in 2002 I was surprised to hear people using the word *black* with such frequency and variety of connotations, running the gamut from prideful to neutral to offensive. I was surprised because many scholars argue that most African-descended people in Latin America reject the label *negro* in favor of other labels such as *moreno* (see W. Wright 1990; Wade 1993, 1997; Twine 1998; Whitten and Torres 1998; Lewis 2000). I soon realized, however, that I could not make any assumptions with regard to what people meant when they used the word *black*. I could not take it for granted that the claiming of blackness entailed an expression of solidarity with others of African descent nor that it indicated any ethnic allegiances. This was made clear by the fact that many people in Ingenio insisted to me that blackness was no more than a skin color, with no cultural or historical implications. Any preference for lighter skin was simply aesthetic. When I asked people in Ingenio what it meant to be black, they consistently told me that it meant having dark skin.

In this book, I explore the ways people in Ingenio talk about blackness in the contexts of Latin American studies and African diaspora studies. When contemplating the meanings of blackness from the perspective of African diaspora studies, we can think about the degree to which either the denigration or the embracing of blackness is common in diasporic communities. From a Latin American studies perspective, we can consider how regional particularities must be taken into consideration to understand fully the meanings of blackness in Peru. Neither perspective alone provides a complete answer to what blackness denotes in Peru. By bringing Latin American studies into a dialogue with diaspora studies, however, we can draw a more nuanced map of the complexities of blackness in Peru.

The local discourse of blackness in Ingenio centers on skin color, with subtexts related to sexuality and physical attractiveness. The existence of this local discourse of blackness raises questions regarding how we can conceptualize and theorize the African diaspora. Specifically, it points to the need for a fluid conception of the diaspora that allows for localized differences in ideas of blackness. In addition, the primacy that people in Ingenio give to skin color when talking about blackness defies the contention that, in Latin America, judgments about an individual's race correlate with social status and cultural features. My argument that the discourse of blackness in Ingenio is primarily a discourse of skin color constitutes a challenge to scholarship on the black diaspora that points to the centrality of slavery for defining blackness in the diaspora and to scholarship on race in Latin America that places cultural and class differences at the core of racial discourses in the region.

The arguments set forth in this book are based on fieldwork and interviews I collected in Ingenio de Buenos Aires and interviews with migrants from Ingenio who live in Lima. Ingenio is a small town that sits on the lands of the former Hacienda Buenos Aires in the state of Piura in northern coastal Peru. The name of the town—Ingenio—refers to a defunct sugar mill that was in operation until the early twentieth century. The majority of the inhabitants of Ingenio are the descendants of African slaves from haciendas in the region. The enslavement of Africans and their descendants in Peru ended in 1854, and the hacienda system came to an end with agrarian reforms in the early 1970s (Cuche 1975). Today, most families in Ingenio own small plots of land from which they eke out meager existences.

Afro-Peruvian Cultural Revival and Social Movements

Ingenio is more than one thousand kilometers from Lima, the capital of Peru. Although most of the residents are of African descent, few residents of Ingenio are aware of the various cultural and social Afro-Peruvian movements that have been based in Lima since the 1940s. Their lack of awareness is a reflection of the low visibility these groups have gained in Peru overall. It is also indicative of the extent to which the overall goals of the movement are out of line with the daily reality of the people of Ingenio.

The beginning of Afro-Peruvian social movements can be located in the black arts revival, which began in Peru in the 1940s. In 1945, the government of José Luis Bustamante y Rivera initiated a program to revalorize national folklore. Most of the funds were directed at indigenous cultural traditions, yet some black Peruvian cultural forms were also promoted. Don Porfirio Vázquez, for example, was hired to teach black Peruvian dance in a government-sponsored Limeño folklore academy. Through connections he made there, Vásquez met José Durand and worked with him to create the Pancho Fierro Company, the first Afro-Peruvian dance company. In 1956, the Pancho Fierro Company made its public debut at the Lima Municipal Theater, bringing black traditions from the homes of black families to the stage for the first time. This marked the beginning of the black arts revival in Peru. The revival was strengthened through subsequent nationalist initiatives of the government of General Juan Velasco Alvarado, and the traditions brought alive through the revival remain at the core of Afro-Peruvian cultural production today (Feldman 2006). The residents of Ingenio are well aware of Afro-Peruvian music and dance, as this genre has come to be called, yet they do not see it as part of their cultural traditions.

The Afro-Peruvian revival consisted of remembering and preserving black cultural forms from Lima and southern coastal Peru—places such as Chincha and Aucallama. These cultural forms are distinct from those practiced by blacks in northern Peru. Thus, although artists such as Victoria and Nicomedes Santa Cruz made great strides in the promotion of Afro-Peruvian culture, their efforts had little relevance for the black people of Ingenio.

The Afro-Peruvian cultural revival was closely followed by Afro-Peruvian social movements that sought to fight against the discrimination and invisibility of blacks in Peru. One of the first movements, Cumanana, was both a cultural revival and a core of black activism. Nicomedes and Victoria Santa Cruz codirected Cumanana from 1959 to 1961, and it continued for many years under the direction of Nicomedes Santa Cruz. Their productions often contested discrimination and celebrated blackness (Feldman 2006).

In the 1960s, Afro-Peruvians found inspiration in the U.S. civil rights movement, and began to form their own organizations. One of the first was Asociación Cultural para la Juventud Negra Peruana (Cultural Association for Black Peruvian Youth, or ACEJUNEP), founded in 1972 by José Campos. It was eventually disbanded due to lack of funding. In 1983, José Campos, José Luciano, and Juan José Vásquez formed the Instituto de Investigaciones Afro-Peruanas (Institute for Afro-Peruvian Studies, or INAPE). With Ford Foundation funding, INAPE carried out several studies of rural Afro-Peruvian communities. When the funding ran out, however, the organization fell apart. It was soon followed by the Movimiento Negro Francisco Congo (Francisco Congo Black Movement, or MNFC), created in 1986 by people from INAPE (Luciano and Rodríguez 1995; J. Thomas 2008).

In the 1990s, black movements in Peru again began to gain access to international funding, and became more stable. Jorge Ramírez Reyna, for example, procured funds from USAID and the Kellogg Foundation to support the Asociación Negra de Derechos Humanos (Black Association of Human Rights, or ASONEDH), which he founded in 1993. In 1999, former members of MNFC formed the Centro de Desarrollo Étnico (Center for Ethnic Development, or CEDET), which successfully secured United Nations funding for economic and cultural development projects in black communities in Peru. By 2005, there were fifteen independent Afro-Peruvian social movement organizations in Peru. Only a handful, however, were financially stable, mostly due to their having secured funds from international donors (J. Thomas 2008).

At various points, leaders of these organizations have traveled to Ingenio in attempts to gain the support of residents and build a grassroots movement. In my conversations with people in Ingenio, I learned that most were unaware that there is a black social movement in Peru. Those who attended workshops sponsored by Afro-Peruvian groups remember them fondly and tell me they learned important things about their history and about human rights. Apart from the occasional workshop, however, few residents of Ingenio have these Afro-Peruvian social movements at the forefront of their minds. Instead, they are much more likely to be concerned about the selling price of rice and their ability to meet their basic needs—especially for food and water. Thus, although many Afro-Peruvian social movements see the people of Ingenio as their constituency, much work remains to be done before the people of Ingenio could be organized as Afro-Peruvians. Similarly, because of their history as the descendants of African slaves, many people would consider blacks in Ingenio to be part of the African diaspora. The residents' limited engagement with diasporic discourses, however, raises questions about the utility of the idea of a diaspora as it pertains to the people of Ingenio. I turn to these questions next.

Locating Ingenio in the African Diaspora

Most scholars of the diaspora fall into one of two camps in the Herskovits-Frazier debates. Those following Melville J. Herskovits have argued that diasporic Africans possess African cultural artifacts, whereas those that follow E. Franklin Frazier have claimed that circumstances in the New World have produced a shared and unique culture among blacks. Most agree that diasporic blacks share something in common, whether it is something from Africa or something produced in the new territories.

Paul Gilroy's text *The Black Atlantic: Modernity and Double Consciousness* (1993) is perhaps the best representative of the idea that diasporic blacks have many common traits as a result of their experiences of enslavement. For Gilroy, diasporic blacks share a "memory of slavery, actively preserved as a living intellectual resource in their expressive political culture" (Gilroy 1993: 39). This memory of slavery is not dormant, but constitutes a resource for the cultural, political, and ideological struggles that breathe life into the global black community.

Although many people who live in Ingenio today have ancestors who were enslaved Africans, slavery does not play much of a role in local conceptions of history. This is in large part because an extensive system of debt peonage was in place both alongside and after slavery. At least 100,000 Africans were brought to Peru as slaves (Bowser 1974). Many of those brought to Piura were manumitted, escaped from slavery, or purchased their freedom and joined the masses of peons who worked as agricultural laborers (Castillo Román 1977; Reyes Flores 2001). Because debt peonage quickly replaced slavery as the primary form of exploitation of agricultural workers in Piura, slavery is not the central way that villagers understand their history.

I am not the first to question the centrality of slavery in the African diasporic experience. Michelle Wright (2004: 3), for example, points out that there is no "cultural trope to which one can link all the African diasporic communities in the West," including those derived from the Atlantic slave trade. As Paul Zeleza (2005) asserts, it is also crucial to complicate the very notion of Africa and of the diaspora. Although fifty-four states make up the African Union today, the borders of Africa are constantly changing. What's more, the African diaspora continues, in that some people leave Africa every day while others return. Thus, there is contention with regard to who is African and who is part of the diaspora. Despite this, the concept of an African diaspora is not vacuous: the forced removal of millions of people from Africa clearly has left its mark on the world, and on Ingenio.

Patterson and Kelley (2000: 65) argue that the "diaspora is both a process and a condition. As a process it is constantly being remade through movement, migration, and travel, as well as imagined through thought, cultural production, and political struggle. Yet, as a condition, it is directly tied to the process by which it is being made and remade." Thinking of the diaspora as both process and condition allows us some flexibility in a conceptualization of the black experience. For if we think of the diaspora as something that just is, we are unable to think about how it has been formed and how it is changing. We are wise to heed Herman Bennett's (2000: 112) suggestion to ask "how, when, why and under what circumstances slavery and racial oppression produced a black consciousness."

My analyses of the way people in Ingenio talk about their history and their blackness reveal it is not the case that simply because people in Ingenio are the descendants of African slaves they logically share cultural attributes and memories with others in the African diaspora. It is also not the case that every individual in Ingenio has the same relationship with the diaspora. For this reason, it is important to consider the interactions and processes that give meaning to being part of the African diaspora.

To gain insight into these interactions and processes that imbue blackness with meaning, I explore how historical experiences interact with present-day conditions to influence the meanings that people in Ingenio give to blackness and Africa. I look at how flows of people, products, media images, and political movements work together to endow blackness with meaning, while taking into account the fact that these meanings are constantly changing and affect individuals differently depending on their social location. I analyze how people in Ingenio talk about Africa and slavery and their connection to them. Conceptualizing the African diaspora as both a condition and a process allows us to broaden our understanding of what it means to be black and of who is or can be considered part of the African diaspora.

People in Ingenio are part of the African diaspora insofar as they are descendants of African slaves. Yet, their weak ties to this history and to other members of the diaspora render problematic many generalizations frequently made about the diaspora. Although many of their cultural practices may have roots in Africa, and many of their social norms may be products of slavery and the slave trade, people in Ingenio do not often perceive themselves to be rooted in a history that derives from Africa and the slave trade.

Mestizaje and Blackness in Ingenio

Just as any treatment of blackness must engage with the idea of an African diaspora, any discussion of race in Latin America must take on the idea of *mestizaje,* an extensively analyzed process of cultural and racial mixing characteristic of Latin America. Mestizaje, often thought of as racial and cultural mixture that involves progression towards whiteness, is one of the central tropes of race in Latin America. Few scholars, however, have paid attention to the ways that mestizaje works differently for blacks versus Indians. Insofar as studies of race in Latin America focus almost exclusively on either blacks or Indians (Wade 1997; Foote 2006), we have limited understanding of how blacks and Indians participate differently in mestizaje.

Scholars of race and mestizaje in Peru have written entire books that make no or only very brief mention of the Afro-Peruvian population (for example, Van den Berghe 1974; de la Cadena 2001; Portocarrero 1993). In Peru, scholars usually have considered the question of race to be an Indian issue. Although the black population in Peru has received some treatment in terms of slavery and abolition, there have been few studies of the contemporary African-descended population, a notable exception being Heidi Feldman's *Black Rhythms of Peru* (2006), which discusses the black arts revival in that country.

In my ethnographic research in Ingenio, I explored the ways that mestizaje works for black Peruvians, and found that processes of mestizaje in Ingenio were quite distinct from those described by scholars who have studied indigenous people. Studies of Peruvians of indigenous descent indicate that identification with labels such as *cholo, indio,* or *mestizo* is determined not by skin color, but by a host of cultural factors, including geographic origin and social standing (see Varallanos 1962; Bourricaud 1975; de la Cadena 2000). The way race is conceptualized in Peru, a person with brown skin and black hair could be labeled white (*blanco*), Indian (*indio*), or either of the two intermediate labels: cholo or mestizo. According to these studies, what determines one's racial status is not skin color, but level of education; cultural markers such as language, dress, and food; and geographic and class location. Because of the flexible nature of these markers, Indians can change their cultural traits and become mestizos through the process of mestizaje. In contrast, blacks from Ingenio cannot become mestizos through this process.

The study of race in Peru has burgeoned in the past two decades. Scholars have argued for the importance of using the concept of race to understand the power divisions among whites, mestizos, and Indians, even when these distinctions are not based primarily on somatic differences. Mary Weismantel and Stephen Eisenman (1998: 121), for example, argue that "despite the absence of strict phenotypical segregation or narrowly color-based hierarchies," race is an important lens through which to understand Andean hierarchies. Yet when these and other scholars point to the lack of genotypic or phenotypic elements in racial discourses in the Andes, their point of reference is the indigenous/mestizo divide, not the black/white binary (Mendoza 1998; Wilson 2007).

Because of tremendous differences between how blackness and indigeneity are defined in Peru, understandings of race developed from studies of indigeneity cannot be applied to blacks in Peru. For example, Orlove (1998) argues that a person is more Indian and less mestizo on the basis of his or her proximity to the earth. Indians are more likely to walk with bare, muddy feet, whereas mestizos are more likely to wear leather shoes. Orlove's continuum of differences from going barefoot to wearing rubber sandals, wearing old shoes, and having new shoes makes little sense in the context of black Peruvians. Blackness is not defined in Peru on the basis of social or cultural attributes; it is a distinction made primarily on the basis of skin color, making it quite distinct from indigeneity.

Scholars of indigeneity in Peru have argued that Indians can be whitened through cultural assimilation (de la Cadena 2000; Ortiz 2001). In contrast, when residents of Ingenio talk about mixture or mestizaje, they are most frequently discussing how light- or dark-skinned the children will be. I did not hear people talking about mestizaje in the contexts of cultural mixture or social whitening. People in Ingenio did not perceive blackness as something that could be erased by virtue of changes in cultural or social features. In addition, people from Ingenio who migrated to Lima did not perceive their upward social mobility as whitening. Cultural and social whitening are not possible for blacks from Ingenio because of the centrality of skin color in definitions of blackness. This, in turn, points to the fact that, in Peru, mestizaje works differently for blacks versus Indians. This is part of a pattern in Latin America whereby mestizaje has fundamentally different meanings for blacks, whites, and Indians.

Because African diaspora studies and Latin American studies talk past each other, Latin American studies scholars are not likely to consider seriously how mestizaje carries different meanings for blacks versus Indians. And, the work of African diaspora studies scholars is not likely to account for Latin American exceptionalism. I bridge these two fields to show the importance of both local particularities and the condition of being black. This engagement with the African diaspora leads me to new ways of thinking about how racial discourses operate in Latin America through a reconceptualization of the relationship between race and color. An analysis of historical and contemporary discourses of race and blackness in Peru shows how global processes and transnational conversations taking place in Latin America change local racial meanings.

Encountering Ingenio

The fact that the population of Ingenio is mostly of African descent differentiates it from most small villages in Peru, where people are primarily indigenous or mestizo. I arrived in Ingenio through a series of contacts, starting in Lima in 2002. There I met with Oswaldo Bilbao of CEDET, a Lima-based nongovernmental organization (NGO). He gave me a list of twelve Afro-Peruvian community leaders in small coastal towns and suggested I visit those towns.[2]

Newton Mori of CEDET has spent the past decade mapping out Afro-Peruvian towns, and now lists eighty-five places along the coast of Peru that have a historical and present-day Afro-Peruvian presence. The two towns with the largest concentrations of Afro-Peruvians are El Carmen in Chincha and Yapatera in Piura. Although El Carmen is known nationally as the "cradle of black culture in Peru," Yapatera actually has the largest concentration of Afro-Peruvians outside of Lima—about six thousand people according to the most recent Afro-Peruvian census conducted by CEDET. I have visited nineteen Afro-Peruvian towns, in addition to all of the barrios in Lima that have a substantial Afro-Peruvian presence.[3] Some of the towns are depopulated, having only a few remaining households. Many of them have a substantial Andean presence because of migration out of the Andes during the civil unrest of the 1980s. Ingenio, with about 2,500 residents, is a smaller version of Yapatera. Ingenio and Yapatera are both in the northern state of Piura, are about sixty kilometers apart, and are about one hundred kilometers from the coast. Many people from Ingenio have relatives in Yapatera. Like Yapatera, Ingenio is primarily African-descended, with a small population of relatively recent migrants from the highlands. Ingenio is also similar to the two neighboring villages, La Pilca and La Maravilla, except that it is larger. Ingenio is different from Afro-Peruvian villages in the south of Peru in that it is more isolated from Lima, has a more visible Afro-Peruvian presence than most (with the notable exceptions of El Carmen, El Guayabo, and San José), and does not have a substantial population of migrants from the Andes Mountains.

Ingenio has about three hundred houses and lies in a valley in the foothills of the Andes. In the early part of the twentieth century, the town was home to a sugar refinery owned by an *hacendado* (plantation owner). In the center of town, a chimney that was formerly used to burn sugarcane stands as a reminder of the sugar era. Notably, the villagers intentionally preserved and protected this thirty-foot-tall brick chimney, signifying their attachment to the history of the town as the seat of the sugar hacienda. Villagers also have built a small chapel containing a statue of the town's patron saint adjacent to the chimney, using funds raised in various festivities organized by the patron saint committee.

With the decline in the profitability of sugar in the early twentieth century, the hacendados converted the fields to rice production. Today, rice remains the primary crop produced in Ingenio. All of the villagers' livelihoods are connected to the growing of rice for the national market. A handful of residents have other ventures, which are also dependent on the success of the rice market. These include stores that sell essential foodstuffs, *chicherías* (where chicha is made and served), weekend stands that sell meat or *mondongo* (soup made from intestines), and local transportation—one minivan and several *moto-taxis* (motorcycle taxis).

Although these ventures are not very profitable, some villagers are reputed to have more money, and a bit more land, than others. The average landholding is about 3.5 hectares, and the largest landowner has around 10 hectares. Thus, although there is some inequality of means in the village, this is not great enough to create a class hierarchy, at least not to the degree described by James Scott (1987) in Indonesia, where some villagers are known as "the rich" and others as "the poor." In Ingenio, some people have greater than average access to consumer goods—mostly because they have family members who have migrated to Lima and send back money and household items. At the extremes, there are a couple of older villagers who live almost entirely outside the cash economy, and there are two families that each own one piece of large machinery, namely, a truck and a tractor. In addition, about ten families own moto-taxis, and young men use these as means of earning money by transporting villagers who can afford the two soles (about US$0.75) fare to Morropón, about seven kilometers away.

I first arrived in Ingenio just after noon on a typically warm day in early August of 2002. I was traveling with my husband, my twin eighteen-month-old daughters, my niece, and my brother in tow. Ingenio was not on my original list of Afro-Peruvian towns—we were directed to Ingenio and to Don Fabio's house by his cousin, Professor Julio, who lives in Morropón. When we arrived in Morropón, I told Professor Julio that CEDET had sent me to him and that I was looking for an Afro-Peruvian town where I could conduct my research. Professor Julio replied, "Well, there are Afro-Peruvians in Morropón, but where you really want to go is Ingenio." He described the town as about 85 percent Afro-Peruvian and thus as a better place to do my research. Professor Julio gave us Don Fabio's name and led us to the plaza whence cars depart for Ingenio. We negotiated with the driver of one, and he agreed to take us across the two rivers to Ingenio.

Luckily for us, it was the dry season and the rivers were passable. As many villagers recounted to us, the rivers run full during the rainy season, and one must cross them in truck-tire inner tubes that serve as makeshift rafts. As we drove along the dirt road into town, I peered out of the dusty car windows at the lines of adobe houses, and decided that Ingenio looked quite similar to most of the other towns we had visited along the coast. Once we got out of the car, however, I was struck by the village's natural beauty. It lies nestled between two immense rivers on one side, and the foothills of the Andes, stretching as far as the eye can see, on the other. In addition, a canal runs right through the middle of town, and Don Fabio's daughters lost no time in taking my daughters to the canal for some respite from the unrelenting sun.

It was easy to locate Don Fabio's house; we simply asked the first person we saw, who pointed us up the hill. Once we got there, he and his wife, Doña Perla, invited us inside. We chatted and I explained to Don Fabio my reasons for coming. He immediately began to recount to me the history of the town and the struggles that the agricultural workers go through, and made it clear that he would be happy to accommodate me were I to choose Ingenio as the site of my research. After a filling lunch and a pleasant day in general, we left Ingenio just before nightfall.

After much deliberation and consultation, I chose Ingenio as the site of my research because of its relative isolation and its notable African-descended presence. I further decided to conduct research in Lima as well, among migrants from Ingenio. Upon making this decision, I called Don Fabio, who agreed to arrange housing for us and told us he was looking forward to our visit. The second time we arrived in Ingenio was a year later, July 28, 2003, and I was to spend six months there with my family. My twin daughters were two and a half years old, and I was five months pregnant.

Fieldwork and Mothering

My pregnancy and my youngest daughter's birth during the course of my field research solidified my status as a mother. For the first three and a half months of my fieldwork, I was visibly pregnant. For this reason, my pregnancy and those of other women was often the main topic of my conversations with other people. Once my daughter was born, childrearing became the primary subject of conversation, particularly because my childrearing practices differed from those of the villagers. For example, the temperature is hot in Ingenio, often above 85 degrees. I would dress my infant daughter in only a T-shirt and cloth diaper. Many villagers swore she would die as a result, because they have the custom of covering every part of the baby except the face for at least the first three months of life. Another example is that local women stay in the house for up to forty days after the baby is born, whereas I was up and about the next day.

Doña Perla, my neighbor, was quite concerned about my well-being during my pregnancy. She insisted on helping me choose an obstetrician and on accompanying me on doctor visits in Morropón. Although Morropón was Doña Perla's hometown, she rarely traveled there. One afternoon in

November 2003, we went together to my obstetrical appointment. That visit gave me an opportunity to see how Doña Perla talked about race and color in Ingenio with people from her hometown, just seven kilometers away.

Upon our arrival at the office, which was in the front part of the doctor's home, the housekeeper, Rosa, greeted us and asked us to sit down and wait for the doctor. Doña Perla recognized Rosa and asked her if she was not the daughter of Don Castillo. When Rosa said yes, Doña Perla introduced herself as Doña Beatriz's sister. Once it had been established that they knew each other's families, they began to chat. Doña Perla remarked that Rosa's two brothers often came to Ingenio on weekends. Rosa agreed and added that they were quite interested in the cockfights that are held there. Doña Perla responded that if Rosa's brothers weren't careful, they would end up with a *negra* (a black woman) from Ingenio. Doña Perla then rhetorically asked why Rosa's brothers, whom she referred to as nice-looking and white, would bother going to Ingenio to look for women, when all the women in Ingenio were ugly (*feas*).

In the doctor's office, Perla, speaking to a woman she barely knew, denigrated the whole town of Ingenio by implying that all the women there were ugly blacks. She further insinuated that Rosa's brothers, since they were white and good-looking, were too good for those women. Doña Perla, in effect, was calling herself and her children ugly, since they too lived in Ingenio. On the other hand, Doña Perla's daughter had recently won the town beauty contest and was the reigning "queen" of Ingenio. Moreover, on other occasions, Doña Perla had described other residents of Ingenio as good-looking. These seeming contradictions—where blackness is sometimes rejected but at other times embraced—is a subject I explore in this book. My status as a woman granted me access to spaces in which conversations about color and beauty were prevalent.

My visible status as a mother influenced not only the types of conversations I had with villagers, but also the people with whom I spent most of my time. I was able to have conversations with unmarried youths and older men, but I would usually have to arrange those conversations intentionally. In contrast, I easily could sit on another woman's front porch and spend hours talking together about life as a wife and mother. And at parties and other social events, I frequently found myself seated in the women's corner, while the youths and the men gathered in their respective corners. On the occasions when I was able to spend time with men in the bars and chicherías, I was accompanied by my husband.

My status as a privileged, married woman allowed me not only to talk to women in their or my kitchen or at the river while washing clothes, but also to enter into primarily male spaces without jeopardizing my respectability. I only went to those male spaces accompanied by my husband, as to do otherwise would have made the villagers uncomfortable. It was easier for me to gain the trust and friendship of the people of Ingenio as a mother and wife than it would have been had I been single or childless. Being a mother and wife normalized my role in the community and granted me access to spaces where other mothers and wives congregated. In addition, by virtue of having and caring for my children, I did not have to worry about being seen as idle. Few women worked outside the home; thus, it was normal for a mother like me to spend most of her days sitting on neighbors' porches and talking about life in the community. In these conversations, my whiteness and my class position both helped and hindered. It helped in that people were generally willing to talk to me, and it hindered in that the villagers were very conscious of my relative privilege.

Privilege in Ingenio meant having cement floors in our house; eating meat, chicken, or fish most days; drinking beer at parties; being able to leave town whenever we wanted; having a camera and a CD player; and being able to hire a young woman to help us with child care and housekeeping. We weren't the only people in the village who could afford those things, but the majority could not. As a result people who associated most closely with us had to worry that others would criticize them for being interested only in our money. When we went out with villagers, many would insist on paying for drinks or giving us food, in order to counter the perception that they might be interested in befriending us for our financial resources.

Villagers would often show up on our doorstep with products from their farms or their kitchens. Although rice is the primary crop produced in Ingenio, corn, cacao, bananas, mangos, cherries, oranges, lemons, yucca, and beans are also grown in much smaller quantities. When each of these is in high season, it is abundant in Ingenio. To our delight, in December our neighbors filled our table with juicy mangoes, and in September we had a seemingly unending supply of sweet bananas. When corn was in season, neighbors would bring us delicious tamales. And, since it is customary to drink cacao made from the cacao plants grown nearby after giving birth and while breast-feeding, a few women brought me delectable balls of toasted cacao when my youngest daughter was born, and I dutifully sipped liquid cacao each morning and night.

Collecting the Data

This book is both interdisciplinary and firmly grounded in sociology. It is based on five years of research, from 2002 to 2007. The primary modes of data collection were ethnography and semi-structured interviews, supplemented with selected historical documents, cultural texts, films, advertisements, and television shows. I conducted participant observation in Ingenio for nine months and in Lima for another nine months (in each case spending six months on my initial visit, with two follow-up visits). I carried out fifty semi-structured interviews in Ingenio and thirty in Lima. In addition, I did eight follow-up interviews in Ingenio, drawing from "collaborative ethnography" techniques (Hinson 2000; Lassiter 2005), where participants were involved in the analysis of the data. I also spent time in libraries in Lima examining historical documents.

One technique I used in the analysis and collection of data is the re-interview. In this procedure the first interview is conducted in the traditional social-scientific way, which involves doing one's best not to ask leading questions or challenge anyone's answers. For example, I did not ask interviewees what their race was, since this would presume that they use the word *race*. Instead, I would say, "People in Ingenio refer to me as *blanca*. How do they describe you?" This question uses a color term (*white*) that is commonly used in Ingenio instead of the word *race*, which is less common and more ambiguous. Similarly, I asked about family history without any leading questions. Thus, if someone told me that her family's roots lay only in Peru, I would not challenge this statement, even if it seemed obvious to me that she had ancestors from Africa.

In the re-interview, however, I would probe deeper, and ask my interviewees to explain their responses in the context of Ingenio. The first set of interviews was semi-structured and I followed a list of questions; the second set was organized around four themes: (1) the interviewees' conceptions of their ancestry; (2) what blackness means to them; (3) their perception of racism in Ingenio; and (4) the presence (or absence) of black culture in Ingenio. The idea behind the re-interview is that informants can also be seen as consultants, and that ethnography can be collaborative (Hinson 2000; Lassiter 2005). That is, black Peruvians are likely to know more about what it means to be black in Peru than I do, and thus, it is worthwhile to analyze the data in collaboration. This exercise cannot eliminate status differentials between the ethnographer and the consultants, but it both allows for a better understanding of the issues at hand and gives more of a voice to the consultants.

To complete the re-interviews, I conducted eight follow-up interviews with people with whom I had formed relationships. Once someone agreed to do a follow-up interview, I provided him or her with a transcript of the initial interview. I explained my analysis with regard to a few key points in order to get the person's feedback. I used this second set of interviews to explore issues that arose during my stay in Ingenio, and to compare my analysis of blackness with the local conceptions.

Re-interviewing entails an ethnographic philosophy that removes the label *expert* from the ethnographer and places it on the study participants. I, of course, have taken on the responsibility of translating my informants' ideas into language that my peers can understand, and of placing my writing into theoretical conversation with other social scientists. In line with the philosophy of collaborative ethnography, you will notice my presence in the ethnography and interviews. The data did not collect itself, and my presence undoubtedly influenced my findings. In addition, my reflections on the interviews are also part of the evidence. For this reason, I analyzed my own reflections, and used them to influence the data-collection process.

My understanding of blackness in Peru is influenced by my status as a person from the United States. I grew up in a primarily black neighborhood in Washington, D.C., and have since come to realize that the understanding of what it means to be black that I grew up with does not necessarily translate well to other contexts, even in the United States. I have also lived in France, Portugal, England, Nigeria, and several countries in Latin America and the Caribbean. In each of these places, I have gotten the sense that blackness has very distinct connotations. Thus, when I arrived in Peru, I knew that I would have to keep an open mind in order to understand how blackness plays out in that country.

My social location inevitably shaped my perceptions of Ingenio. Because of my life experiences, I did not arrive in Ingenio as a dispassionate observer. I did, however, arrive with respect and eagerness to learn. In this vein, I strived to listen and learn, to observe and take notes, and to ask the right questions. In this book, I will ask you to accept that, although Ingenio shares a history with other rural black communities in the Americas, it differs in important ways. I will also ask you to accept that I was able to gain the trust of the townspeople through the common human practices of humility, kindness, patience, and a sincere interest in others. To this end, I begin this book with a presentation of Ingenio and of Lima through my eyes. This allows you to see where I am coming from, and to pass judgment accordingly.

When I have presented my work on Afro-Peruvians to scholarly audiences, members of the audience have often asked how my position as a white North American woman influenced the data I was able to collect. Initially, I resisted this question by responding that, at best, I only could speculate on what sort of data I could have collected had I been a different person. Later, I emphasized my role as a mother and a wife. After many years, I came to realize that this question opens up space for a dialogue about how race works differently in Peru than in the United States. In Peru, I did not experience the same sorts of tensions surrounding issues of race as I have in my home country.

In the United States, a white researcher who plans to study a community of color can expect to have his or her intentions doubted. It is much easier for a white person to gain acceptance in a community of color in Peru. For example, neither the leaders of the Afro-Peruvian NGO in Lima nor the villagers in Ingenio showed suspicion towards me because of my skin color. This absence of suspicion is worthy of discussion, as it sheds light on a fundamental difference between racial politics in the United States versus in Peru. In the United States, we have a long history of struggle for civil rights and racial justice. These struggles often have pitted whites against people of color, and racial conflict has tainted relationships between them. In addition, racism, subtle and overt, institutional and individual, continues to be very much a part of our society, and whites are often distrusted as potential perpetrators of racism. In Ingenio, people of African descent do not encounter individual acts of racism by whites on a daily basis. Although structural racism is prevalent in Peru as a whole, in that a small, mostly white oligarchy controls much of the wealth in the country, most people in Ingenio are not actively aware of this. Although Limeños often hold negative opinions of Peruvian blacks, they rarely express these ideas openly in front of blacks (Golash-Boza 2011). Most people also are not aware of struggles for civil rights that have taken place around the world, or even in Peru. The fight for racial justice in Peru has barely reached Ingenio, and it differs in important ways from its counterpart in the United States.

Leaders of Afro-Peruvian social movements stress inclusion and anti-racism, as opposed to cultural recognition or separatism. The members of CEDET, the organization with which I worked most closely, were not exclusively black, although they did recognize the importance of having a black leader as the face of the group. Although they worked to organize Afro-Peruvians, they welcomed non-blacks into their ranks and invoked an inclusionary rhetoric that emphasized the importance of achieving a more racially democratic society. In Ingenio I was not seen as potentially racist, and in Lima people did not question why a non-black person would be interested in the cause of Afro-Peruvians. The poverty people in Ingenio experience is a product of the Peruvian history of African enslavement; the regional history of labor exploitation of blacks, Indians, and mestizos; and current neoliberal policies in the context of global capitalism. Yet, residents of Ingenio did not implicate me in their exploitation, despite the fact that I am a white North American.

Despite being an educated, white North American woman, I was not regarded with suspicion in Peru; instead, both leaders of NGOs and townspeople were more likely to see me as a person with resources that I might be able to use to their benefit. I, in turn, had to win the trust of people even though I knew that I might disappoint them in terms of my actual access to resources. In Ingenio, my perceived and real access to resources meant that people were likely to engage in impression management when dealing with me. As such, my social location provided an entrée but at the same time may have erected obstacles in terms of the unspoken expectation that I would, at some point, share my resources with people with whom I had contact. In my fieldwork and interviews, I remained conscious of my social location while also endeavoring to establish relationships of trust with the people about whom I would be writing.

Ingenio de Buenos Aires

For my family's stay in Ingenio, Don Fabio arranged for us to rent a house near his, and he and other neighbors lent or gave us a number of household items, including a kitchen table and chairs, as well as a tabletop gas

stove. Don Fabio, his family, and other neighbors were exceptionally welcoming to us as we moved in. At the time, I wasn't sure why they were
being so accommodating. But in hindsight, I think that they presumed
that anyone who was not used to the hard life of *el campo* (the countryside) would have a difficult time adjusting, and they probably felt sorry for
us. It was true, after all, that we did not have much experience washing
dishes without running water, burning our trash in the corral, sweeping
dirt floors, or washing our clothes in the river. They knew that people who
had lived in Lima for a while would come back to Ingenio and would no
longer be able to tolerate life there, and they recognized it wouldn't be easy
for us either. During my first few months, people frequently would ask me,
"¿Usted se enseña aquí?" At first, I didn't understand the question, since
enseñar means "to teach" in traditional Spanish. In Ingenio, however, it is
used to refer to growing accustomed to a place; people were asking me if
I was adjusting to living there. Their surprise at our ability to adapt to life
in Ingenio was likely due to the fact that only one other foreigner, a Dutch
agronomist named Jan, had ever lived there, and that had been a couple
of decades before, as well as to the fact that many migrants who move to
Lima say that "ya no se enseñan en Ingenio," meaning they can no longer
get used to living in Ingenio.

The house we lived in is at the upper end of Ingenio, in what is called
the *parte alta*, or the upper section. This section is on the far side of town,
nearest to the road that heads to the mountain village of Pampa Flores.
The other two roads out of town go, respectively, to Morropón and to La
Pilca, a village even smaller than Ingenio. The road to Morropón is the
most frequently traveled, as Morropón is relatively large and has regular
transportation to other large towns and cities, such as Chulucanas and
Piura.

When traveling to Ingenio from Morropón, you first arrive at the neighborhood called Los Callejones. The structures here were originally built as
workers' barracks during the hacienda times, and currently there are about
thirty houses, all made of adobe bricks and the majority with dirt floors.
A dusty soccer field that serves as scanty grazing grounds for the donkeys
and horses that roam the town separates Los Callejones from the next area
over, Barrio Nuevo. Barrio Nuevo was built in the 1980s to accommodate
the growing village population. Notably, while Ingenio was growing, many
of the other villages I visited, especially in the south of Peru, were los-

ing population. One of those villages, La Banda, had only about a dozen residents when we arrived.

Barrio Nuevo is separated from the center of town by the primary and secondary schools, as well as the Catholic church. The center of town is adorned by a cement plaza, with a gazebo and a few benches where villagers congregate and gossip. Just to the side of the plaza is a grandiose carob tree, which provides shade to people who sit on the tree trunk to wait for a moto-taxi or to sip on Adira's sno-cones. On Sunday mornings, Señora Maria sells *mondongito* (tripe stew) with coffee just next to the plaza. She makes her stew from the tripe that the butcher sells her early Sunday morning, after he kills one of his cattle. Sunday is the only day of the week one can buy beef in Ingenio, as the butcher kills one cow per week and sells all of the meat immediately.

A canal running through the center of town was, up until a few years ago, the only source of water. The waters of this canal once provided power to a hydroelectric wheel, which in turn provided electricity to the mill and to the town center. When the townspeople took over the hacienda during the agrarian reform, they destroyed the mill and the wheel, carting off pieces of it to better their own homes. The ruins of the hydroelectric wheel have left a cement pool where children play when the waters are not too high. Women sit on the cement wall surrounding the pool while they are washing clothes in the canal. Older villagers often lamented the destruction of the wheel and used it to illustrate the lack of interest in community betterment.

The rice mill, another vestige from the hacienda days, stands as a landmark in the center of town. What remains of the rice mill is a large but broken cement floor and about three-quarters of the circumference of the brick wall. The townspeople got together a few years ago and completed the wall with adobe bricks, and now use the old rice mill as an occasional venue for town festivities, such as school fund-raisers, the crowning of the town queen, and Independence Day celebrations. Although villagers often complained "no hay unión" (there is no unity) in Ingenio, this is but one of many examples of community members collectively improving the community. As other examples, Mariana and her friends sweep the entry to the church each Saturday, and villagers frequently organize benefits to raise money for villagers who fall ill.

The side of town past the rice mill and the canal comprises the *parte céntrica* and the *parte alta*, where we lived. These sections of town are primarily made up of adobe houses, similar to the rest of town. On the upper side of town is another square, with a cement platform where the young men often get together to play soccer in the afternoons. Notably, although Ingenio is a small town, some of the young men have gone on to play soccer on national teams. La Pilca, which is the town adjacent to Ingenio and is even smaller with about 150 houses, also had three players on national teams while I was in the area. This, of course, leads many of the young men to aspire to play soccer professionally.

Ingenio first got running water in 1996, and an NGO provided nearly all of the houses with toilets and ten-year septic tanks in 1998. The running water, however, is not particularly reliable. It is supposed to come on every other day at 6:00 a.m. and run for two hours. When the water supply is low or the generator is not working well, it will come for a shorter period or not at all. When the water does come, those people who have running water in their homes collect water in plastic buckets and ceramic pots, which they cover to keep the water clean. Those who do not have faucets installed in their homes must collect water from one of several communal taps outside. Most of these families make do with 5 or 6 five-gallon buckets of water for two days. The poorest people do not collect any water, as they cannot afford to pay the four soles (a little more than US$1.00) per month for the water service. They make do with the water in the canal, as they did before the water service came. When the canal dries up, as it often does at the end of the dry season, those villagers have to walk one kilometer up the hill to the river to fetch water.

From the time the hydroelectric mill was destroyed in 1970 until 2006, there was no communal electricity in Ingenio. Most families in Ingenio have small black-and-white televisions, which, during the bulk of my research period, they powered with rechargeable car batteries. The better-off families had solar panels, which afforded them a constant source of power. A solar panel (or a battery), however, is only sufficient to power either a small black-and-white television, a small CD player, four fluorescent lights, or one 100-watt lightbulb. Electricity finally arrived in Ingenio in 2006, to the elation of the townspeople. During the last two months of my research, some people had electricity. Others, however, continued to use batteries, candles, and kerosene lamps, because they could not afford to pay for the installation of electrical wiring in their homes. Once people saved up the money to install wiring, their power costs were often less, since one sole

(US$0.35) of kerosene was barely enough to provide light for one room for the evening, whereas the electric bill for lighting alone was about fifteen soles a month.

Ingenio is clearly on the periphery of global development, yet is not completely outside of it. The town only recently has begun to experience some of the consequences of globalization, and in some ways more than others. My focus is primarily on cultural globalization—the spread of global discourses through the media, social movements, and internal migration. This focus allows me to think about what happens in a case such as Ingenio where the diffusion of global discourses and images outpaces migration and economic incursions. Media flows are the primary source of global discourses of blackness in Ingenio.

Ingenieros in Lima

Few people from Ingenio engage in international migration, yet migration to Lima is quite common. Many residents of Ingenio migrate to Lima in search of economic opportunities, often immediately upon graduating from the local high school. Young women are more likely to migrate than young men, as they have better opportunities to find a job that pays enough money to meet their basic needs and allows them to send money back home to their families. Most women who migrate to Lima become domestic workers, while men often find jobs as construction workers, security guards, or factory workers. A few men are able to get more coveted jobs, such as those in the police force. Most, however, do not have the connections necessary to secure such positions. Men who stay in Ingenio generally work in seasonal agricultural jobs. There are virtually no economic opportunities for women in Ingenio, apart from selling foodstuffs. Thus, the majority of young women look forward to going to Lima when they finish high school. Those young women who go to Lima usually find jobs as domestics through networks of other young women from Ingenio who are working there.

Since domestic jobs are primarily live-in, women have minimal daily living expenses in Lima. The starting rate for a domestic servant in Lima is 300 soles a month—about US$100. As women gain experience, they can move into wealthier households and make more money. Fiorela, for example, started out four years ago making 250 soles a month. She later changed to another job that paid her 400 soles a month. After two years in her present job, she makes 650 soles a month—nearly US$200—equivalent to the monthly salary of a teacher or a police officer. One of my interviewees, Yraida, who has been working in Lima for sixteen years, makes 1,200 soles a month as the cook for a wealthy family. She has the highest salary for a domestic worker that I heard of during my time in Lima; in fact, her salary is very similar to those of a graphic designer who works at a publishing company and of a skilled construction worker who works under a government contract—two sought-after jobs in Lima. Most of the other experienced young women earn about 600 soles per month. Domestic work allows young women from Ingenio to gain access to material goods that would be inaccessible in Ingenio, and to send some of these items home to their families. Yraida, for example, sends cans of milk, clothes, and toys to her nephew, John, in Ingenio. John thus has a bicycle and is well dressed and well fed. Since his father has only sporadic work, and his mother does not work for pay at all, his life would be very different without Yraida's help. Yraida also installed a solar panel in her mother's house, and has brought her mother to Lima several times for medical treatments.

Even those migrants in Lima who live in substandard housing without amenities still often see themselves as better off than they were in Ingenio. For example, Señora Lorena and her husband, Harold, settled on a sandy hill in the shantytown of Ventanilla eight years ago and recently acquired the title to their land. Harold works as a security guard in a nearby warehouse. Their residence, constructed of plywood, consists of a living room, two bedrooms, a small kitchen, and a corral. Lorena and Harold sleep in one bedroom, and their four children in the other. They keep a couple of chickens and a duck in their small corral. The house has electricity but no sewage system or running water. Nevertheless, Señora Lorena told me that she is better off now than she was in Ingenio. In Lima she has electricity, and her husband has two bicycles. In her kitchen she has a blender and an oven with a stovetop. She has a boom box and a small color television. All of her children have school uniforms and shoes, as well as clothes to wear outside of school. She eats chicken, fish, or meat most days. In Ingenio, they lived in an adobe house with dirt floors and no electricity. Señora Lorena cooked with wood. For music, they had only a small radio, and for light at night, a kerosene lamp. Her children had incomplete school uniforms and worn-out shoes. Every day she asked herself where the next meal would come from. As Señora Tempora, another migrant from Lima said, "At least here we have enough for food."

Organization of the Book

The central argument of this book is that there is a local discourse of blackness in Ingenio that gives primacy to skin color. This local discourse coexists with global discourses yet has its own set of meanings. The existence of this local discourse puts into question the extent to which we can generalize about the black experience across the African diaspora, and the extent to which we can invoke Latin American exceptionalism to reject such generalizations.

Each chapter looks at certain ways that color takes center stage in conceptions of blackness in Ingenio in particular and in Peru in general. I begin with a discussion of the history of Ingenio as a town where the majority of inhabitants are descendants of African slaves yet slavery does not define blackness. From there, I look more specifically at the regional context of Latin America. I discuss how racial categories work in distinct ways for blacks versus Indians in Peru and in Latin America, both historically and in the present day, and how color has been more important for defining blackness than indigeneity. Then, I explore the extent to which theorizations of the African diaspora are useful for understanding the experiences of people in Ingenio, who primarily define blackness based on color. Subsequently, I consider how discourses of blackness spread by global media influence local conceptions of blackness. Following this discussion of blackness in the local and global context, I end with a chapter that explores how contemporary multicultural reforms are influencing discourses of blackness in Peru.

The majority of the people in Ingenio are the descendants of enslaved Africans brought to Peru on ships more than three centuries ago. In the first chapter, I explain why this history of chattel slavery is not central to Ingenieros' identities. The relative unimportance of slavery in the regional economy has meant that chattel slavery has not endured as part of townspeople's collective memory. Chapter 1, "Black, but Not African," discusses the transatlantic and transpacific slave trades that brought Africans to Peru and juxtaposes this history with how their contemporary descendants construct their origins. I argue that the local history of Ingenio explains why slavery does not form part of people's collective consciousness.

This conceptualization of blackness also has implications for ideas of mestizaje in Latin America. Chapter 2, "Locating Black Peruvians in Latin America," traces the transnational discourses of race from the mid-nineteenth century to the present. This analysis reveals that the pattern in Latin America has been for elites to accept indigenous people into the nation through a process of acculturation (or deculturation), yet to accept blacks only through miscegenation. I argue that this difference arose from the different roles of blacks and Indians in the colonies and in subsequent nation-making projects. National projects focused on acculturating Indians and on incorporating blacks through biological dilution. This analysis adds complexity to our understanding of mestizaje, which purports to capture both interracial unions and acculturation, and of *blanqueamiento* (whitening), which also is meant to include both de-ethnicization and physical lightening.

Chapter 3, "Race and Color Labels in Peru," examines how racial categorizations are used in Ingenio and contests generalizations about the construction of race in Latin America. Much of our understanding of race in that region is based on studies of Brazil and the Caribbean. Because of the importance of skin color for defining blackness in Ingenio, these generalizations have limited utility for explaining how racial categorizations work in this case. For example, scholarly reports that racial categorizations are fluid and contextual in Latin America (Landale and Oropesa 2002; Hoetink 1967) do not hold for blacks in Ingenio because blackness is defined in terms of skin color. In addition, the popular and scholarly adage that "money whitens" in Latin America (Wade 1997; Winn 2006; W. Wright 1990) cannot be applied to people from Ingenio. I also explain why there is no "mulatto escape hatch" (Degler 1971) for Ingenieros.

In the fourth chapter, I explain the local discourse on blackness and contrast it with other discourses on blackness. I argue that townspeople differ in their level of access to global discourses of blackness. Chapter 4, "Diasporic Discourses and Local Blackness Compared," makes the case that, although diasporic discourses of blackness are present in Ingenio, black people translate them in multiple ways and do not always see themselves as part of a diasporic community. This counters Gilroy's (1993) assertion that the descendants of African slaves are bound to experience a double consciousness and that the global black community uses the memory of slavery as a resource for cultural, political, and ideological struggles. Instead, I posit that thinking of the diaspora as a process as well as a condition (Patterson and Kelley 2000) helps us to understand better the multiplicity of black identities that exist and the extent to which global and local discourses interact to produce new conditions and processes.

People in Ingenio are not immune to the privileging of whiteness in terms of beauty and desirability. Yet local beauty norms that give preference to brown skin and curly hair coexist with this preference for whiteness. In the fifth chapter, I explore beauty norms, blackness, and whiteness in Ingenio, to shed light on how blackness is viewed there. Chapter 5, "Black Is Beautiful or White Is Right?" considers how the global discourse of "black is beautiful," which derives from black pride movements, and the Latin American discourse of "white is right," which is highly salient in Peruvian media and advertising, translate at the local level. My ethnographic data from Ingenio reveal that at times black is interpreted as beautiful, while at other times white is seen as the right way to be. These countervailing discourses provide us with useful insight into how global, regional, and national "mediascapes" interact with the local context.

In the sixth chapter, I consider the implications of this conceptualization of blackness for multicultural reforms in Peru. Chapter 6, "The Politics of Difference in Peru," describes multicultural reforms that the Peruvian government has recently adopted as part of a project funded by the World Bank. These reforms, which use discourses of cultural and ethnic difference, are a dramatic change from the official discourse that Afro-Peruvian inclusion should be achieved through incorporation as opposed to recognition of differences. Drawing from interviews with Afro-Peruvians, I explain how Afro-Peruvians discuss their inclusion in the Peruvian nation and their desire (or lack thereof) for cultural recognition.

In the epilogue, I return to the African diaspora and argue for the importance of the concept of an African diaspora for understanding blackness in Ingenio. Although local meanings of blackness do not fit neatly into some ideas of what it means to be a diasporic black, the concept of a diaspora is useful in three ways. First, it points to the particularity of the black experience, helping to explain why blackness is constructed differently than indigeneity in Peru. Second, it is clear that, in some ways, diasporic discourses of blackness have reached Ingenio, and a diasporic framework allows us to identify those. Finally, the idea of a diaspora as a process and a condition allows us the flexibility to include people of Ingenio into this conceptual framework.

chapter 1

Black, but Not African

*Negros si, pero, de que sean, de que [mis ancestros]
hayan sido de antecedentes africanas, no sé.*

*Blacks, yes, but that [my ancestors] had been of
African ancestry, I don't know.*

Diana, a young woman from Ingenio

In Ingenio, most people consider themselves to be black. Few, however, think of themselves as the descendants of African slaves. Millions of Africans were displaced from their homelands through the slave trade and dispersed throughout the Americas, as well as into the Middle East and Europe (Segal 1995). Since the slave trade was horrendous and the experience of slavery was dehumanizing and traumatizing, and had lasting effects on the African-descended populations in the Americas and elsewhere, it is not something we would expect people to forget easily. In line with this, Paul Gilroy (1993: 39) argues that the "memory of slavery, actively preserved as a living intellectual resource" is used by blacks in the Western world in their post-emancipation struggles for justice. People in Ingenio, however, do not use the memory of chattel slavery as a resource for collective struggle, and few people trace their ancestries to Africa. In this chapter, I explain the place of Africa and slavery in conceptions of blackness in Ingenio through a discussion of the recorded and remembered histories of the town and the region. This analysis sheds light on the particularity of blackness in Ingenio.

I first describe the racial geography of Piura and explain how this racial-spatial order was created. Then, I discuss the creation of haciendas and the system of slavery that developed in Piura. There were very few slaves in Piura as a whole and often only a handful on each hacienda. The agricultural labor force in colonial and republican Piura was not primarily enslaved, but rather mostly tenant farmers, many of whom were free blacks (Aldana 1989; Castillo Román 1977; Reyes Flores 2001). In haciendas in the valleys of the Río Piura and its tributaries, where Ingenio lies, tenant farmers predominated starting in the late eighteenth century. Because many of them were free blacks, and this system lasted for around two hundred years, the memory of tenant farming has, in most cases, displaced the memory of chattel slavery. In addition, the fact that tenant farming was not exclusive to people of African descent means that Piura did not have a strict racial division of labor. This has diminished the importance of Africa at the same time it has expanded the category of negro to include anyone of visibly African descent.

Racial Geography of Piura

The population of the Department of Piura is primarily composed of the descendants of three groups who found themselves together on Peruvian soil for the first time in the early sixteenth century: (1) various indigenous groups that have populated the region for millennia, (2) Spanish conquistadores and other European settlers and immigrants, and (3) African slaves and freedmen. The three main racial/ethnic groups currently in Piura are whites/mestizos, indigenous people (cholos), and Afro-Peruvians/blacks.

Piura is characterized by a distinct racial geography composed of three regions, each dominated by a particular racial/ethnic group.[1] This racial geography roughly corresponds to the three topographical regions of Piura: Bajo Piura, Medio Piura, and Alto Piura, corresponding to their elevation. These regions run north-south and extend from the Pacific Ocean up to the Andes Mountains. The main exception to this racial division is the city of Piura, which, like most urban areas in Peru, is multiethnic. The racial geography of Piura is an artifact of the Spanish conquest (Schlüpmann 1991) and, although the legal measures taken to achieve this racialized spatial order are no longer in effect, the consequences can be seen to this day.

The low-lying region along the Pacific coast, referred to as Bajo Piura, is primarily inhabited by the descendants of indigenous coastal populations, such as the Sechuras and the Tallanes. The predominance of these groups in this area is due in part to the history of Indian removal in Peru: most of the historic resettlement sites (*reducciones*) are in this region. In the mid-sixteenth century, in light of the massive destruction of indigenous populations and the scarcity of fertile land in Peru, the Crown ordered all surviving Indians to be moved to certain places and restricted these areas to Indians. In these reducciones, the Indians were to work the land, perform the *mita* (obligatory free labor), and pay a tributary tax to the Crown. Their concentration in specific areas also was intended to facilitate their indoctrination into Spanish ways and customs. Starting in the 1570s, Viceroy Francisco de Toledo took up the task of segregating the Indians of the newly established *corregimiento* of Piura into areas set aside exclusively for them. The main resettlement sites in Bajo Piura were Colán, Catacaos, Sechura, and Olmos, and these areas remained almost exclusively indigenous throughout the colonial period (Del Busto Duthurburu, Rosales Aguirre, and Correa Gutiérrez 2004; Ramírez 1986; Schlüpmann 1991). There were very few or no blacks, mulattos, mestizos, or whites in these places. In Catacaos in 1789, for example, there were 1,790 people—1,789 Indians and one priest. In Sechura in the same year, the population was composed of 1,682 Indians, 8 blacks, and 19 *pardos* (people of mixed African and European ancestry), according to the census carried out by Bishop Martínez de Compañón. These areas continue to be predominantly populated by coastal indigenous populations today.

The mountainous eastern part of Piura, known as Alto Piura, is characterized by a white and mestizo population. As in Bajo Piura, in the highlands, indigenous people were relocated to reducciones. The reducción sites in the Andean region included Frías, Ayabaca, and Huancabamba. Indigenous people were sent to reducciones in their region, whether coastal or mountain. The same is true for the mita: Indians were sometimes sent outside of their reducción to work for a certain period of time but remained in the same region (Schlüpmann 1991). We don't know very much about the preconquest indigenous populations in Alto Piura, but we do know that, like the coastal groups, they suffered tremendous population declines. Spanish reports indicate that there were 5,000 Indians in Alto Piura in 1549, but only 2,847 in 1573, and their numbers continued to decline into the seventeenth century (Diez Hurtado 1998). Today, the population is less indigenous-looking in Alto Piura than in Bajo Piura, indicating a stronger history of mestizaje in this area. This increased racial mixing is due in part to the fact that, unlike in Bajo Piura, Spaniards set up towns in the Andes that required the presence of Spanish authorities and administrators. In Bajo Piura, the Indians were segregated and isolated, whereas in Alto Piura, Spanish-Indian mixture was facilitated (Huertas Vallejo 2001). This is particularly the case in the towns of Santo Domingo and Chalaco, which in the 1940 census reported 95 and 98 percent blanco or mestizo populations, respectively. Some Indians in Alto Piura resisted assimilation, notably those of the mountain village of Silahuá. Although they were ordered to relocate to Frías, they refused and were able to maintain their relative independence up until the twentieth century, when they finally were recognized as an indigenous community (Diez Hurtado 1998). Silahuá today stands out as an indigenous community in the primarily white and mestizo region of Alto Piura.[2]

The third region, which is the primary subject of this book, is the territory between Alto Piura and Bajo Piura, in the eastern valleys of the Río Piura and its tributaries, especially the Río Gallega and the Río Corral del Medio. These areas were once home to large indigenous populations, such as the Chimú, Sicán, and Inca (Hocquenghem 2004). However, the Spanish policy of removing Indians into reducciones combined with the destruction of indigenous populations through warfare and disease left much of this area depopulated in the sixteenth century (Hocquenghem 2004; Schlüpmann 1991). For Spaniards and criollos (Peruvian-born Spaniards), this translated into opportunities to form haciendas in the depopulated fertile valleys along the Río Piura. Today, this region has a substantial Afro-descendant population, particularly in those places where large haciendas once existed, such as the Hacienda Bigote, Hacienda Pabur, Hacienda Yapatera, Hacienda Morropón, and Hacienda Buenos Aires. The Afro-Peruvian presence in this area is due to the regional history of hacienda slavery and tenant farming.

Coastal Agriculture and African Slavery in Peru

The African slave trade in Peru was fairly substantial, although much less than in Brazil or the Caribbean. Between 1528 and 1821, more than 100,000 African slaves were brought to Peru (Hunefeldt 1994; Aguirre 2005). The arrival of Africans in Peru dates back to the appearance of the earliest Spanish conquistadores. The first conquistador to arrive in what is today Peru was Francisco Pizarro, who happened upon the northern coastal city of Tumbes in 1528. In this initial visit, Pizarro was accompanied by a man of African descent. When Pizarro returned in 1529 with plans to conquer Peru, he had secured the right to import 52 African slaves. By 1537, the Spanish Crown had issued permits for the importation of 363 African slaves into Peru. The majority of slaves in the sixteenth century came not directly from Africa, but from other parts of the Americas (Bowser 1974).

The African-descended population in Peru grew steadily throughout the sixteenth and seventeenth centuries, fueled primarily by a consistently expanding slave trade. Enslaved Africans were brought directly from Africa, as well as from other Spanish colonies (Bowser 1974). Because were no direct sea routes from Africa to Peru in the eighteenth century, it was necessary to disembark first in Panama. From there, other ships would take passengers and freight to Peru. Slaves were brought into the country through inland routes as well as through ports such as Callao, near Lima, and Paita, in Piura (Schlüpmann 1991).

African slaves were brought to Peru to meet labor needs, principally in terms of coastal agriculture. The native population was the major source of labor in the highland mines, yet attempts to use them for coastal agricultural labor were generally catastrophic, and quickened the decimation of indigenous coastal populations (Bowser 1974; Cushner 1980). The Indians that did survive often were relocated to the coastal reducciones, such as those in Catacaos and Sechura (Del Busto Duthurburu, Rosales Aguirre, and Correa Gutiérrez 2004; Schlüpmann 1994). On the northern Peruvian coast, hacendados had a diverse but limited labor supply. Their laborers often constituted a mix of contracted yanaconas (paid Indian laborers), mitayos (obligated Indian laborers), slaves, and free blacks (Gonzales 1985; Cushner 1980). Rachel O'Toole (2006) argues that these populations had extensive interaction with one another, both on and off the hacienda.

By the end of the sixteenth century, there were 6,690 blacks in Lima, constituting half of the city's population (Cuche 1975). Many of these blacks were not enslaved. Of the more than 80,000 blacks and mulattoes in all of Peru in 1591, only 40,000 were enslaved (Castillo Román 1977). In 1640, there were 20,000 blacks in Lima, both slave and free. In contrast, whereas there were about 1,000,000 indigenous people on the coast when Pizarro arrived, by 1640, there were fewer than 75,000. The continuing epidemics and gross mistreatment of the coastal indigenous population led to their near decimation over the next century (Bowser 1974; Cushner 1980).

The labor shortages on the Peruvian coast made African slave labor an attractive option for coastal hacienda owners (Aldana 1989). By the early eighteenth century, the coastal agricultural sector was heavily dependent on the labor of Africans and their descendants, and blacks played an important role in the urban economy, working as cooks, servants, butchers, wet nurses, bricklayers, blacksmiths, tailors, laundresses, and myriad other occupations (Aguirre 2005). In light of the continual presence of Africans and their descendants in the coastal areas of Peru from the start of the Spanish conquest, by the seventeenth century the operation of the colony without Africans was inconceivable (Bowser 1974).

The Enslavement of Africans in Piura

There is remarkably little historical research on the African-descended population or on slavery in Piura. For example, a single tome summarizes nearly all of the work published on Piura in the twentieth century. This book, *Piura: región y sociedad: derrotero bibliográfico para el desarrollo* (Revesz et al. 1997), contains 2,166 summaries of published works on Piura. Of these, the sole work in the index under "Slavery" is José Castillo Román's 1977 undergraduate thesis on slavery in Piura. There are no references in the index to blacks or Afro-descendants. The fourteen citations under "Ethnic groups" refer almost exclusively to pre-Columbian groups such as the Tallanes or to the mestizos in Alto Piura. The two exceptions are Castillo Román's thesis and an article by Martin Minchom, "The Making of a White Province: Demographic Movement and Ethnic Transformation in the South of the Audiencia de Quito (1670–1830)," which is primarily about the Ecuadoran province of Loja, yet provides some useful contextual information about the demographic decline of blacks in Piura.

The lack of historical work on slavery in Piura is due to the fact that most of the detailed historical work on slavery in Peru has been conducted in the south of the country, where the largest haciendas were concentrated (Aguirre 2005; Bowser 1974; Hunefeldt 1994). Nearly all of the research on northern Peru focuses on haciendas in Chiclayo and Lambayeque, where there is much more extensive historical documentation. For the purposes of this project, I have pieced together the available literature on slavery in

Piura as well as the few early twentieth-century documents I was able to obtain in the library of the Pontificia Universidad Católica in Lima. Particularly useful is the extensive work of historian Jakob Schlüpmann. In addition to his dissertation and several articles, Schlüpmann has posted online a wealth of findings from haciendas in Piura in the seventeenth and eighteenth centuries, including manifests of the port of Paita.[3]

Most slaves brought to Piura came in the mid-eighteenth century (Schlüpmann 1994). Between 1704 and 1773, 170 vessels carrying slaves came through the port of Paita, bringing with them, according to the manifests, 5,517 slaves. All of the vessels came from Panama, except possibly one whose origin is not known. Of the 5,517 African slaves, only 20 were listed as criollos or *ladinos,* indicating they were born in the Spanish colonies. Most of the other slaves were listed as *bozales,* meaning that they were born in Africa and had yet to be Latinized or learn to speak Spanish. The 5,517 figure is most likely an underestimate for a number of reasons. First, the purpose of these manifests was to collect tariffs on imports, so importers would be inclined not to report everything on board. Second, it is possible that there were more unreported ladino or criollo slaves, as they were often not subject to tariffs. Third, the slaves were often listed as "negros bozales piezas de india," literally as "pieces." In some cases, two unhealthy slaves could count as one *pieza de india.*[4]

I do not have complete data on the number of slaves brought into the port of Paita. It is however reasonable to claim that the data I do have, which includes the 1704–1773 manifests, account for much of the Piura slave trade. Schlüpmann (1994) tells us that, prior to the eighteenth century, slavery was still relatively rare in Piura, and that it declined in the nineteenth century. For example, at the Hacienda Yapatera, there were sixty slaves in 1790, but only thirty-two in 1833; the Hacienda Morropón had about thirty slaves at the beginning of the eighteenth century, but only around ten at the beginning of the nineteenth (Schlüpmann 1991).

In Piura, relatively few slaves worked on haciendas. The largest concentration of slaves ever recorded in Piura is sixty slaves on the Hacienda Yapatera in 1790. The next largest slaveholder was the owner of the Hacienda Santa Ana, where there were forty-five slaves in 1800 (Schlüpmann 1991). More typical were the Haciendas Malacasí and Morropón, which had twenty or fewer slaves at that time. By the early nineteenth century, the Hacienda Yapatera had only fourteen slaves, and the Hacienda Morropón only nine (Castillo Román 1977). These haciendas can be compared to the

Jesuit Hacienda La Villa in Lima, which had 433 slaves in 1771, or the Hacienda San Regis in Chincha, which had 302 slaves in 1770 (Schlüpmann 1991).

In 1783, the census carried out by Bishop Martínez de Compañón recorded 5,203 pardos and 884 blacks out of a population of 44,497 people in Piura. Notably, the vast majority of the pardos were not enslaved. Another source indicates that there were 2,503 *pardos libres* in Piura in 1786, and only 894 slaves (Castillo Román 1977). And, Reyes Flores (2001) reports that there were 1,252 slaves and 7,189 free blacks in Piura in 1807. All of these sources indicate that free blacks heavily outnumbered slaves by the late eighteenth century in Piura.

Hacienda owners and operators used various combinations of slaves and tenant farmers, and there is no clear correlation between the usage of either and the production of sugarcane. For example, in 1780, the Hacienda Yapatera had 60 slaves and 13 tenant farmers, and cultivated more than 20 *cuadras* of sugarcane.[5] In that year, Morropón had 137 tenant farmers and about 10 slaves; in 1705, Morropón had 31 slaves and cultivated 20 cuadras of sugarcane. In 1792, Yapatera had 57 slaves and cultivated 25 cuadras of sugarcane. By 1868, when the Hacienda Yapatera no long had slaves because of abolition, and no longer cultivated sugarcane, there were 159 tenant farmers on the land (Schlüpmann 1994).

The sugarcane industry took off in Piura at the end of the seventeenth century, continued to grow throughout the eighteenth century, then began to decline in the early nineteenth century. For example, the Hacienda Morropón produced no sugarcane in 1679, yet had thirteen cuadras dedicated to its production in 1691 and twenty-four at its peak in 1823. In 1856, only six cuadras were dedicated to sugar production. By contrast, Yapatera had twenty-five cuadras of sugarcane at its peak in 1792, and sixteen cuadras in 1833 (Schlüpmann 1994).

The Río Piura haciendas thus rarely relied on slavery as their only or even primary source of labor. Slavery certainly existed and played an important role, but it coexisted with other forms of labor, specifically with tenant farming. The predominance of pardos in the census reports indicates that many of these tenant farmers were likely of African descent. Susana Aldana (1989) also writes that many *colonos* (workers) on the large haciendas in Piura were mulattos. An explanation as to why there were so many free blacks and mulattos in Piura remains elusive. One possibility is the relatively unprofitable nature of the haciendas in that state.

Perhaps it was more economical to have tenant farmers who ensured a constant source of income, as opposed to slaves who would be particularly costly in times of economic hardship for the haciendas. This explanation is supported by two findings. The first is a rental contract from the Hacienda Morropón from 1795. Don Tomás Fernandes de Paredes rented out the hacienda with its sugar processing equipment, yet excluded from the contract the rents from the tenant farmers, yielding an indication of the importance of that income (Schlüpmann 1994). The second piece of evidence comes from Cushner's (1980) study of Jesuit haciendas, where he details the costs associated with making slavery into a profitable venture, particularly the high initial capital investment and the lengthy wait for a return on this investment. Piura's isolation would exacerbate costs associated with sugar production and distribution and reduce potential profitability. As such, slave owners would have been disposed to allowing their slaves to purchase their freedom or even to manumitting them in order to have them pay tenant rents.

The Republican Era and the Long Battle to End Slavery

Although slavery was not central to the rural economy of Piura, it was important to Peru as a whole, and it is useful to discuss briefly the movement to end slavery in Peru. The first major steps toward emancipation were taken after Peru won independence from Spain in 1821. Many of the fifty thousand slaves in Peru at that time hoped that independence would lead to their emancipation. They would however have to wait thirty-three more years before Ramón Castilla would decree an end to slavery in Peru (Blanchard 1992).

The leader of the independence movement, General José de San Martín, introduced a number of legal measures that seemed headed toward emancipation. For example, he instituted the law of the free womb in 1821, by which all children born of slaves after 1821 would be free. These offspring, who came to be known as *libertos*, were to remain under the care of their parents' masters until the age of twenty for females and twenty-four for males. Before twenty years passed however, and thus before this law could take effect, President Agustín Gamarra passed a law in 1839 that maintained libertos under the patronage and control of their parents' masters until they reached the ripe age of fifty. Gamarra also rescinded San Martín's decrees that had ended the slave trade in Peru by mandating that all enslaved persons who arrived in Peru from other countries would become free upon reaching Peruvian soil (Blanchard 1992).

These and other pro-slavery measures that continued to be implemented in Peru up until the mid-nineteenth century reflect the importance, or at least the perceived importance, of slave labor in early republican Peru. There were only fifty thousand slaves in Peru at the time of independence, but they were concentrated in particular valleys along the Peruvian coast, and thus were perceived as essential in those localities. There was also an urban character to slavery in the nineteenth century, especially in Lima, where slaves performed many vital tasks, notably those of water carriers and craftsmen. The concentration of slaves in particular localities, and especially in Lima, combined with the relative political power of slave owners compared to the rest of the population made slavery a hot-button issue that most politicians preferred to avoid. The unwillingness of conservative and liberal political leaders alike to infringe upon the property rights of slave owners meant that slavery continued to exist in republican Peru (Aguirre 1993; Blanchard 1992; Hunefeldt 1994).

The owners of sugarcane and cotton haciendas repeatedly insisted that slavery was necessary and often cited the chronic labor shortages on the coastal haciendas. The hacendados frequently made the case that slaves were vital to maintaining or even reviving Peru's agricultural base. Given the prominence and high social position of these hacendados, leaders of nineteenth-century Peru usually were not willing to enact laws that expanded the rights of slaves. Instead, they were more likely to limit slaves' rights and expand the slave trade in order to curry favor with the hacendados (Blanchard 1992).

In contrast to the relative power of the hacendados, the abolitionist voices in Peru were few and far between. Slaves themselves often worked towards their own emancipation, through rebellions, such as the rebellion in the Chicama Valley in 1851; through court cases, such as when the enslaved José Miranda sued to be freed; or in the numerous cases when slaves purchased freedom for themselves or their spouses or children (Aguirre 1993; Blanchard 1992; Hunefeldt 1994).

Slavery finally ended in Peru at the end of the civil war in 1855, with a decree issued by the leader of the rebel forces, Ramón Castilla. Although Castilla is held up in Peruvian textbooks as the emancipator of slaves, it is likely that he freed the slaves in order to ensure the victory of the rebel forces in the civil war. The president at the time of the civil war, José Rufino

Echenique, offered manumission to any slave who enlisted in the army, in an attempt to recruit slaves to his army and protect his government from Castilla's rebel forces. In response, former President Ramón Castilla declared himself provisional president and pronounced all slaves and libertos freed, with the notable exception of those who had joined Echenique's army. When his forces emerged victorious, this decree came into effect, and the slaves were freed. Whereas there had been fifty thousand slaves when Peru gained independence, there were just over twenty-five thousand at the end of the civil war. The slave owners were compensated for their losses, but the slaves received nothing but their freedom (Blanchard 1992).

Piura Post-Abolition (1854–1969)

There is even less documentation on the post-abolition period than on slavery in Piura. For example, Michael Gonzales's *Plantation Agriculture and Social Control in Northern Peru, 1875–1933* (1985) is primarily about Cayaltí, a plantation in the Saña Valley in the Department of Lambayeque.[6] The other plantations Gonzales refers to are almost all in Lambayeque as well. Although some of his background information on Peru and the north coast is useful for understanding Piura, the departments of Lambayeque and Piura are different in many ways. Lambayeque is home to several rivers that are essential for agriculture in this parched region. The Saña Valley is surrounded by the Lambayeque, Jequetepeque, Chicama, Moche, Viru, and Chao valleys. Piura, in contrast, has only two valleys: the Piura and Chira. Hence the valleys, and thus the haciendas, in Piura are much more isolated. In addition, the smaller size of the Piura valleys means that the plantations and haciendas are smaller. In addition, Gonzales (1985) tells us little about the presence of people of African descent, even though the town of Saña is a well-known center of Afro-Peruvian people and culture. Instead, he focuses primarily on Chinese and Japanese laborers on the Cayaltí plantation. Gonzales (1985: 84) states, "Between 1849 and 1874 over 100,000 indentured [Chinese] servants emigrated to Peru alone, where they replaced blacks on sugarcane plantations." We are left to wonder what happened to those former black workers.

For the vast majority of agricultural workers in rural Piura, life during the ninety-five years between the emancipation of the slaves and the agrarian reform legislation of 1969 likely was not tremendously different from the previous ninety-five years. As mentioned, by the early nineteenth century, there were very few slaves working on haciendas. Much more common was tenant farming, and emancipation would have done little to change that. The most drastic change may have been on the Hacienda Yapatera, where there were thirty slaves in 1848. Yet, the fact that there were 159 tenant farmers there in 1868 indicates that the land continued to be cultivated. Many former slaves likely stayed on in their same position, insofar as their former owners permitted. (Abolition made it easier for former slave owners to rid themselves of disorderly workers; Aguirre 2005.)

The Hacienda Morropón had only seven slaves in 1839, and the majority of the haciendas in Piura no longer had any slaves by this time (Schlüpmann 1991). In fact, there were likely no more than six hundred slaves in all of Piura in 1854 (based on the calculation that the overall Peruvian slave population declined by 50 percent between 1821 and 1855 and there were 1,252 slaves in Piura in 1807; Schlüpmann 1991). Thus, although the long and hard struggle for freedom was an important issue in Peru as a whole, and was certainly important for the slaves themselves, the relatively small number of slaves in Piura meant that emancipation evidently did not greatly affect the lives of most Piuranos in 1854. Unfortunately, there is very little historical information as to what happened to slaves after emancipation that can be used to corroborate these conclusions. As Carlos Aguirre (1993) points out, the end of slavery meant the end of many of the historical documents that could tell us what happened to freed slaves.

Aguirre (1993, 2005) suggests that most of the former hacienda slaves continued to work as agricultural laborers, although not necessarily on the same hacienda, since emancipation did grant former slaves more freedom of movement, allowing them to move according to labor demands. In Piura, more sugar was produced post-abolition, given that the sugar industry there began to expand again in 1870 (Schlüpmann 1994). Between 1870 and 1910, sugar plantations in Piura responded to the increased national and international demand for sugar by augmenting their sugar production. This often involved recruiting workers through a system of *enganche*, literally "hooking." In this system, hacendados or their representatives would promise potential workers an incentive, such as living quarters or a tract of land, in return for coming to work on their hacienda. This is how workers were recruited to work at the Hacienda Buenos Aires, especially in the early twentieth century (CIPCA 1986), a time when Piura continued to experience labor shortages (Paz Soldán 1919).

I found documentation in the work of Hildebrando Castro Pozo that tenant farming existed on the Hacienda Buenos Aires in the twentieth century. On October 17, 1934, the owners or managers of the Hacienda Buenos Aires, Don Celso Garrido Lecca and Don Alfredo R. Colma, signed an agreement with two representatives of the tenant farmers, Don Andrés Manrique and Don Jacobo Arévalo. This agreement prohibited all work without pay, allowed tenant farmers to sell their produce to whomever they wished, limited the workday to eight hours, and called for the hacendado to establish a school in La Pilca, one of the towns on the property. These provisions indicate that, prior to October 17, 1934, some tenant farmers were forced to work without pay, to work long hours, and to sell their products to the hacendado. Similar agreements were signed on nearby haciendas, indicating the widespread nature of these practices (Castro Pozo 1947).

Agrarian Reform

In contrast to emancipation, the agrarian reform of the 1960s and 1970s meant great changes for the population of rural Piura, given the extreme inequality in land tenure in twentieth-century Piura. The process leading up to the agrarian reform was long, and its implementation was drawn out. Agrarian reform also came about in a time of political, economic, social, and ecological crisis. There were continuous droughts along the coast; a military government was in power; and commodity prices were falling. Nevertheless, the reform did transfer much of the arable Peruvian land from large landholders to the formerly landless peasants. President Fernando Belaúnde Terry passed the first agrarian reform legislation in 1964. This legislation had the goal of reducing inequality, but was largely ineffective. Agrarian reform began to become more of a reality with the passage of Legal Decree 17716 on June 24, 1969, by military president Juan Francisco Velasco Alvarado, who is remembered today for his proposition that "the land is for those who till it" (Arce Espinoza 1983; Schirmer 1977).

The agrarian reform led to a reduction in inequality but did not eliminate it by any means. In 1961, in the province of Morropón, Piura, 88.6 percent of landholders had fewer than five hectares of land. Yet, 95 percent of all of the land was in the hands of those 0.3 percent of landholders who had more than five hundred hectares of property. By 1972, with the breaking up of some of the large landholdings, 80 percent of the land was in the hands of the 0.1 percent of all landholders who had more than five hundred hectares of land. Whereas in 1961, 2.5 percent of the land was in holdings of five to five hundred hectares, by 1972, 11 percent of the land was in such medium-sized parcels. Thus, the process initiated in 1960 reduced inequality of land tenure largely through an increase in the number of people with between five and five hundred hectares and a reduction in those who had more than five hundred (Arce Espinoza 1983: 19–20).

Departments in Peru were declared zones of agrarian reform on a case-by-case basis. When Piura was so declared on October 15, 1969, the region was going through an economic crisis in agriculture as a result of recent droughts and an irrigation system insufficient to cultivate much of the land. The agrarian reform was accompanied by new legislation that transferred control of the waterways from private hands to the state. Access to water and irrigation is particularly important in Piura, since most of the land is not cultivable without irrigation (Arce Espinoza 1983).

It was nearly three years after the declaration of the agrarian reform, and of Piura as a zone of agrarian reform, that the peasants of Ingenio were able to take the lands of the former Hacienda Buenos Aires. This *toma de tierras* was made possible by another legal decree—D.L. 19400, passed in April 1972—which facilitated the organization of peasants into cooperatives. The owner of the Hacienda Buenos Aires, like many other hacendados, had broken up his more than one thousand hectares of land into many smaller parcels in anticipation of the land reform. He then sold those parcels of land to twenty-six people (Arce Espinoza 1983). The people in Ingenio refer to these new landholders as *los ingenieros*, presumably because they were agricultural engineers. These new landowners did not last long, as the toma de tierras occurred soon after they purchased the land.

The peasants in Ingenio were successful in taking over all of the land and capital of the former hacienda, and named their cooperative 2 de Enero in honor of the date of their successful takeover—January 2, 1973. The cooperative took possession of the rice mill, the former residences of the hacienda owners, and the administrative offices. The cooperative lasted ten years. By that time, Peru no longer had a military government, and the new president, Fernando Belaúnde Terry had passed another law—D.L. 002—the Agrarian Development Law, permitting the division of collective lands into individual lots. In Ingenio, each worker at the cooperative received 3.5 hectares of land.

Slavery and Tenant Farmers in Ingenio

With this background on the agrarian history of Peru and of Piura, we can now put into context the site that is the main focus of this book—the town of Ingenio de Buenos Aires, which sits on the lands of the former Hacienda Buenos Aires. Buenos Aires was part of one of the largest haciendas in Piura, the Hacienda Morropón, until it was sold off as a separate entity in 1872. It continued to operate as an hacienda until the agrarian reform in 1972, when the former hacienda workers formed an agricultural cooperative and became the collective owners of the land (Leguía y Martínez 1914; F. Helguero 1928; Schlüpmann 1994).

The lands around Ingenio were cultivated long before the arrival of the Spaniards. These lands, which extend between two rivers, were once the domain of pre-Incan cultures and came under the control of the Inca Empire prior to the Spanish conquest (Hocquenghem 2004). Not much is known about this period, as many of the archaeological sites have yet to be excavated. The pre-Incan, Incan, and colonial ceramics and tools that have been extracted from the mounds in the area are more likely to be in the homes of local farmers who happen upon them while tilling their land than in the laboratories of archaeologists or collections of museums. Nevertheless, the abundance of mounds and ceramics clearly indicates the presence of humans prior to the Spanish conquest. Specifically, artifacts from the Chimú and Sicán cultures have been uncovered in the immediate vicinity of the former Hacienda Buenos Aires (Hocquenghem 2004).

The first colonial historical record of this particular valley can be found in 1670, when Francisco de Sojo, of Arsiniega, Spain, acquired the lands around the Río Gallega, the first of the two rivers that today divides Ingenio de Buenos Aires from Morropón (Leguía y Martínez 1914; Schlüpmann 1994). Sojo purchased this land in pieces from various landowners,[7] and the land likely was available for purchase due to the postconquest depopulation of Indians and the subsequent grants made to Spaniards and criollos by the Crown. Sojo's acquisition included what became the Hacienda Buenos Aires and the adjacent Hacienda Morropón as well as other landholdings in the area. Sojo's investment in the sugar industry was probably an attempt to take advantage of the mid-seventeenth-century sugar boom (Del Busto Duthurburu et al. 2004; Ramírez 1986; Schlüpmann 1991).

These lands were to stay in the Sojo family for a little more than one hundred years. Francisco de Sojo's son, Don Juan de Sojo Cantoral, inherited the entire landholding in 1694 (Schlüpmann 1994: 252). Don Francisco de Sojo's will listed among his assets the Hacienda Buenos Ayres, with twenty-six slaves, 1,500 animals, a sugar mill, and other goods. By 1705, Don Juan de Sojo Cantoral had thirty-one African slaves, the largest recorded number of African slaves for this hacienda. In 1733, the property was inherited by Don Francisco Nicolás de Sojo Olabareita, who continued to operate it with about twenty African slaves (Schlüpmann 1994: 254). This decrease in slaves may reflect falling sugar prices in the early eighteenth century (Ramírez 1986).

Forty years later, in 1773, the hacienda passed into the hands of the Paredes family, where it remained for a little more than eighty years. The historical records from the Departmental Archive of Piura (provided by Jakob Schlüpmann in the appendixes to his 1994 dissertation) do not reveal why the land passed out of the Sojo family, but it was likely due to lack of a suitable heir. In any case, Sojo Olabareita willed the hacienda to Don Tomás Fernandes de Paredes, marqués de Salinas, in 1773. In 1795, Don Fernandes de Paredes rented the hacienda out to Don Bartolomé Quiroga y Sotomayor, including the land for sugarcane cultivation as well as the tools and equipment, livestock, and slaves, but excluding the rent from the 137 tenant farmers. The hacienda stayed in the Paredes family until Doña Jacinta Fernandes de Paredes died at the age of thirty-six in 1855, leaving the property to her second husband, Don Pedro de Arrese (Schlüpmann 1994: 253–55).

In 1872 the Arrese heirs divided the Hacienda Morropón into two holdings, one of which took on its former name—the Hacienda Buenos Aires. The other part, which continued to be called the Hacienda Morropón, stayed in the Arrese family until the 1969 agrarian reform. The Hacienda Buenos Aires was first sold to Don Carlos P. López and later came into the possession of the Rospiglossi family. Both of these owners, however, rented out the hacienda to Don Alejandro León Manzares, who operated it well into the twentieth century (F. Helguero 1928; Leguía y Martínez 1914; Schlüpmann 1994).

This is the history of Ingenio according to the archival records and historical reports available to us. This story can be compared with that told to me by the residents of Ingenio. There is consensus among historians that African slaves were brought to Peru and that people of African descent have been in Peru for nearly five hundred years. Scholars would consider the descendants of Africans forcibly brought to Peru in the sixteenth through the nineteenth centuries to be part of the African diaspora in the Americas. Many people in Ingenio do not share this understanding of their history, however, and do not view themselves as diasporic subjects. Specifically, Africa and the slave trade do not figure into their conceptions of their ancestry and of the history of the town.

Oral Histories from Ingenio

Ingenio is unusual among towns in Peru in that it has a visible Afro-Peruvian presence, but it is not the only such village in the area. A twenty-minute walk downriver from Ingenio is another village, La Pilca, that also has a preponderance of Afro-Peruvians. These towns stand in stark contrast to the village twenty minutes' walk upriver, Pampa Flores, which has almost no Afro-Peruvians. As one travels farther up the river into Alto Piura, the villages become primarily white/mestizo. As one travels farther down the valley, one encounters some villages that are heavily mestizo, and others, such as La Encantada, that are nearly all indigenous. Ingenieros as well as residents of other villages frequently describe Ingenio as a town with many negros. Despite this perception that Ingenio is a black town, few villagers linked the presence of blacks in Ingenio with Africa or with a history of slavery. They did, however, strongly identify with a history of agricultural work, with the Department of Piura, and with a regional identity as norteños (northerners).

All but one of the residents I interviewed indicated they or their parents or grandparents had migrated to Ingenio in the early twentieth century to work on the Hacienda Buenos Aires. Those residents of African descent were most likely to report having come in the early twentieth century and to have settled in the central part of town. Most of these residents came from surrounding haciendas that have a history of enslaving Africans, such as the Hacienda Yapatera and the Hacienda Pabur. Residents of indigenous descent generally reported having come from the lowland coastal regions of Piura, such as Sechura or Catacaos, in the 1930s to work on the hacienda; they settled in the lower part of town. Although most residents had only vague recollections of how or why their families had come to Ingenio, many had vivid recollections of the agrarian reform in Piura, and spoke passionately about the takeover of the Hacienda Buenos Aires by the agricultural workers.

In Ingenio, many people remember fondly the years of the Hacienda Buenos Aires, when everyone had work and earned an adequate salary to buy food for all of their children. Señora Olivia, who sells tamales for a living, told me that life was better when the hacienda still existed, and the town was much prettier and more full of life then. On Sundays, there was a market in the central plaza where one could buy food and even clothes and shoes. These days, in the town center, there is a soccer field and a cement plaza, but no market.

Although workers faced mistreatment and low pay, it is true that there was little or no unemployment during the years of the hacienda. After all, the hacendado would not permit anyone to live in Ingenio who did not work for or in conjunction with the hacienda. While the hacienda was in existence, there was electricity in the center of town, a sewage system for the hacienda owner and his employees, and water in the canal all the time. There were two harvests most years and economic prosperity in the town, at least for the hacienda owner. During most of my fieldwork, there was no electricity or sewage system in Ingenio, and the canal had clean and abundant water only from February to June.

Older residents of Ingenio also vividly remembered the punishments inflicted by the hacendado or the *caporal* (foreman) on workers in the early twentieth century. The mantrap in Ingenio that was used to punish workers for disobedience remained in use into the 1930s. Workers who did not show up for work or who drank too much on Sundays were beaten and forced to hang for days in the mantrap. If a worker committed one offense too many, the hacendado would have him and his family removed from the town.

The Hacienda Buenos Aires is now defunct, and the former workers are owners of that land. In 1972, after a series of worker uprisings, the workers threw the owners of the hacienda out of the town and took over the hacienda. The 2 de Enero cooperative they formed at that time barely lasted ten years, before failing due to mismanagement and the changing global and national scene. The worker-owners then decided to distribute the land evenly among the workers, with each worker receiving 3.5 hectares. This story—that of agricultural work, of migration, and of the workers' struggle to gain their land—is the history people in Ingenio most often chose to relate to me, not the story of forced migration from Africa, centuries of slavery, and the selling of human beings in the marketplace. Of the forty-nine African-descended people that I interviewed in Ingenio, only twelve told me that they were of African ancestry, and none were aware of an enslaved ancestor.

Constructions of Ancestry in Ingenio

In the United States, the current racial, political, and social climates make Africa the most important geographical component of African Americans' shared ancestry and collective memory. In Peru, this is not necessarily the case, even though that country is also a product of colonial encounters and the African slave trade. In this sense, my characterization of the people of Ingenio as the descendants of Africans is a product of how I conceptualize the history of the Americas—as that of three populations (whites, blacks, and Indians), each with its own history in these lands. The importance of Africa in African Americans' constructions of their ancestry, and thus of their collective identity, is in line with Evitar Zerubavel's (2003) conjecture that conceptions of ancestry are based on social conventions. Using this understanding of collective memories, we may conclude that perhaps social conventions in Ingenio make it such that Africa has little or no significance in people's constructions of their ancestry.

Social conventions in Ingenio do not include any discussion of Africa. I heard precisely one reference to Africa in the course of nine months of fieldwork in Ingenio. On that occasion, I was riding in a moto-taxi with Don Segundo, a storeowner in his fifties with light brown skin. We were discussing cacao cultivation. I mentioned that a lot of cacao is produced in West Africa, and he responded, "Yes, Africa, that is where we come from." This was the only time anyone volunteered information that would connect them to Africa. When villagers discussed the history of Ingenio amongst themselves, I heard them talking about the agrarian reform and the hacienda era, but never about slavery or their ancestors who had come from other places. To garner information about Africa, I had to ask directly. Because my ethnographic data do not contain any discussions of Africa, the information in this chapter with regard to the memory of Africa comes almost exclusively from interviews.

In my interviews with residents of Ingenio, I asked if they had African, indigenous, European, or Asian ancestry. Of the 49 interviewees whose physical features showed clear signs of African ancestry, 24 denied having

African ancestry, 13 did not know whether they had African ancestry, and 12 said that they did have African ancestry. Notably, only 10 thought they might have Spanish ancestry. Only 2 interviewees had actually heard stories about particular ancestors who had come from somewhere other than Peru. Alfonso had been told that his great-grandfather had come from Spain, and Olivia had been told that her great-great-grandfather had come from Cuba. The rest of my interviewees had specific information only about ancestors who had been born in Peru, and thus constructed their ancestry as essentially Peruvian.

In addition to the in-depth interviews, I conducted a survey of 150 respondents in Ingenio and La Pilca, the neighboring village. Of these individuals 130 appeared to be the descendants of African slaves on the basis of their and their family's physical appearance. Yet only 22 of these 130 people responded yes to the direct question, "¿Tiene usted antepasados africanos?" (Do you have African ancestors?) The results of this survey are indicative of the lack of awareness of Africa in the region.

Claims of African Ancestry

Twelve interviewees told me that they had African ancestry. These individuals ranged in age from twenty to seventy-one, and had varying levels of education—from none to having completed postsecondary education. The respondents' likelihood of affirming that they had African ancestry was not directly related to their level of education. For example, two of the respondents reporting that they had African ancestors had never been to school, five had completed secondary school, two had completed primary school, and three had some school experience but had not completed primary school.

Three of the women, Rosa, Minerva, and Eva, did not know how to read or write. Eva and Rosa are in their fifties, and Minerva, who is known around town as "Señora Negra," is in her early seventies. Eva has been a single mother for many years, although her children have now all grown up, gotten married, and left home. Two of her sons and their children live very close by, and her grandchildren are often around her house. Rosa and Minerva are both married, and their children have also left home. Rosa and Minerva never attended school, and Eva went for only one year.

These women told me that they knew they had African ancestry because their ancestors had been black. For example, Eva said, "La que ha tenido familiar de África ha sido la mamá de mi papá, también ha sido bien negrita." (The one who had family from Africa was my father's mother; she also was quite black.) Rosa and Eva also told me that there had been slavery in Peru, yet they did not know that slaves had been brought over from Africa. When I asked Eva how Africans got to Peru, she told me she did not know. Rosa gave a similar story—her grandmother probably had been from Africa, since she had been very dark-skinned—yet she did not know how Africans had gotten to Peru.

I asked Minerva if she knew how her family had come to live in Ingenio or in this part of Peru, and she told me that she did not know, because "ha sido dejada la gente" (people used to be uninterested). She repeated this assertion several times in her interview, telling me her parents didn't tell her the history of the town or their family because they lacked interest. When I asked her if she had any African ancestry, however, she said yes, she had heard that she had. Nevertheless, she wasn't able to provide me with many details about the Africans in her family. Notably, when I asked Minerva if she had indigenous, European, or Asian ancestry, she assured me that she did not. Thus, she clearly placed her roots in Africa, even if the details surrounding that ancestry were fuzzy.

Rocío, a twenty-five-year old woman who had graduated from high school and gone on to technical college, recounted a slightly different narrative when I asked her whether or not she had African ancestry: "The people who supposedly were the first to arrive in Yapatera were Africans, the first people. And, since we descend from Yapaterans generally, I suppose that yes, then, we have African ancestry."

Rocío traced her ancestry to Yapatera, and hence deduced that she must have African ancestry. Like Rosa, Minerva, and Eva, Rocío did not claim ever to have been told she had African ancestry—she inferred it from other information. This was a common feature in my interviews. Interviewees would say something along the lines of their grandfather had been very dark, so he must have African ancestry. Alternatively, they would say that their relatives came from Yapatera, a place where a lot of Africans arrived, and that therefore they must be of African descent.

This suggests that the stories of African origins are not being passed down in families. Yet some people have had access to information that has led them to conclude that their ancestors were of African descent. For example, someone taught them that Africans are dark-skinned or that Africans arrived in Yapatera, the largest former hacienda in Piura. Others, in contrast, consider themselves to be dark-skinned or black, but do not conclude that their blackness necessarily connects them to Africa.

Claims of Peruvian Ancestry

Diana, Mariana, Antonio, Omar, Alan, Linda, and Reina all graduated from high school in the past ten years, from either the school in Ingenio or the school in Morropón, which, according to some villagers, is better. None of these young people were aware of their connection to Africa or to slavery, despite the fact that most of them learned something about slavery in school. Twenty-five-year-old Mariana, for example, told me she had no idea how her family had come to Ingenio, nor how the hacienda owners or workers had come to be farmers in northern Peru. When I asked her if she had African, indigenous, or Spanish ancestry, she told me she had only Peruvian ancestry. She had no idea that Africans had been brought to Peru.

France Winddance Twine (1998) reports that when she questioned her interviewees in Brazil about their African ancestry, they would sometimes be reduced to tears when asked to talk about their African ancestors. This is not at all the reaction I got in Ingenio. Some of the interviewees were somewhat embarrassed that they could not provide me with more detailed information about their ancestry; they were ashamed of their lack of knowledge, but it did not appear they were trying to hide anything.

A few weeks after my initial interview with Mariana, she came to my house for dinner, and our conversation turned to slavery. I began to recount to her that Africans had been taken from Africa and brought to Peru as slaves. Mariana affirmed that she had never heard that story before. She did not appear upset when I told her that her ancestors were probably among the slaves brought to Peru from Africa. I was a bit cautious in telling her this history, thinking that she might be shocked that her ancestors had been brought to Peru in chains, but she did not seem fazed at all. She just nodded her head, occasionally raised her eyebrows, and continued to eat her soup.

I had a similar experience with Diana. In the initial interview, she denied having African ancestry in response to my question. In a follow-up interview, I questioned her further about her response. (I had given her a transcript of our conversation, and she agreed that the transcript reflected her original intentions.) When I asked Diana if she had African roots, she said no, yet when I asked her if she had black people in her family, she responded, "Negros si, pero, de que sean, de que hayan sido de antecedentes africanas, no sé." (Blacks, yes, but that they had been of African ancestry, I don't know.) I then asked her, "¿Nunca habías pensado que si son negros tienen que haber sido del África, porque, aquí en el Perú no hay . . . ?" (Have you never thought that if they were black, they must have been from Africa, because, here in Peru, there are no . . . ?) Diana interrupted me to say "of course," so I went on to ask her why she had never before thought that her family must be from Africa. She responded that she had just never thought of it that way. Diana, like Rocío, Eva, and Rosa, recognized that her ancestors had been black. Unlike them, however, she did not connect blackness to Africa.

In this conversation, Diana appeared relatively engaged, and her demeanor did not change in any way to indicate that I was making her uncomfortable by pointing out her blackness or by suggesting that, because she and her family were black, she must have African ancestors. She simply got a bit pensive, and agreed that it must be the case that she has African ancestry, but that she had never thought of it before.

If a discourse of shame surrounding Africa and slavery existed in Ingenio, one would expect this to surface at times, especially when people were exchanging insults. Yet in the many hours I spent each day sitting with women on their porches, attending parties and soccer games, and visiting with people in the village, I never heard anyone call someone an African or a slave as an insult. People would call each other dirty or ugly blacks, or use other insults related to skin color or hair texture, but never with reference to slavery or Africa. The insults reveal a discourse of shame with regard to dark skin color, but not with regard to Africa or slavery. It is clearly not the case that people in Ingenio are hiding their affiliation with slavery or Africa; it simply is not part of the local construction of ancestry.

My Great-Grandfather from Spain

Few of my interviewees had direct knowledge of ancestors who had come from outside Peru. The two who did—Alfonso and Olivia—are worth discussing in some detail. Their cases, as exceptions, provide insight into why others construct their own histories as Peruvian.

Alfonso, a retired soldier who never learned to read or write, was eighty-nine when I interviewed him, making him my oldest interviewee.

He recounted the story of his great-grandfather who came to Peru from Spain. Alfonso heard this story from his grandfather, whom he met in 1940, when the latter was 110 years old. Of course, Alfonso may not have had the age exactly right, but even if his grandfather were ninety-five years old in 1940, he would have been able to remember the abolition of slavery in 1854, and could even have met people who had been brought over from Africa. Alfonso however did not mention that his grandfather had told him anything about Africa. In fact, his grandfather told him that his father (Alfonso's great-grandfather) had been Spanish and that his mother had been from Morropón, the village next to Ingenio. Based on Alfonso's physical appearance and that of his relatives, Alfonso's grandfather's mother may well have been an African-descended slave. If his grandfather was born in 1830, as claimed, then we can be fairly certain that his great-grandmother lived during the time of slavery. In addition, Hacienda Morropón at that time had African-descended slaves, albeit very few.

Despite his apparent familial links to Africa, Alfonso told me that his ancestors had not come from Africa. Nevertheless, he was aware that slavery had existed and was connected to Africans. Alfonso told me that he had heard that "antes ha habido el esclavitud de los africanos y se ponían marca." (Earlier there had been slavery of Africans, and they branded them.) He stated that his elders had told him so and also that "los que tenían plata, compraban a los que vienen del África" (those who had money bought people from Africa). Yet, when I asked Alfonso if his ancestors had been among those brought to Peru from Africa, he replied no. Alfonso repeated his story about his grandfather to me, and told me that he had Spanish blood "porque mi bisabuela ha sido morropana y su papá, el padre de mi abuelito, ha sido español; el español se metió con mi abuelita, ya tengo la sangre española" (because my great-grandmother had been from Morropón, and my grandfather's father had been Spanish; the Spaniard got together with my [great]-grandmother, thus, I have Spanish blood).

It is evident Alfonso recognizes that his great-grandmother was not Spanish but Morropana, from Morropón. This is important, because Alfonso does not claim to have purely Spanish ancestry; he recognizes that his great-grandmother was not Spanish. Alfonso did not describe his great-grandmother as Spanish, nor as African or Indian. For him, she was from Morropón. Alfonso's understanding of his great-grandmother's ancestry is based on his grandfather's selective transmission of the family history. Alfonso's grandfather was aware that his father had been born in Spain but evidently knew only that his mother had been born in Peru.

Why did Alfonso's great-grandmother not tell her son her origin story? One possibility is that she was unaware of her own African ancestry. Transported slaves would not have referred to the continent from which they came as Africa if they came over to the Americas before the term *Africa* was prevalent where they came from. Second, if their journey to Peru involved a long layover in the Caribbean, perhaps lasting a generation or more, then the Pacific passage may have erased Africa from their historical memory. African slaves began to be brought to Piura in large numbers at the end of the seventeenth century. In fact, there had been slaves in Piura since the early sixteenth century (Schlüpmann 1994). This means that Alfonso's African-descended ancestors could have been in Peru for four centuries. Over the course of four hundred years, it is not surprising that Africa would or could be forgotten. Alfonso's claim to Spanish ancestry is based on his grandfather's story that his great-grandfather had emigrated from Spain to Peru. Alfonso's African ancestors most likely were brought to Peru centuries before his great-grandfather came.[8]

The only other interviewee who claimed to have direct knowledge of ancestors who had come from another country was Alfonso's cousin's daughter, Olivia. When I asked Olivia, a woman the color of coffee with tightly curled hair, if she had Spanish ancestry, she said no. Apparently, she was not aware that her great-great-grandfather came from Spain. (She shares this relative with Alfonso, on her maternal side.) Her father, a man the color of coffee with coarse black hair, however had told her "that we have Cuban ancestry." Olivia learned from her father that her great-great-grandfather had come over to Peru from Cuba. Yet, she was never told why or how he had come over. In fact, when I asked her why he had come, she replied that she did not know and speculated that perhaps he had come to Peru as a tourist and decided to stay. This is significant, as it suggests that Olivia is unaware of the involuntary nature of her family's migration to Peru. Of note, Olivia also believed that most Cubans were dark-skinned blacks. One day, she recounted to me a story of a black Cuban man and his white wife who arrived on a ship in the port of Paita. She said that the woman was not from Cuba, because she was white, but that the man was.

Olivia's father had told her that there had been slavery in Ingenio, and that this involved the mistreatment of blacks. The fact that Olivia's father was willing to discuss the enslavement and mistreatment of blacks in Ingenio indicates that his story about Cuba was not intended to deny African origins. It seems more likely that Olivia's father, and perhaps even his father before him, was unaware of his African ancestry. African slaves brought to Peru rarely came directly from Africa. After the Atlantic passage, there was always a stop prior to making the Pacific passage. It is conceivable that Olivia's ancestors were slaves brought to Peru from Cuba, and for this reason, only the Cuba story got passed down. Olivia also told me that her last name, Cienfuegos, comes from Cuba. (Cienfuegos is, in fact, a city and a surname in Cuba.)

The selective forgetting I witnessed in Ingenio differs from other similar cases of collective amnesia in Latin America. Losonczy (1999), for example, found in her research in an Afro-Colombian community that the residents there were not aware that they were from Africa nor that they had been enslaved. Losonczy (1999: 17) recounts that the villagers she worked with had invented a new myth of origin that depicts Afro-Colombians as being autochthonous Colombians. She cites as evidence the local mythology, which situates the origin of the distinct racial groups in Colombia in time immemorial. Losonczy's story fits well into the framework presented by Irwin-Zarecka (1994: 120), who writes that "when we speak of forgetting, we are speaking of displacement (or replacement) of one version of the past by another." In contrast to these depictions, the villagers of Ingenio had not created an origin story of how their ancestors got to Peru. Many of my interviewees simply stated that they did not know how or why their ancestors had come to live in Peru.

Twine (1998: 116) found in her study of Afro-Brazilians what she termed "willful forgetting," a strategy of whitening the family tree to disassociate oneself from the shame of slavery. Twine's Afro-Brazilian informants did not wish to divulge their African roots to her because they chose to "willfully forget" slavery. In order to maintain a sense of dignity, her informants intentionally distanced themselves from "the degradation of slavery" by claiming that their ancestors had not been subjected to it. Twine documents that her informants first claimed not to have any African ancestors, or not to have had any enslaved ancestors, then later reluctantly admitted on further questioning that they in fact were aware of having enslaved African ancestors.

The Peruvian case differs from the cases discussed by Twine and Losonczy in that the residents of Ingenio have not made up a story to account for their origins, nor do they seem to be feigning ignorance of African or slave origins in order to gain prestige. Unlike Twine's informants, who pretended to be unaware of their African origins, my informants appear to lack the knowledge that would lead them to conclude that some of their ancestors had been enslaved Africans. Instead, they construct their ancestry as Peruvian. In addition, in both the Brazilian and Colombian cases, both Africa and slavery have disappeared from collective memory, whereas in Ingenio, slavery is very much a part of collective memory. This memory of slavery in Ingenio, however, takes a particular form that is not connected directly to blackness or to Africa.

Remembering Slavery

Slavery is part of the collective memory in Ingenio, yet the discourse surrounding slavery does not refer to chattel slavery in particular. The majority of Ingenieros were not aware that their ancestors came from Africa, and even fewer were aware that chattel slavery was an institution peculiar to Africans and their descendants. This lack of knowledge appears to result from the fact that many residents of Ingenio conflate slavery with sharecropping and other forms of exploitation. When I asked Ingenieros about slavery, most of them told me that slavery had existed well into the twentieth century, but did not define slavery as the ownership of one human being by another. Instead, they defined it as exploitation, as working for little or no wages, as corporal punishment, or as forced labor. These are all conditions that existed in Ingenio well into the twentieth century. They are also conditions that were not particular to African-descended peoples.

When chattel slavery was outlawed, many former slaves continued to work on the same plantations, and their conditions of life changed little. This seems to have been common across Peru: Cuche (1975) presents evidence that some slaves were unaware of manumission and that their lives continued as they had prior to emancipation, and Aguirre (2005) contends that conditions for slaves did not change dramatically after abolition. In Ingenio, this means that the abolition of legal slavery does not appear to be a significant part of the collective memory.

The racial nature of slavery also is not part of the story that villagers told me. In interviews, residents told me that, during the cotton harvests in the 1930s, the hacendados recruited large numbers of indigenous people to pick cotton, since they had experience in that domain. These cotton-pickers largely came from the Peruvian coast and moved into the area of Ingenio closest to the fields and therefore infested with mosquitoes during the rainy season. Despite this residential segregation that to a certain extent persists today, my interviewees never mentioned race in connection with exploitation, or indicated that indigenous people and African-descended people experienced distinct forms of exploitation.

For example, Rosa and Eva were not able to provide me with much information regarding Africa, yet they had vivid stories about what they referred to as slavery. Eva, for example, explained that her grandfather had told her that there had been slavery in Peru, and that it had been very cruel: "This is what my grandfather used to say, that here, people used to like to have people as slaves . . . so that they would work without pay." Rosa had also heard of severe corporal punishment, as the following quotation illustrates:

> Here in this plantation they also say that there was slavery before. . . . They made them work for free. . . . If the plantation owners wanted something, . . . if they wanted you to go and get a stick from the other side of this hill, you had to go do it. And, this was free; and if you didn't go, they would put you in the stockade. . . . They say [the stockade] was a piece of wood, . . . with holes. They made some holes here where your arms fit; it had another hole here where your legs fit, and you would put your leg in there, and then they would close it up and you couldn't get out any more. Here in the neck too. There were two big pieces of wood for the neck, two big boards. . . . They would stay there in the stockade. They say that they would hang them by their legs and their wife had to bring them food, to spoon-feed them. They were there as prisoners.

Rosa and Eva were both born around 1950, and their grandparents had told them these stories in the 1960s. These memories are in all likelihood not from slavery in the 1850s, but from hacienda life in the early twentieth century, when the conditions that Rosa describes were prevalent for tenant farmers. Since they are describing the cruelties that existed under tenant farming up until the 1930s, and are calling that system slavery, it makes sense that they would not connect this story to the African slave trade. In the early twentieth century, this system where workers were treated like animals and forced to work without pay was not exclusive to people of African descent.

For some people, the memory of slavery serves mostly as a way of contextualizing or understanding global capitalism. Felipe, an agricultural worker from Ingenio in his fifties told me that his grandfather had told him that slavery used to exist on the Hacienda Buenos Aires. During that time, the boss would make people work up to fifteen hours a day, and would inflict severe punishments or even kill workers for infractions. I then asked Felipe if he had ever witnessed slavery. He replied that slavery still exists today:

> I think that slavery perhaps still exists because, sometimes, people in the countryside plant their produce, yet the one who has greater benefits is the intermediary, the businessperson, the middleman. In this way, we are practically slaves of others, we plant but we don't sell, and if we do sell, we sell cheaply and others make more profit than we do.

Felipe understands slavery as hyper-exploitation and uses this understanding of slavery and of his past to discuss the hyper-exploitation that currently exists in global capitalism. Notably, he does not use the memory of slavery to identify with other people of African descent in the Americas. Instead, he draws from the memory of slavery to contextualize his current position in the global economy.

In Ingenio, the system of slavery created a particular form of racial domination, yet this is overshadowed today by the history of tenant farming that coexisted with slavery, as well as more than one hundred years of sharecropping that followed chattel slavery. As a result, when people in Ingenio speak of slavery today, they primarily refer to the years prior to the agrarian reform, especially those years before 1934 when the abuse of workers on the hacienda was flagrant.

The way that people in Ingenio remember slavery and the lack of salience they give to Africa reveals the importance of local understandings of race, exploitation, ancestry, and history for the creation of collective memory. A collective memory of abuse and exploitation takes precedence over other possible collective memories, and this is the story most likely to be passed down. The Pacific and Atlantic passages as well as the lives of their ancestors in Africa have not been passed down in families and are not the subject of discussion in the village square.

Conclusion

Ingenio presents an intriguing case insofar as the memory of slavery is alive and well, but for many people, it does not serve to connect them to other blacks. This is because slavery typically is not remembered as something particular to blacks. In the U.S. case, slavery created a unique system of racial domination that is the forerunner of conceptions of race and racism in the contemporary United States. Anthropologist Audrey Smedley (2007: 143) posited that "slavery was seminal to the creation and the development of the idea of race in the North American colonies." The memory of slavery in the United States has played a vital role in the formation of African American collective identity (Eyerman 2004). France Winddance Twine (1998: 123) likewise argues that "memories of African slave ancestors have been an important means for African Americans to establish an antiracist identity in the United States."

People in Ingenio are much more likely to discuss the tenant farming system than chattel slavery. Although most villagers have a remote ancestor who was enslaved, this aspect of their history has faded from their memories. This situation is very different from rural Brazil where Twine (1998) did her fieldwork; slavery was abolished there in 1888, and nearly all of the people she interviewed had a grandparent or great-grandparent who had been enslaved. In Ingenio, no one could remember a family member of theirs who had been enslaved. This is not surprising, given that the Hacienda Morropón had only seven slaves in 1839, and there were likely no more than six hundred slaves in all of Piura at the time of abolition. Thus, although the people of Ingenio could rightly be called descendants of African slaves, their ancestors likely had been freed since the eighteenth century, and more than two hundred years of a different form of exploitation has nearly eliminated the relevance of chattel slavery for locals' understandings of their past.

Within the local history of Ingenio color differences are more salient than ancestral differences. Ingenieros do not think of themselves as being divided into groups depending on whether they have African ancestors, Indian ancestors, or Spanish ancestors. Instead, people are more likely to recall a particularly dark- or light-skinned grandparent and highlight color rather than geographic origins.

In addition, very few residents of Ingenio seemed to be aware that chattel slavery had been particular to Afro-descendants, or that forced labor had worked differently for Africans versus indigenous people in Peru. The fact that my informants conflated slavery with exploitation means not only that they do not think slavery ended in 1854, but also that they do not think that only blacks had been slaves. As such, it makes sense that they would not be aware that Africans had been imported to Peru as slaves, even if they were aware that slavery had existed in Peru. The particular way that ancestry and local history are constructed by residents of Ingenio is a reflection of their particular history, their allegiance to Peru, and their local customs and practices.

This construction of ancestry and its relation to blackness is rooted in the diasporic experience as well as in Latin American discourses on race and racial mixture. In the next chapter, I explore the trajectory of racial discourses at the regional level. Specifically, I consider the distinct roles blackness and indigeneity have played in national discourses across the region.

chapter 2

Locating Black Peruvians
in Latin America

> *su nariz, ligeramente roma, sus labios anabelfos, adelgaza-*
> *dos, . . . y aquellos cabellos suaves, delgados, y discretamente rizos*
> (his nose slightly Roman, his fine, thin lips . . . and those soft,
> thin, discreetly curly locks)
> Enrique López Albújar, describing José Manuel, a mulatto slave

> *de chimpanesco mentón. Su negrura y fealdad al lado de la arro-*
> *gante figura de José Manuel resaltaba enormemente*
> (with an apelike chin. His blackness and ugliness stood in
> marked contrast next to the arrogant face of José Manuel)
> Enrique López Albújar, describing Congo, a black slave

In the first chapter, I explored the presumption that the history of slavery
in Ingenio would give rise to a collective memory of slavery. In this chapter, I consider another common assumption: the presumed importance of
cultural and social (as opposed to physical) attributes for defining race in
Latin America. I argue that, although cultural and social attributes have
been crucial for defining what it means to be Indian in Peru, the same is
not true for blacks. Over the course of the twentieth century, skin color
and facial features, as shown in the epigraphs, have been central to definitions of race for Afro–Latin Americans.

My finding that in Ingenio blackness is understood primarily in terms
of skin color, not in terms of a common history or shared cultural attributes, led me to ask to what extent the same was true for the rest of Peru

and for other countries in Latin America. Notably, the primacy of skin color in Ingenio seems to contradict the widely accepted idea that, in Latin America, nonwhites can be whitened through mestizaje.

In the Peruvian context, mestizaje is described as the process by which Indians can be included in the nation through an abandonment of indigenous cultural forms; there has been very little analysis of blacks' participation in this process. Within Latin American studies more generally, few scholars distinguish between black and Indian participation in mestizaje. Some even insist that these processes are not distinct. For example, Carol Smith (1991), in her insightful essay "The Symbolics of Blood," equates mestizo (white/Indian) with mulatto (white/black) mixture by including both of them under the same rubric of mestizaje. She posits that "a publically identified mestizo can be virtually any biological mixture—from all Indian/African to all European—but must have acquiesced to the dominant 'national' culture, severed kinship ties with community members of non-European culture, and speak Spanish" (505). Her suggestion that a person of primarily African descent can acquiesce to the dominant culture and thereby become mestizo seems implausible in Ingenio for two reasons. First, blackness in Ingenio is defined in terms of skin color, not cultural attributes such as dress or language. Second, most blacks in Ingenio share in the dominant (criollo) culture in Peru, leaving cultural assimilation with little meaning in this context.

How true is this for all of Peru? How do we locate black Peruvians within national discourses when little attention has been paid to them? Does the national discourse on blackness give the same primacy to skin color as the local discourse in Ingenio does? What about in the rest of Latin America? Can we distinguish between the participation of blacks versus Indians in mestizaje in other Latin American countries?

In this chapter, I approach these questions through a historical analysis of nation-making discourses in the late nineteenth and early twentieth centuries, and a discussion of the role of blacks in cultural production during the same period. I argue that, in Peru, blacks and Indians have participated in mestizaje in dissimilar ways, and that this distinction is crucial for understanding how blackness is conceptualized there. In addition, I contend that this situation is not unique to Peru: across Latin America, blacks and Indians have played different roles in mestizaje. Whereas mestizaje for Indians has been more likely to involve acculturation, for blacks it has meant intergenerational whitening.

This chapter highlights the importance of skin color for defining blackness and of cultural attributes for defining indigeneity. Revealing this distinction is important not to uncover a hierarchy of oppression, but to clarify that processes of mestizaje and exclusion work in different ways for blacks and Indians. At the same time, it is crucial to keep in mind that the idea of race is always dependent on notions of both culture and skin color. The idea that an Indian can become a mestizo through education relies on the notion of color even as it denies the importance of color, because being Indian continues to be defined as being nonwhite, and whiteness is based on ideas of skin color. The fact that a light-skinned black can be accepted as a mulatto is also related to culture. The disdain many whites hold for blacks is not attributable to skin color per se, but to the association between dark skin color and certain cultural and social attributes. Thus, color and culture are interdependent and form crucial parts of the idea of race. Nevertheless, discourses of difference for blacks and Indians differ in the extent to which color and cultural differences are made explicit.

The broad overview in this chapter permits me to make some claims with regard to the place of blacks in Latin American national narratives. The analyses in this chapter focus on a particular time—roughly 1870 to 1940—the period of nation making in Latin America. Across Latin America during this time, intellectual and political elites preoccupied themselves with building national unity and attempting to present their countries as modern nations (Knight 1990). In this project, they had to contend with European scholars who denounced the racial degeneracy of these fledgling nations (Stepan 1991). Their response to these claims was that their nations were progressing towards whiteness through mestizaje. This consideration of how political and intellectual elites talked and wrote about blacks and Indians in the late nineteenth and early twentieth centuries uncovers the different ways that blacks and Indians have been viewed as potential participants in mestizaje in Latin America during the time when national elites were conceiving their ideas of nationhood. Indian participation in cultural mestizaje usually has meant either the exaltation of ancestral Indians or the acceptance of Indians without their indigenous cultures. For blacks, mestizaje has meant either the elimination of blacks or their progressive whitening through interracial unions.

The prominence of the mestizaje discourse in Latin America was a response to the importance given to racial differences in scientific thought at the time. As Latin American intellectuals were engaging in transnational debates about modern nation building, European intellectuals were developing theories of racial difference based on novel scientific techniques and modes of analysis. Latin Americans could not simply ignore these debates, in part because Europeans such as Paul Broca and Gustav le Bon used Latin American racial hybridism as proof of the degenerative effects of miscegenation, and also because these debates were central to scientific and medical discussions as a whole in the late nineteenth and early twentieth centuries (Stepan 1991). Latin Americans countered European intellectuals' insistence on their racial degeneracy with claims that racial mixture would lead to progress.

Latin American intellectuals argued that mestizaje not only was beneficial, but also was the hallmark of Latin American nations. According to this logic, the felicitous mixture of Iberians with other races is what made countries such as Mexico, Cuba, and Brazil great nations. This mixture, embodied in the trope of mestizaje, played out differently in terms of the inclusion or exclusion of blacks and Indians in national imaginaries. I discuss these discourses of race and race mixture in a variety of Latin American settings, starting with Peru, the central focus of this study. This comparative approach is useful for understanding the dynamics of racial exclusion in Latin America because it highlights the polysemic nature of mestizaje. This comparison of the situation of blacks in Peru versus other Latin American countries sheds light on the extent to which national storylines of race and racial mixture affect the position of citizens of African descent in Latin America.

Peru: The (Un)importance of Skin Color

Peru gained its independence from Spain in 1821. Efforts to build this new nation after independence often were troubled by what came to be known as the "Indian problem." The presence and lack of integration of a very large indigenous population gnawed at intellectuals and politicians intent on cobbling together a unified nation. Juan Bustamante, a mestizo politician from Puno, for example, urged the state to build schools in the highlands in order that Indian children would learn Spanish and adopt modern ways. Although Bustamante was stoned to death in 1868, his "civilizing program soon became the centerpiece of reform under Manuel Pardo (1872–6). This new 'civilista' coalition of coastal oligarchs, intellectuals, and politicians launched the first state-directed civilizing project in the

Indian sierra" (Larson 2004: 159). This project, aimed at de-Indianizing Peru through the Hispanicization of indigenous people, was unsuccessful insofar as it did not gain enough support to have a widespread impact. It did, however, lay the "discursive groundwork for the prevailing 'assimilationist paradigm' that later would drive Lima-based projects of *indigenismo* in the 1910s and 1920s" (Larson 2004: 161).

The severity of the Indian problem became clear to Peruvian leaders after Peru's defeat in the War of the Pacific against Chile (1879–1883). Many elites became convinced that, had Indians been better incorporated into the nation, Peru would not have lost the war. In addition, the war was followed by a series of indigenous uprisings that threatened Peru's sovereignty. These two factors led to debates among the Creole elite concerning the indigenous population. Some Creole intellectuals drew from biological determinism to point to the irredeemable nature of Indians, while others argued that Indian backwardness could be overcome through assimilation programs. The latter group of intellectuals, known as neo-positivists, proclaimed that Peru would be able to move forward as a nation only if Indians were assimilated (Davies 1973; Larson 2004). In response, in the early twentieth century, the Peruvian government poured funds into the Ministry of Education and Health to "civilize the countryside and improve their lives by incorporating [Indians and mestizos] into the national community" (de la Cadena 2005: 271). The state investment in rural education increased 16.5 times between 1900 and 1929. These funds may have reached rural black communities, but the explicit intention of these projects was to civilize Indians through education (de la Cadena 2005). Peruvian elites perceived Indians to be potential citizens of Peru who, with education, could participate in the modernization of the state. Scholars of race and culture in Peru characterize these assimilation programs as cultural mestizaje, as they were designed to transform indios into mestizos.

The debate surrounding the black population in Peru did not indicate that blacks could become citizens through education, and although many blacks lived in the countryside, they were not the targets of these reform projects. Instead, blacks were "imagined out" of the nation over the course of about one hundred years. In 1790, 46 percent of the Limeño population was of African descent. In 1884, there were 18,320 blacks and mulattos in Lima—18 percent of the population (Cuche 1981), yet by 1908 there were 6,763 blacks in Lima—less than 1 percent of the Limeño population (Stokes 1987). Although there may have been declines in black fertility or increases in black mortality, this precipitous decrease in the black population was not simply a product of demographic decline but a consequence of efforts to downplay the numbers of blacks in Peru. More importantly, it was indicative of very different discourses surrounding the place of blacks and Indians in the Peruvian nation. Indians were to be educated; blacks were to disappear.

The idea that Indians could or should integrate culturally entailed the assumption that Indians were culturally distinct from other Peruvians. In contrast, Peruvian intellectuals saw blacks as culturally proximate to whites. For example, leading modernist thinker Manuel González Prada noted the historical sexual and cultural alliances between blacks and whites, which contrasted with whites' relations with Indians. Whereas blacks lived on the coast, close to whites, Indians lived far away in the highlands. González Prada saw Indians as the future of Peru, whereas he viewed blacks as a relic of the colonial past. For González Prada, Indians were in need of cultural improvement, whereas the nation would be better off without blacks, culturally improved or not.

Peruvian intellectuals engaged in a series of debates in their efforts to better the nation by improving its racial composition, which they equated with solving the Indian problem. The role of blacks in the nation was notably absent from nearly all of these debates. Peruvian intellectuals used the analytical tools available to them in the early twentieth century—namely, positivism, social Darwinism, and scientific racism—to take stock of the Indian problem. Within Peru, the debates were often between the Cuzqueños (highland intellectuals) and the Limeños (Creole elite). Cuzqueño elites were proud of their Incan heritage and racial purity (de la Cadena 2000). Rather than endorsing racial mixture in hopes of whitening the nation, as other Latin Americans did, Andean cultural nationalists emphasized the "redemptive renderings of racial purity . . . in the 'authentic Indian'" (Larson 2004: 68). In contrast, Limeño elites typically believed that Indians should discard their "backward culture" in order to become Peruvians (de la Cadena 2000; Larson 2004). Peruvian scholars have described the process advocated by Limeño elites as cultural mestizaje where, through education and socialization, the Indian became a Peruvian. For Limeño elites, the alleged backwardness of Indians could be solved through educational programs. Thus, for Indians, race was redefined in cultural terms. And, cultural features could be changed.

Andean intellectuals and Creole elites agreed that skin color was not a key determinant of racial status in Peru. In 1909, Javier Prado, a well-known Limeño positivist philosopher declared, "Thanks to education, the contemporary man can transform his physical milieu and even his race" (quoted in de la Cadena 1998: 146). Prado was voicing what was a popular conception at the time—that individuals could overcome their racial origins through education, that intellectuals could become racially unmarked and thereby whitened. Similarly, Manuel González Prada, also a Limeño, contested the ideas of Gustav le Bon in his work *Nuestros indios* (1986 [1904]). González Prada found unconvincing and even unscientific the idea that white skin conferred intellectual superiority. He also pointed out that, in Peru, white skin did not mean racial purity, since Peruvian Creoles were mixed with Indians and blacks, even if their white skin would suggest otherwise. In a similar fashion, Luis E. Valcárcel (1891–1987), a well-known social scientist who graduated from the University of Cuzco in 1913, posited in 1914 that "receiving a professional degree is a dignity that erases stigmas of origin" (quoted in de la Cadena 2000: 44). These conversations were ostensibly about race, yet the primary focus of racial betterment was Indians, and the focus of the debate was cultural, not phenotypical. Cuzqueño and Limeño elites were in agreement that education could serve to unmark Indians racially, and thus to whiten them.

This idea that Indians were in need of cultural and moral uplift also could be seen in the realm of state policy and investment. In the early twentieth century, the Peruvian government poured considerable sums of money into indigenous education, with the hope that education would uplift the moral standing of the Indian population (de la Cadena 2005). Similar programs were implemented in Mexico and Ecuador. Nowhere in Latin America, however, was money invested in improving the education of Afro–Latin Americans. Instead of being the beneficiaries of educational outlays, blacks across Latin America were proclaimed to be disappearing. Lima and Buenos Aires saw substantial declines in their black populations, and similar predictions were made for Brazil and Cuba, among other countries.

Imagining Mestizaje

The intellectual debates about Indians that I review here have been extensively analyzed by a series of scholars, including anthropologists like Marisol de la Cadena and historians like Brooke Larson. These scholars describe the modernization programs directed at Indians as part of Peruvian cultural mestizaje. The position of blacks is rarely mentioned; the absence of debate regarding blacks during the nation-making period in Peru is thus reinforced in the scholarly literature. To the extent that blacks are mentioned in academic debates, it is usually to mention in passing that blacks were not included in nation-making discourses in Peru.

There is a notable presence of blacks in cultural production during the same period. Unfortunately, we do not have the benefit of a series of intellectual debates on the place of blacks in literature during this time. A notable exception is Marcel Velázquez Castro's *Las mascaras de la representación* (2005). Although Velázquez Castro only analyzes texts up until 1895, his work is very useful insofar as it pays particular attention to the place of blacks in the white Peruvian imaginary.

Without the benefit of existing scholarly analysis of the role of blacks in early twentieth-century Peruvian literature, I have had to rely on primary sources for this era. A review of turn-of-the-twentieth-century cultural production assures us that Peruvian elites were in fact concerned about the presence of blacks in the nation, as literary figures often engaged with the Afro-Peruvian population in their writings. These texts show some of the subtler ways that blacks existed in the elite imaginary. This use of literary texts alongside scholarship must however be done with caution, as the texts are, after all, fictional representations of Peruvian life. Nevertheless, to the extent that we can uncover patterns in these narratives, the texts provide us with unique insights into how blacks were imagined in the late nineteenth and early twentieth centuries. As Néstor García Canclini points out in *La globalización imaginada* (1999), to understand the complexities and intricacies of modern life, we must analyze cultural texts in addition to intellectual production, since life itself is not only lived but also imagined in many different ways.

One tendency in the works of Peruvian literary figures of the time is an idealization of mulattos alongside the denigration of blacks. For example, in *Salto atrás* (1888), by José Antonio de Lavalle, the main character is a young marquis who does not know that his biological father was a slave. His birth was the consequence of his mother having been raped by a slave, a secret she had never revealed. After the marquis marries, his wife gets pregnant and their child is black. When the marquis sees the child, he "violently throws the horrible creature" down (cited in Velázquez Castro 2005: 160). This act is at once a rejection and a denial of the marquis' hidden blackness. When the marquis goes to tell his mother what happened, she tells him, "Si ella ha parido un negro es porque tú eres un mulato: ha habido salto atrás y nada más." (If she gave birth to a black, it is because you are a mulatto: there was a leap backwards, and nothing more) (cited in Velázquez Castro 2005: 160). *Salto atrás* is the term used in eighteenth-century *casta* paintings and hierarchies to describe one of the many possible mixtures of Africans and Spaniards. The language José Antonio de Lavalle uses is revealing in that his denigration of the dark-skinned baby can be contrasted with how he describes a quadroon (person with one-quarter black ancestry) in another story as "a refined product of the mixture of the black and white races" (cited in Velázquez Castro 2005: 163). Similarly, Ricardo Palma (1833–1919), author of *Tradiciones peruanas* (1872), gives preference to mulattos in his works. In fact, only mulattos, never blacks, are central figures in Palma's works, and only mulatto men, not black men, are the objects of white women's desire (Velázquez Castro 2005).

In Velázquez Castro's (2005) analyses of literary works from this time, he finds a fascination among Peruvian writers with the slaves' physicality, which both seduces and evokes fear, as well as with the alleged sexual vigor of black men and women. There is much less emphasis on blacks' cultural or social differences—in large part because blacks and whites shared similar cultural attributes. According to Velázquez Castro, blacks' cultural life in Peru was part of the popular culture of the time, and thus not very different from the cultural traditions of the white elite.

Moving into the early twentieth century, the preference for mulattoes over blacks does not fade. Moreover, this preference continues to parallel the distinction between unacculturated slaves directly from Africa (referred to as bozales) and those that had been raised in Spain or the Americas (referred to as criollos). This remains evident in Peruvian literature well into the twentieth century. Velázquez Castro (2005: 181) argues that Ricardo Palma's "La emplazada" (1874) "is a direct predecessor to *Matalaché*. In *Matalaché*, when José Manuel [a mulatto] is described, the author highlights his physical beauty, which distinguishes him from other blacks." *Matalaché* (1928) is particularly relevant for my purposes, as the author, Enrique López Albújar, is perhaps the best-known novelist from Piura, and certainly one of the few Morropanos who have risen to national fame. In fact, one of the butcher shops in Morropón today bears the name Matalaché.

The central character in *Matalaché* is José Manuel, a mulatto slave, and the novel is set in Piura at the end of the colonial era, in 1816. López Albújar describes José Manuel as follows:

> Física y espiritualmente José Manuel era el negro menos negro de los esclavos de La Tina. Su tipo, su porte, cierto espíritu de orden e iniciativa y un marcado sentimiento de altivez diferenciábale grandemente de la negrada. (Physically and spiritually, José Manuel was the least black of the blacks among the La Tina slaves. His appearance, his comportment, a certain spirit of order and initiative and a notable feeling of self-worth differentiated him greatly from the other blacks.)

López Albújar also describes him as being physically attractive, and as generally conforming to European standards of beauty: "su nariz, ligeramente roma, sus labios anabelfos, adelgazados, . . . y aquellos cabellos suaves, delgados, y discretamente rizos" (his nose slightly Roman, his fine, thin lips . . . and those soft, thin, discreetly curly locks) (López Albújar 2005 [1928]: 52). In fact, José Manuel's physical and intellectual closeness to whiteness—his *cumananas* (poems) were a work of genius, for example— is what allowed María de la Luz, his master's beautiful young daughter, to fall in love with him. José Manuel's good looks and intelligence are further highlighted in contrast to another slave, referred to only as "Congo." Congo is described as "de chimpanesco mentón. Su negrura y fealdad al lado de la arrogante figura de José Manuel resaltaba enormemente" (with an ape-like chin. His blackness and ugliness stood in marked contrast next to the arrogant face of José Manuel) (López Albújar 2005 [1928]: 28). Unlike José Manuel, who was the wonderful product of mixture, this other slave was a pure Congo, who could barely speak Spanish and had an "ignoble, bestial" voice compared to José Manuel's "pure" voice. Notably, Congo not only serves as a constant reminder of the distasteful nature of pure blackness, but also is responsible for letting María de la Luz's father know about the forbidden love affair. Upon finding out about the intimate relations between José Manuel and his daughter, Don Juan Francisco throws José Manuel into a vat full of burning lye. The symbolism of this ending episode is clear. It is José Manuel's blackness, represented in the figure of Congo, that makes this affair unacceptable; thus Congo is the one to reveal this secret. By throwing José Manuel into a vat of soap mixture, Don Juan

LOCATING BLACK PERUVIANS IN LATIN AMERICA ⤮ 69

Francisco not only saves his daughter from disgrace by killing her mulatto lover, but cleanses, even whitens, José Manuel in his last moments.

This representation of blacks as repulsive and of mulattos, quadroons, and octoroons as having some redeeming qualities is evident in *Matalaché* and *Salto atrás*, as well as in the works of Ricardo Palma. The fact that blacks of unmixed African heritage are consistently portrayed negatively whereas blacks of mixed parentage are sometimes depicted in a positive light points to the importance of mixed blood for a positive perception of blacks. This importance of miscegenation contrasts with portrayals of Indians, who can be redeemed through education alone.

In all of these works, the main subject of mestizaje is male. Education and cultural improvement are primarily intended for Indian men. The most salient differences between blacks and mulattos are between men. Congo, a black male, is juxtaposed to José Manuel, a mulatto male. Both are portrayed as threatening to María de la Luz's purity—embodied in her white sexuality. Gender and sexuality provide prominent subtexts to these discussions, as is common in discussions of race and ethnicity everywhere (Nagel 2003).

Living Mestizaje

In addition to these fictional representations, there were two well-known men of African descent in nineteenth- and twentieth-century Peru who would seem to provide evidence for the claim that skin color was not necessarily an obstacle to upward mobility. The first was José Manuel Valdés, the "light complexioned mulatto" (Romero and Cook 1942: 301) who despite his African ancestry was able in 1806 to obtain a *real cédula*, a license from the king of Spain, to practice medicine. The second was Ricardo Palma, a canonical figure in Peruvian literature whose mother was a quadroon, making him an octoroon (one-eighth black). Marcel Velázquez Castro (2005) tells us that it was well known at the time that Palma had black ancestry, yet that it was not given much importance.

This idea that skin color was not important for determining racial status continued to be promulgated throughout the twentieth century. Jorge Basadre (1903–1980), a renowned Peruvian historian, wrote in 1948, "In Peru, . . . color does not prevent an aborigine, *mestizo*, or negroid from occupying high positions if they can accumulate wealth or achieve political success" (quoted in de la Cadena 1998: 143). Notably, even though Basadre and others write that skin color is not important, the only individuals of African descent who have risen to prominence in Peruvian literature and politics have been light-skinned men. These examples render evident the importance of (light) skin color for people of African descent in Peru. Although it may be the case that physical appearance was not important for assessing the intellectual and moral characteristics, or even the racial status, of people of indigenous descent in nineteenth- and twentieth-century Peru, the fascination and repulsion associated with black skin color have ensured that this was not the case for black Peruvians. Black Peruvians, or those individuals of visible African descent, have not been found among the political and intellectual elite of Peruvian society, at least not until very recently, and then only in very limited capacities.

The trend in literary works to portray only light-skinned blacks favorably, alongside the fact that only light-skinned people of African descent have risen to prominence in Peru, provides evidence that skin color does matter in terms of passing judgment on African-descended Peruvians. Thus, for most blacks, whitening through racial mixture is possible, but whitening through cultural mixture alone is not. This situation is quite distinct from the case of indigenous Peruvians, who can be racially unmarked through education alone.

Peru in the Context of Latin America

In Peru, indigeneity is defined by culture: speaking Quechua and wearing rubber sandals make you an Indian. Thus, a person can become "de-Indianized" (de la Cadena 2000) through acquiring dominant cultural norms. Blackness, in contrast, is not defined through these sorts of cultural tropes, but in terms of physical appearance. Blacks cannot become de-blackened through adopting dominant cultural forms. This fundamental difference between the ways that blackness and indigeneity are defined in Peru points to the need to reconceptualize the idea of mestizaje in order to distinguish between black and Indian incorporation and avoid conflating cultural assimilation with miscegenation.

Moreover, since mestizaje is a central trope in racial discourses in Latin America, it is also necessary to explore the extent to which mestizaje works differently for blacks and Indians across the region. The following discussion builds on the work of scholars who argue that Latin American countries can be divided into Afro–Latin America, mestizo America, and Euro-America. Afro–Latin America includes countries where blackness has played a prominent role in constructions of national identity, including Brazil and Cuba. Mestizo America encompasses those countries, such as Peru, Ecuador, and Bolivia, where the national discourse focuses primarily on the distinction between Indians and mestizos. Finally, Euro-America refers to countries such as Argentina, Uruguay, and Chile that do not include blacks or Indians as part of their national discourses, despite having historical and contemporary presences of these populations (Andrews 1980; Harris 1964; Mörner 1967; Sue and Golash-Boza 2009; Wade 1997).

An examination of late nineteenth- and early twentieth-century racial discourses in Latin America reveals that Latin American elites generally accepted the idea of white superiority and black and indigenous inferiority, and that questions of race mixture were at the forefront of intellectual thought at the time. This analysis also provides evidence for a lack of consensus with regard to the value of black and Indian contributions to the nation; yet, to the extent that blacks were accepted, it was as mulattos, whereas Indians were sometimes heralded for their racial purity and at other times accepted as mestizos (whitened Indians). The discussion of the differences and similarities between racial discourses shows that mestizaje and blanqueamiento were indeed widespread but did not mean the same thing for blacks and Indians. This, in turn, demonstrates the importance of distinguishing between mestizaje as assimilation or acculturation (as seen for indios in Peru) and mestizaje as interracial unions and whitening through intermarriage (as seen for blacks in Brazil and Cuba).

Locating Afro–Latin Americans in Discourses of Mestizaje

Across Latin America, blacks have been imagined out of most nations. This process has happened in two distinct ways. The first is the construction of national statistics to show an absence of blacks in the country. The second is to claim that, through mixture, blacks have been incorporated into the nation as mulattos. Both of these strategies allude to mestizaje, understood as racial mixture that usually leads to whitening.

In the Caribbean countries and in Brazil, discussions of blacks as contributors to the nation have been much more prevalent than in the rest of Latin America, reflecting the demographic realities and the history of large slave plantations in these nations. Nevertheless, these discourses have been accompanied by racelessness agendas, which have downplayed African contributions to national identity, as well as whitening agendas, which have presented whites as the superior component of the race-mixture recipe.

Cuba gained its independence from Spain in 1898 only to be occupied by the United States until 1902. The U.S. occupation and the prominence of discussions about the race of Cubans among U.S. officials made it very difficult for Cubans to ignore the scientific racism prevalent in its northern neighbor at the turn of the twentieth century. U.S. intellectuals decried both the high level of racial mixture and the large percentage of blacks in Cuba. For them, these factors were inimical to progress. Cuban intellectuals responded with positive assessments of Cubanness. These claims took two forms: (1) the allegation that Cuba would be whitened through immigration, and (2) a valorization of the black contribution to Cuba (de la Fuente 2001).

The politician Francisco Figueras promulgated the idea that Cuba would be whitened through immigration. In his 1907 work *Cuba y su evolución colonial,* he argued that blacks eventually would be absorbed by the superior white race, although this process might take several generations. Figueras's work is one example of how Latin American intellectuals adapted the positivist and scientific racist thinking of their time into a discourse that allowed for progress in their racially mixed nations. Figueras proposed that Cuba would be able to move forward as a nation primarily because blacks eventually would disappear. This process was put into action by promoting immigration from Spain to Cuba.

The first Cuban government after independence subsidized immigration from Europe to whiten the Cuban population. Between 1902 and 1907, 128,000 Spaniards migrated to Cuba (Helg 1990; Bronfman 2003). Although by 1929 approximately 900,000 Spaniards and Canary Islanders had migrated to Cuba, these immigrants did not succeed in outnumbering the black and mulatto populations. As it became increasingly evident that the whitening project was bound to fail, there began to be more evidence of a valorization of blackness in Cuba. This valorization, however, tended to take the form of a celebration of mixed race and of the contribution of blacks to the *mulatto* nation. The emergence of the *mulato* (or *mulata*) as Cuba's symbol of national identity did not occur until the 1920s, with the writings of Fernando Ortiz and Nicolás Guillén (Arnedo 2001; de la Fuente 2001; Helg 1990).

The Afro-Cuban writer Nicolás Guillén exalted the mulata and mulato as fundamental assets to *cubanía*. Guillén wrote in 1931: "I believe that we won't have a well-developed Creole poetry if we forget the black. The black—in my judgment—provides essential ingredients in our cocktail" (cited in Miller 2004: 48). This reference to a cocktail is, importantly, a reference to mestizaje (or *mulataje,* in this case). In much of his poetry, Guillén makes positive references to racial mixture, although he does so without denigrating the black element. For Guillén, the mulata (more than the mulato) served as an icon of national identity (Arrizón 2002). This can be seen in his 1934 poem *Los dos abuelos,* in which he pays homage to two grandfathers—one white, the other black. This representation of two different racial extractions leading to mulatto offspring is indicative of the fact that mulataje is not a reference to cultural mixture but to interracial unions.

In contrast to the acceptance of mulattoes, any efforts to put forth Africanness or pure blackness as the symbol of cubanía were unsuccessful. The mulato and mulata were much more palatable to the Cuban public. Guillén plays on this a bit in his 1930 poem *Mulata,* where he tells a mulata he knows she is not interested in him because of his blackness, but that she need not worry because he is happy with his negra. His references to the mulata's physical appearance in this poem again point to the importance of physical features for defining blackness. Notably, although Cuba mounted programs to expand education in the early twentieth century, Cubans did not argue that these programs would whiten or de-blacken Cuba, as Peru did for its indigenous education programs.

In Brazil, the pattern was similar—efforts at whitening though immigration were followed by an acceptance and celebration of racial mixture. After the abolition of slavery in 1888, with a large ex-slave and free black and mulatto population, and under the specter of scientific racism, the Brazilian government openly promoted whitening through European immigration. In addition, the government put its money where its mouth was by paying immigrants' passage to Brazil. In the four decades after emancipation, more than two million European immigrants arrived in São Paulo alone, nearly a million of whom had their passages paid for by the national government (Andrews 1991: 54).

Despite substantial immigration, Brazil never transformed itself into a white nation. North American and European intellectuals lamented Brazil's large nonwhite population and predicted a dim future for the country. In response, Brazilian intellectuals developed ideas of racial progress. This new ideology put forth the mulatto as Brazil's hope for the future. Through whitening, Brazil would be able to progress from black to mulatto to white. By the early twentieth century, Brazilian scholars were confident in reporting that the whitening of Brazil was well under way and that concerns about inferior racial elements could be quelled (Skidmore 1990).

Brazilian intellectuals accepted European ideas of white superiority, but rejected the notion that racial mixture was degenerative and argued that Brazil was becoming a white nation through mestizaje. Sílvio Romero (1851–1915), one of Brazil's foremost literary critics of the late nineteenth century, was heavily influenced by European positivism. Romero thus had to deal with the paradox of believing in the possibility of Brazilian progress while accepting European theories that consigned Brazil to doom on the basis of its racially mixed population. To resolve this, Romero adapted positivism to the Brazilian reality and did not fully adopt the tenets of scientific racism, particularly those that deemed interracial unions to be degenerative. Instead, Romero proclaimed the mestizo—the mixture of the black, white, and Indian—to be the prototypical Brazilian and the person best suited to Brazil's tropical climate. Nevertheless, Romero could not fully escape scientific racism insofar as he predicted that hybridity would lead to whiteness. Many Brazilian thinkers embraced this whitening theory, as it provided them with an ideological framework for the nation-building project (Eakin 1985). At the same time, scholars such as the lawyer and historian Oliveira Vianna were able to demonstrate that the white population was increasing. Comparing the 1872 and 1890 censuses, Vianna argued that whites had increased from 38 to 44 percent of the Brazilian population, while blacks fell from 20 percent to less than 15 percent (Skidmore 1990).

This self-appraisal as a whitening nation was accompanied by the rise of some individuals of African descent into the elite, including the writer Joaquim Maria Machado de Assis and the scientist Juliano Moreira. Some prominent Brazilians saw the mulatto element as acceptable insofar as it was a temporary waypoint on the road to racial whitening, whereas others, such as Octavio Domingues, argued that the success of some mulattos was proof that constructive miscegenation was viable and that mulattos were not inferior to whites (Stepan 1991).

One of the first Brazilian literary works to celebrate mixture was *O mulato*, by Aluisio Azevedo, published in 1881. Marchant (2000) argues that this novel is a reflection of Azevedo's efforts to reconcile Brazilian social reality with European scientific racism, similar to Cuba's efforts to reconcile its situation with U.S. biological racism. Azevedo's main character, Raimundo, is a mulatto who is in all ways an admirable person and who does not realize he is a mulatto until he reaches adulthood. Whereas Azevedo describes Raimundo as being refined and of elegant stature, he refers to a black woman (*uma preta*) in the novel as tragically ugly, and several times describes blacks as dirty. Raimundo's physical attractiveness and educational achievements, despite his origins, demonstrate the possibility that Brazil can become whitened through racial mixture. This celebration of mixture became the hallmark of Brazilian-ness and reached its apex in the work of Gilberto Freyre. By the time Freyre published *Casa grande e senzala* in 1933, he was able to affirm that the racial heterogeneity of Brazilian society was a tremendous benefit to the country and should be a source of pride.

In both Brazil and the Caribbean, the positive assessments of blackness appear primarily in the literary arena, rather than in official government policies or institutions (Wade 1997). Like Nicolás Guillén, the Puerto Rican Palés Matos and the Dominican Manuel del Cabral often portray the mulato and mulata positively in their writings, although "intellectuals in the islands . . . [f]requently focus on the body of the mulatta as the quintessential site of felicitous mixture" (Miller 2004: 47), indicating that these portrayals certainly are not free from stereotypes of black female sexuality. In any case, the presence of the mulata as the "synonym of *mestizaje*" and even perhaps as the "symbol of national identity" (Miller 2004: 46) in some parts of the Caribbean (and to some extent in Brazil) makes those regions very distinct from the rest of Latin America, where people of African descent are typically invisible.

The Colombian and Venezuelan cases are also worth mentioning here, as they do not fit neatly into the paradigm of Indian or mulatto exaltation, yet the mulatto and the black were not completely excluded from considerations of nation building, as they were in countries such as Mexico, Nicaragua, and El Salvador. In Colombia, the work of Manuel Zapata Olivella is clearly part of the *mulatez* literary movement, as is the work of the Venezuelan Ramón Díaz Sánchez. Zapata Olivella differs from other writers in this movement in that he is more prone to write about the indigenous element in his work, given the relatively strong indigenous presence in Colombia and his personal familial connections to the European, indigenous, and African roots of Colombia.

Notably, in Colombia, blacks and Indians are both included in the nation-making project, but only as potential recruits for the racial mixture that is the essence of the country (Wade 1993). Indians hold a slightly privileged place in elite conceptions of national identity insofar as the mestizo manifestation of mixture is preferable to the mulatto. Nevertheless, Indians are not emblems of national identity in Colombia, as they are in Mexico and Peru. By the same token, African origins have not been valorized in Colombia (or in Venezuela) to the extent they have been in Brazil and Cuba. Similar to Peruvians, Colombians are likely to consider blacks to be fellow Colombian citizens who share a common culture with most Colombians, whereas Indians are perceived as having a distinct culture.

Argentine intellectuals were less likely to embrace mixture. Most leading intellectuals in late nineteenth- and early twentieth-century Argentina were proponents of positivism and used those theories to develop their ideas. Domingo Faustino Sarmiento (1811–1888), an Argentine writer and statesman, fully embraced nineteenth-century European positivism and developed his own ideas for improving the Argentine race. Notably, Sarmiento saw racial mixture as regressive when it involved whites and Indians, yet progressive when it involved whites and blacks. This is in line with the thought of Carlos Octavio Bunge (1875–1918), an Argentine sociologist who argued in *Nuestra América: ensayo de psicología social* (1903) that African blood "blends admirably with the Spanish" (quoted in Martínez-Echazábal 1998: 26). The Argentine intellectual José Ingenieros (1877–1925) had less confidence in the redeeming powers of mestizaje and believed that inferior races would simply die out (Martínez-Echazábal 1998). These writers shared a desire to improve Argentina and saw the presence of nonwhites as a fundamental problem for the future of the nation. None of them believed that blacks or Indians could be incorporated culturally into Argentina. Those who believed in constructive miscegenation argued that blacks could blend with whites to improve the (black) race.

The White Ideal: Moving toward Whiteness in Latin America

Some Latin American countries have been willing to embrace their indigenous pasts. Others have celebrated mulataje. In contrast, leaders in countries such as Argentina and the Dominican Republic have made their best efforts to present themselves to the international community and to themselves as white nations. For demographic reasons, Argentina was much more successful than the Dominican Republic in this endeavor.

Argentina was not unique in its aspirations to become a white nation in the early twentieth century—but it was unique in its ability to convince itself as well as onlookers of its having become a white nation. In 1906, the U.S. President Theodore Roosevelt lauded Argentina's economic success, attributing it to both "the 'purity of the blood' and the 'superiority of the race'" (Zimmerman 1992: 30). The Argentine minister at the time, Joaquín V. González, also espoused the view that Argentina had the "enormous advantage of not having inferior ethnic elements in her population" (cited in Zimmerman 1992: 30). One wonders how the African and indigenous elements could have disappeared from the Argentine population in fifty years. In Buenos Aires in 1852, 34 percent of the population was labeled black or colored. In the same year, 125,000 Argentines out of 816,000 were classified as black or colored (Hoetink 1967). This case bears striking parallels to the situations in Nicaragua and El Salvador, where the indigenous populations were imagined away over the course of a couple of generations, and in Peru, where the black population precipitously declined between 1884 and 1908.

As in other Latin American countries, Argentine national elites promoted the whitening of the country through massive immigration from Europe. What distinguished Argentina from Brazil and Cuba, however, was their apparent ability to whiten their population. Their relative success was in part imagined, but in part real—more than three million European immigrants arrived in Argentina between 1880 and 1930, predominantly from Spain and Italy (Helg 1990). In proportional terms, this was the largest influx experienced by any country in the Americas during that time, and Europeans soon outnumbered blacks. Even though some Argentine elites would have preferred Nordic or Anglo-Saxon immigration, the eugenicists in Argentina eventually were able to come to terms with their Latin identity, and focused their criticisms on other unwelcome elements—Jews, Syrians, Asians, and people of African descent. It is worth noting here that a distinction was also made between undesirable eastern Europeans and unwanted mulattos and zambos. For example, the Argentine eugenicist Carlos Bernaldo de Quirós spoke out against the inclusion of eastern

Europeans on the basis of cultural incompatibility, yet referred to the racial incompatibility of mulattos and zambos (Stepan 1991: 140–42).

Cultural mestizaje in Argentina primarily involved the fusion of Spanish and Italian culture into Argentine criollo culture. Yet there is one famous example—the tango—that was once associated with Afro-Argentine culture but has come to be the epitome of what it means to be Argentinean. At this point, tango has lost all acknowledgment of its origins as a product of African cultures and has been "refashioned as the elite global signifier of white" Argentina (Miller 2004: 94). This shows that cultural mestizaje is possible insofar as it succeeds in erasing the African elements and whitening their cultural forms, just as the nation itself has been whitened. Whereas this whitening is possible for black cultural forms, it is not necessarily so for black individuals, who cannot be whitened through assimilation alone.

The Dominican Republic shared with Argentina the aspiration to present itself as a nation with no "inferior" ethnic elements. Despite a long history of a slave economy, political leaders in the Dominican Republic claimed to have no blacks. The Dominican Republic had more trouble convincing onlookers of its whiteness than did Argentina. In 1871, a commission of inquiry reported to the U.S. president that "white blood preponderates largely in Dominica, but pure whites, in the popular sense of the word, are not numerous. The majority are of a mixed race nearer white than black" (quoted in Robarge 2004: 126).

The leaders of the Dominican Republic in the late nineteenth century embarked on a campaign to make the nation whiter. One aspect of this effort was immigration, and the government sent ambassadors to Europe in 1879 and 1880 to promote immigration. In 1908, President Ramón Cáceres, in an address to the nation, put forth the argument, "We need immigrants, healthy, intelligent, and hard workers, . . . as a biological element that will increase the vitality of our race with a contingent of new blood that will activate and strengthen that which now circulates in our veins" (quoted in Robarge 2004: 137). The Dominicans met with some success in convincing the U.S. public that they were white. In the early twentieth century, one U.S. writer argued that "the refusal of the white Dominican to be governed by the black Haitian" was the reason behind the split between the two previously joined countries (quoted in Torres-Saillant 1998: 129).

The contrast between a white Dominican Republic and a black Haiti became crucial under the dictatorship of Rafael Trujillo, after his successful coup in 1930. In 1937, Trujillo launched a genocidal campaign against the Haitians, triggering international condemnation. Then Trujillo started up another European immigration campaign. Not too long thereafter, Trujillo declared the Dominican Republic to be a white nation (Robarge 2004: 163). The only blacks in the Dominican Republic were allegedly Haitians. These claims were echoed by Trujillo's advisor Joaquín Balaguer, who would later state that the Dominican people were "the most Spanish people of America" (quoted in Robarge 2004: 169). These efforts led to a situation where Dominicans became "deracialized" in a way that "precluded ethnic self-affirmation" (Torres-Saillant 1998: 138).

A contrast between the Dominican Republic and El Salvador is revealing. Both claimed to have rid themselves of a population through mestizaje—blacks in the case of the Dominican Republic and Indians in El Salvador. However, mestizaje in the Dominican Republic meant that blacks had become indios or whites through miscegenation, whereas in El Salvador, Indians had become mestizos by abandoning their culture. Today, in El Salvador, when someone says "se te salió el indio" (the Indian in you came out), it means that you have demonstrated your cultural backwardness or your inability to control your emotions. In the Dominican Republic, when someone says that you are "negro tras de la oreja" (black behind the ears), you allegedly have a black grandparent. These idioms provide yet another example of the distinction between the black and the Indian contribution to Latin American mestizaje.

Our Great Incan, Mayan, and Aztec Heritages

In Mexico as well as Central America, we can uncover examples of the ancestral Indian being portrayed as an important symbol of national identity in the early twentieth century. This portrayal contained a lot of variation, however; in some cases the ancient Mayas or Aztecs were heralded, and in others, it was the mixture that was lauded. Gerardo Rénique (2003: 218) argues that, in Mexico, "During the postrevolutionary years *mestizaje* became the dominant paradigm of national and racial formation, while the *mestizo* was consecrated as the unquestioned symbol of Mexican national culture." To counter the European critics of hybridism, some Mexican intellectuals thought it would be useful to recast the Indian component as the ideal counterpart to the Spanish. The Mexican anthropologist Manuel Gamio, for example, likened the Indian to bronze and the Spanish to iron, and used these metaphors to idealize the mixture between these two great races (Tilley 2005a: 57–58). Although the Aztecs were recognized as having been a great civilization, many intellectuals reduced the contemporary Indian presence to a folklorized element that made only a cultural contribution to the nation.

Although the colonial regime in Mexico endeavored to create caste-like divisions between Indians and Spaniards, generations of intermarriage and interculturation made it difficult to maintain any sort of racial apartheid in Mexico. By the early twentieth century, most Mexicans self-identified as mestizos, rather than Indians or Spaniards. Although Indians were perceived to be darker than whites, light skin color was not a prerequisite for being considered mestizo or even white. "Indians could become *mestizos*" and "upwardly mobile individuals were 'whitened' . . . therefore, the process of *mestizaje*, sometimes seen as basically racial, is in fact social; 'mestizo' is an achieved as well as an ascribed status" (Knight 1990: 73). *Mestizo* thus stands in contrast to *mulatto* in Cuba and Brazil, where it refers to the progeny of blacks and whites, not to upwardly mobile blacks.

In Mexico, *indigenistas* advocated for a rural education program that not only taught literacy, but also incorporated customs associated with indigeneity, such as music, dance, and rituals. Notably, the rise of indigenismo coincided with genocide carried out against the Yaqui and civil war in Mexico. Intellectuals such as Manuel Gamio and Andrés Molina Enríquez hoped that, by incorporating Indian values and history into a new nationalism, Mexico would be able to re-create itself as a unified nation. For both of them, mestizaje and the cult of the mestizo were essential to nation building in Mexico. Through the work of intellectuals such as Gamio and Molina Enríquez and the much better known writing of José Vasconcelos, the "*mestizo* thus became the ideological symbol of the new regime" (Knight 1990: 86), just as the mulatto became the ideological symbol of Brazil and Cuba.

In the 1920s, both Gamio and Vasconcelos hailed the virtues of the mixture between the great Aztec and Spanish civilizations, which they claimed had produced a virile bronze population (de la Cadena 2000; Tilley 2005a). Tilley (2005a: 58) argues that "Gamio's re-imagining of an ennobled (Spanish-Indian) *mestizaje* galvanized imaginations not only in Mexico but throughout those parts of Latin America where 'whitening' appeared hopeless: especially, the middle Isthmus and the Andes."

In contrast to Mexico, in El Salvador and Nicaragua national elites were able to convince the general population that Indians had disappeared from the country entirely by the 1920s (Gould 1998;   Tilley 2005b). Gould (1998: 10) argues that the myth that Nicaragua is an ethnically homogenous mestizo nation is a "cornerstone of Nicaraguan nationalism." Not only does this discourse of ethnic homogeneity ignore the indigenous communities that Gould describes, but it also renders invisible the Afro-Creole communities that Edmund Gordon (1998) discusses extensively in his ethnography.

In most Central American countries, with the notable exception of Guatemala, national elites promoted the mestizo as the national symbol, and proclaimed the Indian to be merely a relic of the past. Like in Mexico, in El Salvador the indigenous *past* is often glorified in national rhetoric—through textbooks, the census, and public symbols and discourses. Two important symbols are Cuscatlán (a former Nahua city) and Atlacatl (a legendary Nahua prince who fought against the Spanish). Yet, when Atlacatl is represented in public symbols, he is often misrepresented; for example, on cigarette packs he looks more like a North American Indian than a historical Nahua figure. Notably, the Nahua did not go to war bare-chested, yet Atlacatl is often so portrayed, which infantilizes and exoticizes him. The historical inaccuracy of this portrayal also reinforces the myth that there are no Indians left in El Salvador, since there are no bare-chested, feather-wearing Indians in the country. In El Salvador, indigenous cultures are portrayed as having been shattered by the conquest, and the contemporary rural population as having no real cultural identities. This allows Salvadorans to claim that there are no Indians in El Salvador, with the explanation that the Indians disappeared in the 1932 *matanza* (Tilley 2005b).

Ecuador, although much smaller than Peru, is quite similar to it in racial and geographical makeup, as also is Bolivia. Like Peru, Ecuador has coastal, Andean, and Amazonian regions in terms of physical geography, and blacks, whites, mestizos, and Indians in terms of racial geography. The percentages of these populations are also somewhat similar, although exact estimates are difficult insofar as neither country records racial categories in its census. In addition, in both Ecuador and Peru, blacks are concentrated on the coast, and indigenous people in the highlands. Despite these similarities, there are certain differences, such as the fact that Ecuador has some black settlements in the highlands, which Peru lacks.

The Ecuadoran government promoted immigration in the late

nineteenth century with the hope of whitening the nation through racial mixture. This plan failed miserably however, as the majority of the im-migrants who came to Ecuador at this time were from the West Indies and China. Black West Indian and Chinese immigrants were explicitly denied citizenship rights in Ecuador. The descendants of slaves who were native to Ecuador were cast as foreigners, as Colombians, to reinforce the idea that there were no blacks in Ecuador. Despite the historical and con-temporary presence of people of African descent in Ecuador, few leaders recognized either the history of slavery or the migration of West Indians to Ecuador (Foote 2006).

Intellectuals in Ecuador described blacks as biologically unfit and un-desirable, in contrast to Indians, who were portrayed as merely lacking education. Indians could be transformed into citizens through education, but blacks had no such prospects for improvement. The state enacted this ideology by providing highland Indians with educational opportunities while largely excluding blacks from them. This process was facilitated by the isolation of many blacks in the province of Esmeraldas on the Pacific coast (Foote 2006).

In 1916, Alfredo Espinoza Tamayo published *Psicología y sociología del pueblo ecuatoriano*, perhaps the first sociological analysis of the Ecuadoran population conducted by an Ecuadoran, although Espinoza admits that his study was not based on as much empirical evidence as he would have liked. Nevertheless, this work provides unique insight into elite percep-tions of blacks and Indians insofar as Espinoza devotes considerable space to issues of racial difference. He discusses the extent to which Indians are wanting for educational opportunities. He criticizes the state for not creat-ing schools where they can learn Spanish, as learning Spanish "levanta ya mucho su condición moral" (greatly elevates their moral condition) ([1916] 1979: 149). In his discussion of Ecuadoran Indians, he notes several times that they are capable of moral uplift through education, even writing "una sola cosa puede levantar el estado moral del indígena y es una educación" (only one thing can improve the moral state of the indigene and that is ed-ucation) (155). He also contrasts blacks to Indians by calling the imagina-tion of blacks "simiesca y burda" (apelike and coarse) yet pointing out that Indians' low intellect can be remedied through education. When referring to blacks in Ecuador, he remarks that blacks and mulattos predominate on the coast whereas Indians and mestizos are more common in the Andes. He laments the black race is "la menos apta para incorporarse a la civilización y tiende a desaparecerse mas fácilmente que la raza aborigen, absorbida por las demás" (the least apt at incorporating itself into civilization and tends to disappear with greater ease than the aboriginal race, being absorbed by others." Thus, for Espinoza, Indians need education, whereas blacks are en route to extinction in Ecuador. In his writing, he clearly is concerned with the progress and future of the nation and cites Gustav le Bon as well as Argentine thinkers such as Sarmiento and Bunge, all of whom have quite negative opinions of blacks and Indians and believe in the superiority of white Europeans. Given the inability of Ecuador to attract European immigrants and the preponderance of blacks and Indians, Espinoza exhorts the government to provide educational programs for Indians but does not make explicit suggestions for blacks. He also does not venerate the positive qualities of pure Indians, as do the Andean cultural nationalists in Peru.

Other Ecuadorans, however, did romanticize Indians. One example is Pedro Fermín Cevallos in his work *Customs,* completed in 1887. In it, Cevallos argues that the Indian is the only pure race in Ecuador and chides his compatriots for not valuing their purity. Notably, Cevallos not only insists that there are no pure whites, but also that there are no pure blacks in Ecuador, only mulattos and zambos. In contrast, thirty years later, Espinoza estimates that there are between twenty and thirty thousand pure blacks in Ecuador. Cevallos also asserts that, although the mixing of Europeans and Americans can result in "perfect forms," "it takes considerably longer to improve the offspring of Europeans and Africans." Yet he does concede that this improvement is possible (cited in Guerrero 1997: 571).

Nicola Foote (2006: 265) argues that it was so difficult for elite Ecuadorans in the early twentieth century to "reconcile the negative conceptions of blacks with the national self-image that it was easier to simply ignore their presence." Thus, although there is considerable discussion of blacks and mulattos in Peruvian literature of this period, we find few parallels in Ecuador. The lack of discussion of blacks in Ecuadoran literature may also be due to the relative isolation of Ecuadoran blacks in the coastal region, far from the highland capital of Quito. This contrasts with Peru, where blacks have been a visible presence in Lima practically since the moment of colonization. In any case, in both nations Indians were presented as being "capable of cultural transformation," whereas "blacks were not viewed in the same terms" (Foote 2006: 267). Foote (2004: 271) posits that this tendency to exclude blacks from educational projects "reflects the extent to which blacks were not seen as part of the newly expanded vision of the nation, and underlines that this was based on a conception of them as non-transformable."

The first Afro-Ecuadoran writers to rise to national prominence are Nelson Estupiñán Bass and Adalberto Ortiz, who began writing in the late 1930s (García-Barrio 1981). Ortiz's book *Juyungo* was published in 1942. Some other exceptions to the lack of attention to blacks in Ecuador are *A la costa* (1904) by Luis A. Martínez and some of the short stories in *Los que se van: cuentos del cholo y del montuvio*, written between 1928 and 1932 by the Grupo Guayaquil. In *A la costa*, Martínez portrays two families—the Ramírezes and the Pérezes. More fully embracing positivism and biological determinism than his contemporaries, Martínez describes the struggles of the ill-fated Ramírez family, which has some Afro-Ecuadoran roots and all of whom end up meeting their deaths. Emmanuelle Sinardet (1998: 299) argues that the death of the protagonist from this family, Salvador, represents a happy ending for Martínez insofar as it announces the symbolic death of "a badly adapted and backwards world and the beginning of a better society." Sinardet (1998: 300) further posits that this work reveals Martínez's belief that "la población negra tiene por su substrato biológico una propensión irreparable, incluso a pesar de una buena educación, a los vicios: lascivia, liviandad, holgazanería, alcoholismo, socarronería" (the black population has, because of its biological lowliness, an irreparable propensity towards vices: lasciviousness, lewdness, laziness, alcoholism, sarcasm, even despite a good education). This idea that blacks cannot be improved even through education and are destined to disappear for the good of the nation is a discernable theme in Espinoza's work as well as in works across Latin America at this time.

The renowned Mexican writer José Vasconcelos was one of the forerunners in the development of the discourse of mestizaje in the Americas. Although he exalts the mixing of races in general, he points out the undesirability of too much mixing with blacks. In *The Cosmic Race*, he argues that one of the problems the United States faces is its large black presence and celebrates the idea that "in the Ibero-American world, the problem does not present itself in such crude terms. We have very few blacks, and a large part of them is already becoming a mulatto population. The Indian is a good bridge for racial mixing" (Vasconcelos [1925] 1997: 26). This passage makes clear the undesirability of the Afro-Mexican population for Vasconcelos's racial mixing schema. Also noteworthy in Vasconcelos's work is his implication that Indians can be culturally assimilated, but that blacks must be biologically assimilated, and thus physically whitened through miscegenation. For example, he states that "even pure Indians are Hispanicized" (Vasconcelos [1925] 1997: 16), but that blacks must become mulattos in order to become Mexican. Through this reading of Vasconcelos's work, we can detect a trend in Latin American thought at the time: the national project cannot be realized as long as inferior races are present (that is, blacks and Indians), but it can with Latinized Indians and whitened blacks.

In present-day El Salvador, Indians are claimed no longer to exist, and blacks are said never to have been present (Tilley 2005b). Whereas most Salvadorans are willing to admit an Indian ancestor a few generations back, they find the insinuation that they might have black ancestry insulting. There are even national myths that explain why there are no blacks in El Salvador, none of which hold up to scrutiny. "According to colonial documents, African slaves were imported into the Salvadoran region in small but significant numbers during the early colonial period" (Tilley 2005b: 209). Despite claims that blacks were banished from El Salvador, there is no evidence that these blacks ever left. What is notable here for our purposes is that blacks hold a very different place in the national imaginary than Indians do. Through mestizaje, Indians have become Salvadorans. This option is not available to blacks, who have been imagined out of even the nation's history.

At the beginning of the nineteenth century in Honduras, 30 percent of the population was of African descent (Euraque 2004). This mostly mulatto population was ideologically incorporated into the mestizo majority over the course of the nineteenth century. In this process of mestizaje, Hondurans reinvented their history to exclude their African past. The only people in Honduras marked as black and of African descent were depicted as foreigners—the Garifuna and the West Indians—who were excluded from the mestizaje process. Darío Euraque (2003) explains that the black populations in Honduras were perceived as a "threat" to "Indo-Hispanic *mestizaje*" (239) in the early twentieth century. Striking evidence for this claim comes from President Miguel Paz Barahona's (1925–1928) claim that "Honduras needs 'serene races' which are essential for peace and necessary for the permanence of democracy. Blood is a commodity of utmost necessity. We must import it" (Euraque 2003: 244). Euraque attributes the perception that Honduran blacks are a threat to the mestizo nation to their participation in the growing banana enclave. This case also fits into the perceived need to biologically dilute the black race in order to approximate more closely the mestizo ideal, and the tendency to include mulattos in but exclude blacks from nation-making processes.

Jeffrey Gould (1998) argues that the "myth of *mestizaje*" has made the indigenous population of Nicaragua largely invisible to most Nicaraguans. According to the myth, Indians used to exist, but they have all now become Nicaraguans or mestizos, and Nicaragua is an ethnically homogeneous society. In the cases of El Salvador, Mexico, Nicaragua, and Honduras, the possibility for cultural mestizaje is restricted to indigenous peoples. Blacks, in contrast, are generally rendered invisible.

In Andean countries such as Peru and Ecuador, as well as in Mexico and Central American countries, the indigenous presence often has out-weighed the African presence, in ways both real and imagined. In these countries, leaders intent on building nationalism have reclaimed their great indigenous pasts as part of this effort, yet have been unlikely to highlight black or African elements in this endeavor. Leaders and intellectuals in these nations are apt either to deny any African presence in their coun-tries, despite historical evidence to the contrary, or to imply that blacks are rapidly headed toward extinction. Whereas Latin American thinkers hailed mestizaje in opposition to European critics of miscegenation, the desired outcome of mestizaje ranged from a whitened nation to a brown nation, but no intellectuals advocated for a black nation. In fact, the upris-ings in Haiti, which led to French expulsion by the African-descended slaves, served as a constant reminder to onlookers of the undesirability of a black nation. Haiti stands apart as a nation which embraced its blackness at independence, and it has paid heavily for doing so.

Conclusion

In this chapter, I have argued that, across Latin America, mestizaje has meant very different things for whites, blacks, and Indians. Whitened peo-ple and whitened (or Latinized) culture have been the desired outcome of mestizaje in most cases. Indian participation in cultural mestizaje usually has meant either the exaltation of the ancestral Indians or the acceptance of modern Indians without their indigenous culture. For blacks, the focus and concern have been biological rather than cultural mestizaje.

In Mexico, for example, light skin color was not a prerequisite for being seen as mestizo, and mestizos became the ideological symbol of Mexican-ness. Blacks, in contrast, had to be de-blackened to become part of the Mexican mestizo nation. In Cuba, blacks had to become mulattos to be considered fully Cuban. Cuba and Brazil both encouraged whitening through immigration, and the mulato or the mulata became a symbol of national identity. It is worth emphasizing here that the mestizo differs from the mulato in that mestizos are understood to have culturally incorporated themselves into society, but do not have to be products of interracial unions. The mulato, in contrast, is the product of intermarriage or coupling between blacks and whites or Creoles. This is a very different form of whitening.

So, why has blanqueamiento meant different things for blacks versus Indians in Latin America? Why is it that in Mexico and Peru, Indians have to be civilized in order to become Mexicans or Peruvians, but black people have to become mulattoes? These are complex questions that have yet to be fully answered. Yet we can begin to answer them for the Peruvian case.

The scientific racism produced in Europe classified both blacks and Indians as inferior to Europeans and assumed that racial mixture was degenerative. In light of the large numbers of Indians in Peru, and the generations of racial mixture of whites and Indians with blacks in Lima, Peruvian intellectuals had to reinvent and reinterpret European ideas to incorporate their emerging nation into the modern world.

In Peru, there had been a long history of racial mixture between blacks and whites, in many cases resulting from white men taking advantage of the subordinate status of black women. The proximity of blacks to whites in the context of slavery meant that there was frequent contact between these two groups over the course of more than two centuries. The closeness of blacks to whites in coastal Peru also led to sexual liaisons and, thus, to a large mulatto population. In addition, the cultural differences between blacks and whites became increasingly less pronounced. For example, Creoles and blacks ate the same food, danced to the same music, and spoke the same language. For this reason, the idea of acculturating blacks would not have resonated much.

In contrast, indigenous communities in Peru frequently lived in isolation from whites. The Peruvian systems of exploitation of indigenous labor often did not require the constant presence of whites. The Incas had organized systems of labor, of which the Spaniards were able to take advantage. In Peru, the contact between whites and Indians was not as close or as intimate as that between whites and blacks. In addition, some indigenous communities were able to remain outside the reach of colonizers. For these and other reasons, indigenous people in Peru held a different set of cultural traditions than mestizos, including language, dress, and food. In contrast, by the end of the nineteenth century, it would not have made much sense to distinguish between acculturated and unacculturated blacks. The differences in skin tone among people of African descent were however much more prominent. Among indigenous people, skin color differences were much less evident than differences between Indians who lived in indigenous communities, did not speak Spanish, and did not wear Western clothes, versus those who shared many of the cultural traits of whites or mestizos.

Latin American intellectuals who were engaged in conversations about the future of their nations had to reconcile the demographic realities of their countries with the scientific racism which declared that the racial hybridity of Latin America had doomed it to failure. Their solutions were very much in line with the options available to them. Blacks could become mulattos through interracial unions and Indians could become mestizos through education. With mestizos and mulatos, Peru could become a modern nation.

Race still figures prominently in national imaginaries across Latin America, and Indians and blacks continue to play distinct roles in constructions of the nation. It is crucial, then, to take this conversation beyond the elite imaginary and the historical setting to think about how race is lived today. In the next chapter, I discuss how ideas about whitening through mestizaje continue to figure in contemporary conversations about race in Latin America yet have limited utility for understanding the way residents of Ingenio conceptualize race and color differences.

chapter 3

Race and Color Labels in Peru

In the United States, he who is born black, dies black, whereas,
in Peru, your social status can change your racial classification.
Alejandro Ortiz, Peruvian anthropologist

If I was born black, I have to stay black.
Mirella Campoverde, a young single mother from Ingenio

Mirella Campoverde and Alejandro Ortiz are both Peruvian, yet inhabit vastly different worlds. Mirella is a dark-skinned, poor, single mother whose future holds little possibility for upward mobility. Dr. Ortiz is a fair-skinned, well-known anthropology professor. Their understandings of the meanings of blackness in Peru seem as distinct as their stations in life. Ortiz is making a general statement about how race works in the United States versus in Peru. Mirella is making a statement specifically about herself. They are both right. It is very probable that Mirella will always be black and will always be referred to as black by others; strangers will assume she knows how to cook and dance; and she will have trouble obtaining employment in positions reserved for whites, such as reception-ist or bank teller. Ortiz's world is filled with options and possibilities, not only for him, but also, in his view, for Mirella. How do we reconcile these two different maps of the Peruvian racial landscape? This is not simply a question about race in Peru. It raises a broader set of questions about the roles of class, gender, color, geography, and biography in understanding race in Peru, in Latin America, and in North America. These are the questions this chapter sets out to answer.

In this chapter, I explore the disjuncture between Ortiz's and Mirella's views and experiences. For Ortiz (2001), blackness in Peru is contextually dependent and subject to change. For Mirella and other residents of Ingenio, blackness is determined by skin color and descent, and does not change over the course of one's life. Ortiz's statement that social whitening is possible for blacks in Peru resonates with widely accepted conceptualizations of race in Latin America and with the well-known adage "money whitens." Over the past fifty years, students of race relations have described racial hierarchies in Latin America in three ways: (1) there is an intermediate racial category in Latin America between black and white that serves as a buffer between these two categories; (2) social whitening is a way for a person to become less black; and (3) racial classification in Latin America constitutes a continuum of racial categories. I examine the extent to which these three claims about race in Latin America can be used to understand the racial hierarchy in Ingenio.

This chapter contributes to the arguments in the first two chapters through a consideration of the particularity of racial discourses in Ingenio. In the first chapter, I discussed how memories of slavery and Africa are not salient in discourses of blackness in Ingenio. In the second chapter, I pointed out that discourses of race have typically been distinct for blacks and Indians, and that concepts of race in Afro–Latin America versus mestizo Latin America have been highly divergent. The two preceding chapters drive home the point that localities matter a great deal, and that skin color has been crucial for determining the status of Afro–Latin Americans. In this chapter, I build on these arguments by demonstrating the ways in which generalizations about race in Latin America, and even in Peru, fail to account for the way blackness is conceptualized in Ingenio. Before I begin this discussion, however, it is important to clarify the distinction between race and color.

Race versus Color

Race and color labels are conceptually distinct. Race is an externally imposed social categorization. A racial category is applied to a group of people thought to share physical and cultural traits and a common ancestry. Racial categories are mutually exclusive. The most common markers associated with race are skin color, facial features, and hair texture (Smedley 2007; Wade 1997). Color labels describe gradients of skin color, yet do not refer to mutually exclusive categories of people. In some cases, one word can be used as both a color label and a racial category, as can, for example, the word *black* in Spanish and English. *Black* can be used as a color label in Spanish when someone says, "Me pongo bien negra cuando estoy en el sol todo el día," or in English as "I get quite black when I am in the sun all day." In these instances, black is a color, not a racial identifier. The person making this declaration does not necessarily consider herself (or himself) to be a member of the black race.[1]

I use *category* to refer to races following Richard Jenkins's (1994, 2000: 8) distinction between externally imposed "categories" and internally recognized "groups." Racial categories in the United States are used by state actors, social scientists, and others to distinguish between people collectively understood to be black, white, Asian, or Native American. These categories have, in turn, produced race-based group identifications: people often understand themselves to belong to one (or more) of these groups (Brubaker and Cooper 2000; Nagel 1994). In Peru since 1940, racial categories have not been used in official recording efforts such as the census. Nevertheless, the long history of racial categorization has influenced how Peruvians talk about themselves and others.

This discussion of race and color requires a further layer of complexity, which I draw from McPherson and Shelby's (2004: 175) analysis of labels. Classificatory labels can refer to groups or categories. They also can refer to descriptors that are not groups or categories. I will argue that color labels do not refer to categories or groups, whereas racial labels refer to both. Racial categories lead to race-based group identities. Color labels, in contrast, do not create group-based identities.

Conceptualizations of Race in the Americas

The following exploration of how race and color labels are used permits a consideration of the extent to which group-based identities form part of the local parlance in the Afro-Peruvian community of Ingenio. This discussion sheds light on the utility of generalizations about race in Latin America for understanding race and color distinctions in this community. I begin by discussing these generalizations.

Mulatto Escape Hatch

The "mulatto escape hatch" (Degler 1971), also called the "intermediate mu-latto stratum" (Safa 1998), refers to the notion that someone can be born black, yet become mulatto through an increase in social status, or their children can achieve higher status through intergenerational whitening. This intermediate category emerged from the large free colored population in many Latin American countries during the time of slavery (Safa 1998; Skidmore 1990; Smedley 2007). The creation of the mulatto category, which possessed some benefits over the black one, was a mechanism of social control insofar as the possibility of moving out of the black category inhibited alliances among people of African descent (Daniel 2006). Peter Wade (1997) contends that in Latin America, racially mixed children are recognized as socially distinct from their parents. Eduardo Bonilla-Silva (2004) explains that Latin American countries have a tri-racial system, in which an intermediate group buffers race conflict. Luisa Schwartzman (2007: 944) similarly claims that, in Brazil, "browns serve as a buffer zone between blacks and whites."

Whitening

A related process that scholars argue tones down race conflict is whitening. Whitening can occur in three ways: (1) In intergenerational whitening, a black and a white person have a child, and the child is considered whiter than the black parent. (2) Social whitening is when a person is born black, but through an increase in class status is considered to be white or at least whiter in some situations. (3) Cultural whitening is when a person is born Indian, but acculturates to the dominant culture and becomes white or at least whiter in some instances. Intergenerational whitening can apply to blacks or Indians; social whitening is more commonly used with regard to people of African descent; and cultural whitening is more frequently used to describe processes of incorporation for people of indigenous descent. The whitening process works at the level of practice and ideology; people hope to "improve the race" through marrying lighter-skinned partners, and the governments of many Latin American countries have promulgated mestizaje for the purpose of whitening the nation (Graham 1990; Skid-more 1990).

The possibility of whitening is dependent on a definition of race that is not based solely on color or descent, but includes other, changeable factors. Many scholars contend that, in Latin America, race is not always based solely on color or descent, but that social and cultural characteristics also come into play (Rodríguez 2000). Jorge Duany (1998: 150) argues that in the Caribbean, "Phenotype and social status rather than biological descent define a person's racial identity." Similarly, Landale and Oropesa (2002: 233) posit that in Latin America "definitions of race are more fluid and ambiguous than is the case in the U.S." According to these scholars, the lack of rigidity in racial classifications allows a Latin American to change his or her racial status.

Social Whitening

Scholars of Afro–Latin America have argued that blacks can be whitened through a change in social status. Winthrop Wright (1990), for example, claims that, in Venezuela, "when a black escaped poverty, he or she ceased to be socially black." Wright goes on to explain that "occasionally, financial and political success socially whitened black Venezuelans. For them and their white counterparts, clothes, education, language, social position, and the accumulation of wealth combined to make an individual whiter in the social context" (10). Peter Wade (1993: 339) argues that, in Colombia, the trope "money whitens" does not mean that very dark-skinned people are actually classified as white, but that "rich black or mulatto people are treated as if they were white (or nearly white)."

Cultural Whitening

Studies of Peruvians of indigenous descent indicate that classifications such as cholo, indio, or mestizo are not determined by skin color but by cultural factors, including geographic origin and social standing (see Varallanos 1962; Bourricaud 1975; de la Cadena 2000). The way indigeneity is conceptualized in Peru, a person with brown skin and black hair could be labeled as white (blanco), Indian (indio), or either of the two intermediate labels: cholo or mestizo.[2] According to these studies, what determines one's racial status is not skin color, but level of education, cultural markers such as language and dress, and geographic and class location. In Peru, descendants of indigenous people can change their racial status from indio to mestizo by abandoning indigenous cultural forms, obtaining a formal

education, and migrating to the coast (which entails leaving highland Indian villages). Highly educated Peruvians are considered white and acculturated Indians are considered mestizos. Recent work on indigenous
identities in Peru contests the simplicity of this framework; however, these
studies do not address the absence of African-descended Peruvians in discussions of cultural whitening in Peru (de la Cadena 2000; García 2005;
Weismantel 2001).

Intergenerational Whitening

Scholars of race in Latin America have found evidence of intergenerational whitening in Brazil and Colombia. One study found that highly
educated nonwhite Brazilians were more likely than their less-educated
counterparts to label their children white (Schwartzman 2007). Data
limitations did not allow Luisa Schwartzman to discern whether this is
because class status directly influences racial self-identification or because
upper-class brown Brazilians are typically lighter in skin tone than their
lower-class counterparts, and thus closer to the boundary between white
and brown, which facilitates their "boundary crossing." Research by Peter
Wade (1993) in Colombia and Edward Telles (2004) in Brazil would support the latter claim, as they argue that only racially ambiguous people have
the option of shifting racial categories. As I will argue later, in Peru, people
of black ancestry are considered white only when their African ancestry is
no longer discernable.

Bipolarity versus Continuum

When discussing how people of African and European descent are classified, scholars frequently contend that the United States is marked by a
"rigid bipolar" construction of race, whereas Latin America has a "racial
continuum based on phenotype" (Safa 1998: 4–5). Peter Wade (1997: 14)
states that, in Latin America, race is a continuum and that "only people
who look quite African in appearance will be identified as black." According to Clara Rodríguez (2000: 9), U.S. racial categories are "few, discrete,
and mutually exclusive," but in Latin America, there are "many, often over-
lapping categories." Livio Sansone (2003: 8) claims that throughout Latin
America, we find "a color or racial continuum, rather than a polarized system of racial classification." These scholars concur that, in Latin America,
black is a relatively narrow category used to refer to only a small portion

of the descendants of African slaves and that there are a variety of other classifiers used to refer to people who are "neither black nor white" (Degler 1971: 110). They contrast this with the U.S. system, where black is a wide category used to refer to people of a variety of skin tones.

More recent scholarship, however, contests these generalizations and posits that bipolar conceptions of race do exist in Latin America, alongside color continua. Robin Sheriff (2003), for example, cites the Brazilian colloquial expression, "If you do not pass for white, you are black," as well as other evidence to argue that many Brazilians see white and black as separate categories, with no intermediate category. Sheriff posits that Brazilians use a variety of color terms, such as *moreno, mestiço,* and *mulato,* not as intermediate categories between black and white, but as a way to avoid the more loaded term *negro.* Stanley Bailey also distinguishes between race and color and posits that the Brazilian census terms—*white, brown,* and *black*—"may in fact represent primarily color categories rather than robust racial groups" (2009: 60). This important work in Brazil points to the value of distinguishing between race and color for understanding social inequality in Latin America.

I now turn to exploring the extent to which these ways of thinking about race are useful for understanding the African-descended community in Peru. I argue that, if we consider race and color to be conceptually distinct, there is no mulatto escape hatch, no social or cultural whitening, and no continuum of racial categories in the African-descended community I studied.

Research Methodology: Asking about Race in Ingenio and Lima

In my interviews in Ingenio, I did not ask people directly what their race was or whether they considered themselves to be black, as I wanted to understand local systems of classification. To that end, I asked, "People in Ingenio refer to me as blanca; how do you think they refer to you?" Throughout the subsequent discussion of race and color, I probed interviewees about labels they offered. Toward the end of the interview, I asked interviewees more direct questions about the most common labels I had culled through my ethnography—*negro, cholo, blanco, zambo,* and *moreno.* I also asked about the label *mestizo,* since it forms part of the official discourse, but found most interviewees were not sure what *mestizo* refers to.

In Lima, I asked questions that allowed me to understand how migration to Lima affects the identity of people from Ingenio. Specifically, I considered whether or not better wages, access to amenities, and a cosmopolitan environment influence patterns of racial identification among Ingenieros. Comparing the use of race and color labels in Ingenio and in Lima provides a way to gauge the extent to which African-descended Peruvians can experience social whitening, as migration to Lima nearly always leads to upward mobility.

I was granted permission to record all of the interviews I conducted. I transcribed and coded the interviews while I was in Peru, allowing my interview analyses to inform my ethnography in both Ingenio and Lima. Coding consisted of selecting themes that emerged from the interviews and categorizing interview excerpts according to these themes.

Conceptualizations of Race and Color in Ingenio and Lima

In Ingenio, the most common race and color labels were, from lightest to darkest, *blanco, trigueño, moreno,* and *negro.* In local usage, only *negro* and *blanco* can be directly translated into English, as "black" and "white," respectively. The other terms do not have English equivalents. Spanish *negro* shares a common root with the English word *Negro,* which applies only to people; like *black,* however, *negro* can refer to anything that is black in color, including cats or cars. In Peru, *blanco* is used to refer to people who are very light-skinned, but not necessarily only to people who have exclusively European ancestry. Similar to *white, blanco* can be used to describe animals or objects. The other two labels refer exclusively to people. *Moreno* could be translated as either "black" or "brown," and is used in Peru to refer to people who have dark skin, usually with some evidence of African descent in their facial features or hair texture. *Trigueño,* literally translated as "wheat-colored," was occasionally invoked in my interviews in both Ingenio and Lima to refer to very light-skinned people of African descent. *Trigueño* is also used in Lima to describe people of European or indigenous ancestry who have tan skin.

I will also make brief mention of two labels that refer more to hair texture than skin color—*cholo* and *zambo. Zambo* derives from colonial classifications and historically has referred to the progeny of black-Indian unions. In Ingenio, however, *zambo* is used to refer to people who have curly or kinky hair. It is used in opposition to *cholo,* which refers to people with very straight hair, usually Indians. *Cholo* nearly always is used to refer to indigenous people from Bajo Piura, and has physical as well as cultural connotations. It is worth pointing out that I rarely heard the labels *mestizo* or *mulato* mentioned in the course of this research.

Is There a Mulatto Escape Hatch?

In Ingenio, the word *mulatto* has fallen into disuse. There is evidence that this label was used in colonial Peru to refer to the offspring of blacks and Spaniards, and that mulattos were perceived differently than blacks or Spaniards; witness the mulatto figure of José Manuel in *Matalaché* (discussed in chapter 2). In this text, José Manuel is arguably an intermediary figure insofar as the author portrays him as superior to pure blacks, yet not good enough for the master's daughter.

Mulatto does not however form part of the local parlance in Ingenio today. The very few times I did hear this word used, it was in reference to someone who was very dark-skinned. Today, mulatto does not serve as an intermediate category between black and white, but there are other contenders for this role: moreno, trigueño, and zambo.

To determine whether or not there is an intermediate category that serves as a buffer group between blacks and whites, I consider how my interviewees in Lima and in Ingenio use the labels *negro, moreno, zambo,* and *trigueño* to describe people. An analysis of these labels reveals that they refer to color rather than race. As I have discussed, color labels are not group classifications but descriptors of individuals, disqualifying them as intermediary groups.

Is Moreno an Intermediary Category?

Moreno and *negro* were used interchangeably, indicating that they are not mutually exclusive categories. My interviewees often made references to both the *raza morena* and the *raza negra* in the same sentence to talk about the same group of people. Some of my interviewees stated that negros and morenos are of the black race. For example, Roberta, a woman who self-identified as morena and negra, said, "Mi papá ha sido así moreno, zambo. Ha sido negrito, zambo." (My father was moreno, zambo, like that. He was negro, zambo.") Roberta's phraseology indicates that *negro* and *moreno* are synonyms and that they are color descriptors, as she is describing her father's appearance, not placing him in a particular category.

I asked my interviewees in Lima to clarify the difference between *negro* and *moreno* for me. Consider this dialogue I had with two young people from Ingenio who had moved to Lima. I was interviewing Mirella, a young honey-colored woman with long curly locks who had come to Lima to work as a nanny. We were in Fiorela's room, and she also participated in the interview. Fiorela also worked as a domestic, was the color of cinnamon, and had long, tightly curled hair.

TGB: What does *moreno* mean?
Fiorela: It is a color, right? . . .
TGB: And, what kind of color is it? The color . . .
Mirella: negro . . .
Fiorela: Let's say negro, because [if I'm] negra, then yeah, I am morena.
Mirella You are negra, then.
Fiorela It is a color, negro, of course, negro, that's it.
TGB: *Negra* and *morena* are one and the same color?
Fiorela: Of course. It is one and the same color.

Fiorela and Mirella concur that moreno is a color and is the same color as negro. I then ask questions to probe whether *moreno* and *negro* are mutually exclusive groups:

TGB: Any person who is morena is also negro?
Mirella: Of course, because there are morenos that are called negros or negros that are called morenos.
TGB: But is there a difference? Are there people who say, "I am morena but I am not negra?"
Mirella: There are people who *say* that.
TGB: But is it false, or no, it's true?
Fiorela: For me, it is false.
Mirella: Of course, because . . .
Fiorela: Sometimes, when I walk by, they call me "morena" and . . . other times they call me "negra," but I don't get offended. I have thought about this, and if they call me morena and negra . . .
Mirella: It's the same.
Fiorela: It's the same, one and the same color.

I had interviewed Fiorela the week before and had asked her about the meanings of *moreno* and *negro*. Thus, her reflection may well be a product of my questioning her about issues she had not heretofore considered. Nevertheless, Fiorela concluded that *negro* and *moreno* mean the same thing, and Mirella agreed. Later in the interview, I asked them again if *negro* and *moreno* meant the same thing, and Mirella responded, "Si salimos morenos es porque venimos de negros ¿di? ni modo que vamos a venir de blancos." ("If we come out morenos it is because we come from negros, right? No way that we would be coming from whites.") Here, Mirella is invoking descent, and contrasting both *negro* and *moreno* with *white*. This means that she sees negros and morenos as belonging to the same group, a group that clearly is not white. In addition, by mentioning descent, Mirella is assigning a group-based identity to blackness, distinct from a color descriptor.

This conversation is reminiscent of a discussion anthropologist Robin Sheriff had with her interviewees in Rio de Janeiro. Sheriff (2003: 92) asked one interviewee "what does *preto* [black] mean?" Her interviewee responded "*preto* is *preto*," then went on to equate *preto* with *moreno* and *mulato*. In addition, Sheriff's interviewees told her that people who were not white were part of the black race, and that all of the well-known intermediary terms in Brazil that do not refer to whiteness refer by default to the black race. I heard similar arguments in Ingenio—that morenos are part of the black race. In Peru, however, unlike in Brazil, the presence of a large indigenous population means that there are many people who are neither black nor white—they are mestizo or indigenous.

Janelly and Lorena also concurred that morenos are part of the black race. Janelly, a woman the color of coffee in her late teens who at the time I interviewed her had recently moved to Lima from Ingenio, told me that morenos are part of the black race. When I asked what *moreno* means to her, she responded, "Que somos negritos, pues, que somos de raza negra." (That we are black, that we are of the black race.) Her response implies that she sees morenos and negros as belonging to the same (black) racial category and that *moreno* and *negro* refer to the same group-based identity. I heard a similar response from Lorena, a housewife in her forties who lives in Lima and is the color of milk chocolate. Lorena self-identified as morena, then told me that not only is she part of the black race (la raza negra) but her children are as well, even though they are not very dark-skinned.

As a final example, consider Vicente, a construction worker from Ingenio in his forties, who used *negro* as both a color and a racial label.

Vicente's comments show how color and race both differ and are interdependent. When I asked him what it means to be black, he used *black* in a racial sense, although without invoking the word *race* in this excerpt. At other times in the interview he stated that there is a white race and a black race:

> TGB: Here in Peru, people would say that I am blanca. How would people refer to you?
> Vicente: People call me, more call me negro.
>
> . . .
>
> TGB: And, what does *negro* mean to you?
> Vicente: Well, for me negro is a color that really is, as they say, so beautiful that it has no comparison. And I feel proud because, really, it is an appealing color. And I have no reason to be offended by what I am.
> TGB: And, if you see another person who also is negro, do you feel any brotherhood or camaraderie with him?
> Vicente: Actually, I call other morenos *familia*. Most people from Chincha[3] call each other *familia*.
>
> . . .
>
> TGB: *Moreno* and *negro* mean the same thing?
> Vicente: No, they are more, well, here, we distinguish by color, because there are some that are *very* mulato,[4] negro mulato, nearly blue, and I am more like moreno.

In these comments, Vicente strongly identified as negro and referred to negros as belonging to a fictive family, indicating a group-based identity. He also associated positive traits with blackness. Nevertheless, he described himself as moreno, in contrast to others who were darker than him. In this sense, he was using *negro* as a racial label, and both *negro* and *moreno* as color labels. *Negro* qualified as a racial group in this case, since Vicente used the term to refer to heritable traits that have a cultural element, and he identified with this group in the collective sense (Smedley 2007). Vicente also, like other interviewees, used *moreno* and *negro* interchangeably on some occasions, as when I asked him about negros and he responded using the term *morenos*.

Vicente distinguishes between colors, pointing out that he is not as black as other blacks and thus is actually moreno. Vicente uses *moreno* as a label that identifies a brown skin color, but that does not mean he sees *moreno* as a separate group from *negro*. He in fact emphatically defines himself as negro and then goes on to point out that his skin color is not black but brown. Notably, although he describes *negro* as a color, he attaches meaning to it: "I feel proud because, really, it is an appealing color." This statement reinforces the notion that, although negro as a color is distinct from negro as a race, both are value-laden. Although interviewees at times insist that *negro* is "just a color," it is a color with meanings attached to it, meanings that are intimately related to ideas of race.

Vicente and Lorena's insistence that they are morenos not negros in terms of skin color is reflective of the idea that it is better to be brown- than black-skinned. It is also a point of fact: they are not as dark as some blacks. Some people, however, did refer to themselves as negros. One was Minerva, who has skin the color of dark chocolate, has kinky hair, and is known around town as "Señora Negra." When I spoke with her, she described herself as negra and told me that she prefers to be called Señora Negra than by her name.

Vicente and Mirella also volunteered that they were not ashamed of being black, without me asking them a question that would seem to provoke that response. I simply asked them what *black* meant to them. Their responses indicated that they were aware of negative connotations associated with blackness, yet chose not to believe them. As Vicente's and the other cases make clear, some Peruvians who self-identify as black or moreno understand blackness as both a color and as a collective group. Since morenos are part of the black/negro collective, moreno cannot be an intermediate racial group.

Are Trigueño and Zambo Intermediary Categories?

Although moreno was the most likely candidate for an intermediary group, it is worthwhile to consider other contenders: trigueño and zambo. In an interview, Jeremy, a young man who did not appear to be of African descent and worked in a garment factory in Lima, told me that he had black blood and black family members, yet his skin color was trigueño. His mention of consanguinity indicated that he saw himself as a member of the black racial group, and used *trigueño* merely to describe his skin color.

Similarly, I had a conversation with a woman named Olga in Ingenio whose sandy skin led others to label her as white. When I asked her if she was white, she replied, "Yo no soy tan blanca" (I am not that white). I then asked her if she considered herself to be black, and she said that she did. She also described herself as zamba, due to her tightly curled hair. In general, zambo/a was used to describe hair texture, in that a zambo could be light- or dark-skinned. Since some zambos are negro in color, others are moreno, and still others are trigueño or blanco, zambo cannot be an intermediary category. Likewise, villagers used trigueño to describe the color of people they also considered to be negros. The fact that villagers do not use these categories in a mutually exclusive fashion indicates that they are color not racial descriptors and that there is no intermediary racial category between black and white. There is no escape hatch, mulatto or otherwise.

Social, Cultural, and Intergenerational Whitening

I now explore the extent to which social, cultural, and intergenerational whitening are possible. The possibility of whitening is predicated on the idea that definitions of race in Latin America are "more fluid and ambiguous" compared to the United States (Landale and Oropesa 2002: 233; Rodríguez 2000), allowing for the possibility of moving from one category to another over the course of one's life or across generations. These ideas have their origins in the whitening theories of the early twentieth century (discussed in chapter 2), yet continue to be prevalent today. In an August 29, 1999, article in the prestigious Limeño newspaper El Comercio the Peruvian scholar Alejandro Ortiz argued that in the United States, he who is born black, dies black, whereas in Peru, your social status can change your racial classification.

If one can become less white by virtue of an increase in social status or a change in cultural attributes, then race and color classifications cannot be fixed. In order to discern the extent to which blackness in Peru is fixed or fluid, I asked interviewees in Lima if a black person could become white. Here is how Fiorela and Mirella responded:

> TGB: If a black person from Ingenio comes here to Lima, does this person continue to be black, or can they become white?
> Mirella: There, no (laughs).

Fiorela: Unless they are Michael Jackson (laughs).
Mirella: If I color myself (laughs).
TGB: (laughs), so, for you, Michael Jackson . . .
Mirella: If I was born black, black I have to stay.

Fiorela and Mirella find the idea that a black person could become white laughable. In this excerpt, they are using blackness as a color, and mention how Michael Jackson changed his skin color. Neither Mirella nor Fiorela, nor any of my other interviewees, mentioned financial status in connection with whiteness. In their view, Michael Jackson was whitened due to skin bleaching not his wealth or phenomenal status. Despite the fact that people in Ingenio and in Lima generally agreed that migration to Lima led to a relative improvement in one's socioeconomic status, I did not interview any people in Lima who indicated that they had become less black by virtue of moving to Lima, even if they did mention that their financial status had improved. I also directly asked people if it were possible to become less black by moving to Lima, and most gave similar responses to Fiorela, that if you were born negro, negro you would remain. When discussing blackness as a color, some people did mention that one could become physically lighter because the sun is not as harsh in Lima as in Ingenio. But becoming less black meant a change in color gradation (physical lightening) not becoming white or mestizo (social whitening). As Renata's comments illustrate, blackness as a racial category is not something that can be changed:

> TGB: If a black person comes here to Lima from Ingenio, can they become white or mestizo, or will they always be black?
> Renata: No, no, there can't be a change. That is our origin, our nature; there won't be a change, even if we bleach our hair. No, no, (laughs). Even if we dye ourselves, no, that is our race, our origin. No one can take that away; it does not change.

In this excerpt, Renata is using *black* as a racial category, insofar as she focuses on race and origin. The interview excerpts in this section point to the fact that people from Ingenio generally see blackness as a fixed quality that does not change over the course of one's life. Thus, racial and color classifications are not fluid for them. The lack of fluidity makes social and cultural whitening unlikely, as I explore next.

Social Whitening

Social whitening is the process whereby an improvement in social or class status results in a person being classified as white (or whiter). If social whitening were possible for blacks in Peru, we would expect that blacks from Ingenio who migrate to Lima would become less black as a result of their consequent increase in financial status. Migration to Lima means entry into the cash economy, and nearly all migrants in Lima have more access to cash and consumer items than those they left behind.

To assess the social whitening prospects for Lima migrants, I compared the use of race and color labels by my interviewees in Ingenio versus in Lima. Charles Gallagher (2000), Ruth Frankenberg (1997), and bell hooks (1989) agree that, in the United States, whiteness is an unmarked status. To be white means that one can either safely ignore race (hooks 1989) or decide for oneself what whiteness means (Gallagher 2000). In the United States, whiteness is also a gendered status that implies racial purity. Richard Dyer (1997) argues that the equation of whiteness with the Virgin Mary in the Western world implies that white women are imagined to be the pinnacle of purity and cleanliness.[5] To determine whether or not black Peruvians can become white in a racial sense, I asked my interviewees what their racial categorization means to them. If they would prefer to dispense with their black group identity, that would suggest that they wished to become white, to become ethnically or racially unmarked.

Most interviewees in Ingenio said that blackness referred above all to skin color. For example, when I asked Mariana, a young single woman the color of cacao why people called her negra, she said it was because she was morena. When I then asked her what negra meant, she said it referred to color. I asked if it had any other meaning, and she replied that it did not.

In contrast, interviewees in Lima were more likely to give blackness a more politicized tinge, as the following interview excerpts reveal. These interviewees displayed more attachment to their black group identity than did my Ingenio interviewees. The first example, Dariel, was a man in his early twenties who was the color of milk chocolate and worked in a clothing factory in Lima. Dariel considered himself to be black. He used negro and moreno interchangeably, and said that he found morenos to be attractive:

TGB: Does being black have any meaning for you?

Dariel: Being black has meaning. Yes, for me, yes because now all morenos are, perhaps for me have something appealing about them.

Dariel's assertion that his blackness was meaningful to him contrasted with responses given by my interviewees in Ingenio, who often responded that being black just meant having dark skin. Gustavo, a young carpenter in Lima, also indicated that his blackness was meaningful to him. His statement that he did not feel either superior or inferior to whites indicated that he was aware of discrimination yet refused to internalize it. As the following quotation demonstrates, Gustavo was well aware of his status as a black man:

Gustavo: Because what the white does, I do, and what the black does, the white can do, because we are all equals, we are all the same. The only difference is the skin, nothing else, the color, as they say, right?

TGB: The color, but is there more discrimination here for blacks than for whites?

Gustavo: Yes, here, yes.

TGB: Why? How does it work?

Gustavo: Well, I am not going to feel inferior to others just because I am black, right? No. The truth is that I feel neither inferior nor superior. I feel equal, normal.

Almost the only people in Ingenio who invoked such a politicized definition of blackness had either been to Lima or been active in the Afro-Peruvian social movement. A comparison of two women—one living in Ingenio, the other in Lima—demonstrates this contrast. Georgina, a young mother of a three-year-old boy who lived in Lima and had worked as a domestic but was unemployed at the time of the interview, began the interview lamenting her current financial situation. She told me she left Ingenio before finishing high school because her parents fought a lot and she saw no other choice. Upon arriving in Lima, she found a job, but it paid less than half the minimum wage for more than twelve hours of work a day. Now, she does not work and her partner barely makes enough for them to get by, a challenge exacerbated by his drinking problem. Her life contrasts with Alexandra's: she was born in Ingenio, married a baker in town, and their business is sufficient for the whole family to eat well. Alexandra rarely leaves town, as she and her husband are open for business every day. Alexandra has two sons, whom she described as "morenito" and "zambito."

Alexandra's understanding of race was depoliticized. She freely used color terms to describe her family members, but did not imbue these labels with meaning beyond descriptors. She was not aware of her own ancestry, nor of the history of African slavery in Peru. When I asked her if she had ever been discriminated against, she recounted a story of a boy who had disrespected her husband, and with whom she had had a few negative encounters. There was no racial undertone to these events. When I asked her how she described herself, she responded "zamba," on account of her tightly curled hair. When I asked her what *moreno, blanco,* and *negro* meant, she replied that they were color descriptors. Alexandra had never heard of the Afro-Peruvian social movements and did not view cultural production from Ingenio as being "black" in nature. She did, however, say that sometimes calling someone "negro" could be an insult, although she thought people were being overly sensitive if they were offended by that, as it was simply a descriptor.

Georgina, in contrast, perceived racism as a problem in Peru. When I asked Georgina if her boss had ever insulted her because of her skin color, she responded that she had not experienced racism, but that her boss sexually harassed her. Unlike Alexandra, she offered up the word *racism* to describe what it would have meant for her boss to mistreat her for being black. Then, Georgina told me that in Ingenio people could have relationships with whomever they pleased, whereas in Lima people had criticized both her and her partner because she was black and he was not. She also told me that sometimes she was offended when people called her black, but her feeling depended on the context and how they said it.

> TGB: Has anyone ever offended you because of your skin color?
> Georgina: I think so, but I haven't paid them any attention.
> TGB What did they say, for example?
> Georgina Ugly negra, zamba. No, they don't offend me if they say that . . .
> TGB: Do people say "negra" in an affectionate way or more in an offensive way?
> Georgina: My husband calls me "negra" affectionately, and I don't get offended because of that. And if they just call me "negra" in the street, I don't get offended. I don't get offended anymore.

TGB: Does it depend on how they say it?

Georgina: Of course.... At the market, one of my friends calls me "negrita," and it doesn't bother me. Why would I get mad if I am black? No, for what? I am proud of my color, and everyone would like to have this color, don't you think?

Georgina, because of her experiences of discrimination in Lima, attributed new meaning to her blackness. She indicated that she was proud to be black, and later in the interview, said that everyone should be proud of their color, since that was who they were. She also said she did not get offended "anymore," indicating a change in her sense of self. Instead of downplaying her blackness, Georgina's experience of migration gave her blackness new meaning.

A comparison of Georgina's, Gustavo's, and Dariel's comments to those made by people in Ingenio indicates that migrating to Lima and consequently experiencing new forms of racial discrimination leads some people to heighten their racial consciousness rather than to attribute less meaning to their blackness or reject their ethnic identity. Thus, if we understand whiteness to mean having an unmarked identity, migration from Ingenio to Lima is clearly not a whitening process. Rather, migrants in Lima are more likely to develop a group-based identity as black. Social whitening does not appear to be a possibility for blacks from Ingenio.

Cultural Whitening

Cultural whitening refers to the process whereby acculturation allows a person to be classified as white (or whiter). In Peru, scholars have contended that Indians can become mestizo or even white through acquiescence to the dominant culture. Marisol de la Cadena (2000) argues that, in Peru, whiteness is a status that implies cleanliness and moral decency, and does not entail a white skin color. In both Peru and the United States, whiteness is construed as the superior racial category. Yet unlike in the United States, in Peru, indigenous people can become white by virtue of adopting dominant cultural forms and gaining an education (Bourricaud 1975).

In Peru, whitening through acculturation is not possible for blacks, as they generally participate in dominant cultural forms. For example, criollo music, food, and dance are cultural forms associated with coastal whites and blacks. Blacks are seen as the "authentic" producers of these criollo cultural forms, and criollo culture is dominant. For example, domestic workers from Ingenio told me that their employers preferred them to indigenous women, because they already knew how to cook criollo foods and were accustomed to criollo culture and language. So, there is no way for blacks to acculturate by participating in dominant cultural forms, given that blacks are already the producers of cultural forms associated with Peruvian-ness.

Intergenerational Whitening

Many of my interviewees used a descent-based definition of blackness, which indicated fixity, not fluidity, of the black group, even across generations. One example of this was Yraida. Yraida was in her thirties and had been a cook in a wealthy Limeño household for about fifteen years. Yraida described her father as white, her mother as black, and herself as black. When I asked her about her self-description as negra, she responded, "Sí, soy negra, sí. Pero, sé que tengo sangre serrana, pero sé que soy negra, pero con sangre serrana." (Yes, I am black, yes. But I know that I have mountain blood, but I know that I am black, but with mountain blood.) Yraida uses *serrana* here to refer to her white father, since in Ingenio being from the mountains is associated with whiteness. It is noteworthy that Yraida invokes race or blood when referring to both her serrana ancestry and her black ancestry, and that she gives primacy to her black ancestry. In the following conversation, she describes herself as both negra and morena, and contrasts these terms with whiteness:

TGB: How would people describe you?
Yraida: Me, they would call me negra. . . .
TGB: And, what does *negra* mean to you?
Yraida: Negra, raza negra, well, that I was a slave, that I was, I don't know, negra, that I was not white. . . .

Yraida insists she is not white, even though she describes her father as white. This is similar to a U.S. discourse of hypo-descent, where black ancestry trumps white ancestry. It is also important to note that Yraida is quite certain of her racial classification, of belonging to the "raza negra." This contradicts Suzanne Oboler's (2005: 84) claims that in Peru "one drop of white blood makes you white" and that "the ideology of *blanqueamiento* [whitening] has 'confused' . . . Peruvians' racial identifications." Yraida does not appear the least bit confused, nor does she subscribe to the whitening ideology. Because Yraida sees her blackness as based in her ancestry, it is unchanging, even across generations.

Yraida claimed black ancestry yet acknowledged her white father. Yraida's claiming of blackness was related to the fact that her black ancestry was visible through her skin color. Other, lighter-skinned people in Ingenio also claimed blackness, however. As I mentioned, Olga told me she considered herself to be black, even though some people referred to her as white because of her light skin. Olga's black ancestry was also visible in her coarse, kinky hair. Another young woman, Yanice, who had white skin and straight, light brown hair was identified by other villagers as white. Yanice's father, who had light brown skin and coarse black hair, told me he considered himself black. In Yanice's case, intergenerational whitening had rendered invisible any trace of African ancestry. Thus, she was identified as white. The fact that Yanice was identified as white supports my main argument: that blackness in Peru is primarily a discourse of color. When blackness is no longer visible, a person of African ancestry will be considered white.

Bipolarity or Continuum?

In Ingenio, people use a variety of labels to describe others' skin color and hair texture. In this section, I argue that not all of these labels are racial classifications, in that they do not refer to mutually exclusive groups of people thought to share physical and cultural traits and a common ancestry. The only two categories that fall into this definition are black and white. The other labels are descriptors not references to collective groups. Therefore, there is not a continuum of racial categories, but rather a continuum of color labels.

It was clear that *negro* was used as a racial label in Ingenio. In my participant observation, people often referred to themselves, their family, or the whole town as black. In many cases, villagers would use the descriptor *negro* as a racial label, meaning that they would contrast it with the category *white*. One occurrence of this was at a cockfight, a frequent source of entertainment in Ingenio. Whenever there was a cockfight, villagers from nearby towns would bring their roosters to compete with the local roost-ers. On this occasion, the competing cockfighters came from a town a few hours up the road, well into the highlands. Like many of the people in the northern highlands of Peru, some of the visitors had blond hair and blue or green eyes. I asked Mariana where the competing cockfighters came from. Mariana replied that they had come from the mountains. I asked her if the people in the sierra were white, as I had noticed a lot of the visitors were white. She laughed, and said, in reference to Ingenio, "Sí, porque aquí hay puros negros." (Yes, because here there are purely blacks.) The other women near us nodded and chuckled in agreement.

On another occasion, my brother and his family came to visit us in In-genio, bringing their nine-month-old son with them. Perla and her family came to welcome them upon their arrival. Perla and her children, both the men and the women, all wanted to hold my nephew, Dante, who has blond hair and blue eyes. Tired from a long trip and puzzled by the new faces, Dante became a bit fussy. At that point, Perla said that Dante must be thinking, "¿Quienes serán esas negras feas?" (Who are these ugly blacks?), referring to herself and her family members. She and her children laughed at this and continued to entertain Dante. In both of these situations, villag-ers were using blackness in a way that could be construed racially, insofar as they were contrasting blackness with whiteness as mutually exclusive descriptors of people.

In some cases, people used *black* to refer to color. One afternoon in Lima I was walking to the market with Fiorela to purchase some things we needed for lunch. Fiorela and I were talking about life in Ingenio. She mentioned that, when she went to Ingenio and stayed in the sun for too long, "me pongo bien negrita" (I get very black). She laughed after saying this. By saying that she *gets* black, Fiorela is using black as a color identifier. Her ensuing laughter is akin to Donna Goldstein's (2003) suggestion that much racial signifying is done through coded, joking language. By laughing after saying that she gets black, Fiorela smoothes over the negative conno-tations that go along with the label *black* and the widespread belief in Peru that it is better to be light.

Not all labels that describe people can be considered race or color labels. Labels may, for example, be used to refer to one's physical size. In Peru, people commonly call one another *gorda* (fat), *flaco* (slender), *ojona* (big-eyed); and other similar labels. These clearly do not refer to race, as they do not form part of the "real and sometimes imagined somatic cultural characteristics" that people see when they think they are seeing race (Miles and Torres 1999: 32).

People used *lacio, trinchudo,* and *cholo* to describe straight hair, and *enrulado, zambo,* and *ñuto* to describe curly or kinky hair. Only *zambo* and *cholo* were used as nouns to refer to people, whereas the other descriptors were used as adjectives to modify the word *pelo* (hair). *Ñuto* meant kinky hair, whereas *trinchudo* was used to describe abundant straight hair, associated with Indians. Notably, *trinchudo* and *ñuto* have somewhat negative connotations. The preferred hair textures in Ingenio are wavy or curly hair (enrulado) or fine straight hair (lacio). European facial features are also more highly valued. People in Ingenio occasionally insulted others by referring to them as *picuda* (big-lipped) or *ñato* (flat-nosed).

All of these descriptors are value laden, and local practices reinforce the preference for European features of straighter hair, lighter skin, thinner lips, and pointier noses. These preferences do not necessarily mean however that any of these descriptors are intermediate racial categories. They are indicative of a color, not a race, continuum. They are applied to people who fall into other generally agreed upon racial groups—blanco (white), cholo (Indian), and negro (black). The labels *moreno, trigueño,* and *zambo* point to skin color and hair texture variations within the black group. They are thus more akin to color classifications such as light-skinned or brown-skinned than to racial classifications such as black or white. This is similar to the Brazilian case, where terms such as *moreno* can be used descriptively, whereas *negro* takes on categorical meaning (Sheriff 2003).

My interviewees' comments indicate that color-based classifications can and do exist alongside race-based classifications. African Americans use *dark-skinned, brown-skinned, light-skinned, red-boned, high yellow,* and other terms to denote differences in skin tones among people considered to be black. In Peru, people use color-coded terms such as *moreno* and *trigueño* to distinguish darker-skinned from lighter-skinned blacks. The primary difference is that these skin color indicators are not nearly as commonplace in the United States as in Peru. In the United States, when non-blacks refer to blacks, they almost exclusively will call them "black," almost never naming their skin tone. In Peru, blacks and non-blacks alike use the categories negro, moreno, zambo, and trigueño to describe people of African descent.

Conclusion

In this chapter, I have argued that broad claims about race in Latin America do not hold for the Afro-Peruvian community I studied. Clarifying the distinction between race and color labels, as they are used in this African-descended community, has allowed me to demonstrate three things: (1) There is no buffer group between whites and blacks, as the color labels serve as descriptors, not intermediary categories; (2) social and cultural whitening are not possible because of the fixity of the black category; and (3) the continuum that exists is not of racial categories but of color labels.

My interviewees made it clear that blackness is a product of skin color and descent, not social status or cultural attributes. In some cases, they used *negro* to refer to a collective group, mutually exclusive from the white group. In this sense, *negro* qualifies as a racial label, whereas other labels such as *trigueño, moreno,* and *zambo* are color labels that do not refer to mutually exclusive groups of people. These findings point to the importance of distinguishing between race and color in analyses of racial categorization in Latin America and beyond.

Returning to Mirella Campoverde's and Alejandro Ortiz's statements at the beginning of this chapter, it is clear that Mirella will always be black. Ortiz's argument that racial status in Peru is fluid does not apply to blacks from Ingenio. It may continue to apply to Indians, as previous studies have indicated. And it may apply to middle-class blacks in Lima—a group that has not received much scholarly scrutiny. To make this determination, it would be necessary to conduct research in these communities and pay close attention to the distinction between race and color in the analyses.

The absence of a mulatto category in Ingenio points to the importance of conducting qualitative research with African-descended populations in countries with relatively small black populations in order to evaluate the persistence of the mulatto category in the post-slavery era. During the era of slavery in Peru, there were legal distinctions between free blacks and slaves. There is not enough historical research on different social statuses of people of African descent in Peru to determine whether or not there was a mulatto category that enjoyed special benefits during this time. Rachel O'Toole's (2006) recent work on castas in Peru suggests that the system of social identification in colonial Peru was complex and belied such simple characterizations. In Ingenio, it is clear that, if a mulatto buffer category ever existed, it no longer does. One reason for the disappearance of the mulatto category is that in the demographics of Peru a mulatto category is not necessary to prevent black solidarity. Blacks make up less than 10 percent of the population, and therefore do not pose a collective threat to the social order. The possibility that there may be other communities where the mulatto escape hatch may not exist points to the need for further research on the mulatto escape hatch and social whitening in countries where blacks are a small minority—countries such as Mexico, Bolivia, Ecuador, and Colombia.

In the next chapter, I consider the meanings people in Ingenio gave to blackness. This chapter moves away from Latin American discourses of racial categorizations and toward a consideration of diasporic discourses. In this and the preceding chapters, I questioned the extent to which Latin American exceptionalism works to explain racial categorizations for blacks in Peru. Next, I turn to questioning the extent to which global discourses of blackness make sense in the isolated rural village of Ingenio.

chapter 4

Diasporic Discourses and
Local Blackness Compared

> *A mí, no me gusta que me digan negro, porque dicen negro con asco, y me caliento.*
> *(I don't like when they call me black, because they say disgusting black, and I get worked up.)*
> Arañita, a character in the movie *Juliana* (1988)

> *Me gusta que me digan negro porque soy orgulloso de ser negro.*
> *(I like to be called black because I am proud to be black.)*
> Don Esteban, fifty-year old agricultural worker, Ingenio

> *Negro es una [sic] color, nada más.*
> *(Black is a color, nothing more.)*
> Doña Perla, fifty-year-old housewife, Ingenio

When these three Peruvians use the word *black*, what are they referring to? Can we presume that their willingness to use the word *black*, instead of *moreno* or *brown*, implies solidarity with people in other parts of the world who identify as blacks? Or, is the relationship between these uses of *black* and those in other parts of the diaspora purely semantic? Doña Perla insists that blackness is no more than a skin color. Could this be true? Why does Arañita—albeit in a fictional representation—reject the label as having only negative connotations? And, why is Don Esteban proud to be black? The label *black* seems to evoke a history of colonialism and slavery; of oral, musical, and literary production; of exploitation, oppression, and racism. But must it? Is there a global discourse of blackness that is

necessarily conjured up by the word *black?* Could Perla use the word to refer to her skin color in an act unrelated to the historical and contemporary
experiences of people in the African diaspora? Could a term with such a
violent history (and present) ever be divorced from social meaning? These
questions center on the extent to which a global discourse of blackness—
defined as one where *black* carries the same connotations across various
contexts—influences how people talk about being black in Ingenio.

I address these questions through a discussion of the gendered nature
of access to global and local discourses of blackness in Ingenio, where the
majority of residents self-identify as black. As I discussed in chapter 1,
many people in Ingenio refer to themselves as black, but do not see themselves as part of a broader community of people descended from African
slaves. In Ingenio, blackness is not necessarily tied to African ancestry or
to a history of slavery. What, then, do people in Ingenio mean when they
say they are black? What is the local discourse of blackness in Ingenio,
and how is it related to the global discourse of blackness? In this chapter,
I explore the meanings people give to blackness and place those meanings
in the local and global contexts. These analyses permit me to examine the
extent to which there is continuity across contexts and the extent to which
we can use the global to understand the local.

As in the previous chapters, this chapter highlights the centrality of
color in understandings of blackness in Peru. Specifically, I consider how
color is at the core of local discourses of blackness, while also exploring
how global discourses that stress ancestral roots in Africa, the history of
slavery, and a common experience of oppression among blacks interact
with local discourses of blackness in Ingenio.

Drawing from Patricia Hill Collins (2004), Charles Briggs (2005), and
Michel Foucault (1990), I conceptualize discourse as public and private
conversations, sets of ideas and practices, and mass-media messages that
shape both societal conceptions and social power. The ideological dimensions of discourses on blackness work in both hegemonic and counterhegemonic fashions to influence the ways people think and talk about
blackness. I explore discourse primarily at the level of interpersonal conversations, and consider mass media in more detail in the next chapter. Because of the gendered division of social roles and public spaces in Ingenio,
men and women participate in different ways in public and private conversations and have varying levels of access to these conversations, especially
to those that occur outside the community. Local discourses are those that

are particular to Ingenio. Global discourses have a wider dissemination and purported sphere of influence.

In Peru, between 6 and 12 percent of the population of about 28 million can be identified as being descendants of African slaves. The nongovernmental organization CEDET estimates the Afro-descendant population to be 2.5 million. It is hard to say exactly what percentage of this group self-identifies as black, as there have been no nationally representative surveys that ask for racial self-identification. From my research, it is clear that some African-descended Peruvians self-identify as black, and the objective of this chapter is to understand what self-identifying as black means in Ingenio through an exploration of the discourses that people draw on when identifying themselves as black. The first step is to clarify what a global discourse of blackness is.

Global Blackness

As a social category, blackness is endowed with meaning through processes of identification. It is the product of both identifying as black and being identified as black by others (Nagel 1994; Jenkins 2000). In this chapter, I probe the meanings embedded in the process of identifying oneself or someone else as black. I argue that these meanings are shaped by global and local discourses on blackness, and that access to these discourses varies by gender.

The act of labeling a person black involves associating that person with a set of ideas about what it means to be black. This set of ideas is different for each individual and is influenced by the person's geographical and social location, local realities, national discourses, popular culture, and political movements. The meanings we give to blackness are produced through social interactions and encounters with the media and popular culture. To uncover what it means to be black in Ingenio, Peru, it is necessary to consider the global discourses as well as the local realities and possibilities for engagement with global discourses. Thus, when thinking about the black diaspora, we are not talking about a population that exists simply by virtue of its history, but as an interaction between people and a set of ideas about who is black and what blackness is. We have, thus, two constantly changing phenomena before us. One is the set of people who belong to the black diaspora and the second is the aggregate set of ideas about blackness. The set of ideas is constantly changing in the media, in popular culture, at academic conferences, and in writings such as this one. The group of people is also constantly changing, through births, deaths, migration, and shifting conceptions about who is black and who is not.

The idea that a person can be black has its roots in the Enlightenment, in the African slave trade, and in colonialism. The notion that there is a black race distinct from a white race is the product of a particular historical moment: the colonial encounter. While some Europeans were enslaving and colonizing Africans, others were developing elaborate systems of human (and other) classifications. The perception of Africans as black and Europeans as white was formulated by some of the most esteemed Enlightenment scholars (Eze 1997; Smedley 2007). To the extent that it resonated with colonial realities, this classification became part of how people talked about differences across populations around the globe. In the contemporary Anglophone world, it is unnecessary to clarify in lay conversation what one means by *black* or *white*. With the spread of mass media, people around the world are familiar with popular connotations of blackness in the "Black Atlantic" (Gilroy 1993: 38). Thus, although there are local meanings of blackness in communities around the world, based on their own particular histories, these meanings are connected to Black Atlantic discourses of blackness in two ways: (1) they share a similar history, as the idea of blackness was created through colonial encounters; and (2) they share an understanding of blackness as it is portrayed by global mass media.

As discussed in the introduction, scholars of the African diaspora often imply that the descendants of African slaves in the Americas share a common experience, and relate that shared experience to blackness. Some scholars, such as Melville J. Herskovits, have argued that diasporic Africans share African cultural artifacts, while others, such as E. Franklin Frazier, have claimed that the circumstances in the New World have produced a shared and unique culture among blacks. Most scholars of the diaspora fall into one of these two camps, and most agree that diasporic blacks have some type of common cultural repertoire, whether that shared culture is from the "homeland," produced in the new territories, or a combination of both (Zeleza 2005).

Paul Gilroy's book *The Black Atlantic: Modernity and Double Consciousness* (1993) is representative of the idea that diasporic blacks share a common background as a result of their experiences in the New World. The astute reader will notice immediately that Peru is actually located on the

Pacific Ocean not the Atlantic. It is however arguably part of the Black Atlantic, insofar as African-descended Peruvians share African "roots" and their ancestors arrived in Peru via the same Atlantic "routes" as the ancestors of African-descended people in countries with Atlantic shores. Notably, Gilroy's assertions that the African diasporic experience is essential to modernity draw from a long line of scholars, including C.L.R. James and W.E.B. DuBois. In *The Black Atlantic*, Gilroy criticizes African American claims to particularity on the basis that African American culture, like other black cultures, transcends national particularities. Gilroy carefully points out the syncretic nature of black cultures and highlights the unresolved nature of the concept of a diasporic culture. Nevertheless, his analyses essentialize the notion of the black diaspora. For example, drawing from DuBois, Gilroy points to the "fundamental antinomy of diaspora blacks" (30), meaning they have a divided sense of consciousness as transnational blacks and as citizens of a particular country. The use of the word *fundamental* here indicates a fixed attribute. In addition, Gilroy attributes much of black diasporic cultural production not only to the slave heritage, but also to the "memory of slavery, actively preserved as a living intellectual resource in their expressive political culture" (40). Gilroy's text thus leaves little room for diasporic blacks who do not experience their blackness as a fundamental contradiction with their national origin and do not draw from the memory of slavery as a living intellectual resource.

For Gilroy, diasporic blacks are bound to experience a divided sense of self. As he points out, this "doubleness . . . is often argued to be the constitutive force giving rise to the black experience in the modern world" (1993: 38). Gilroy draws extensively from DuBois's concept of a double consciousness, even including this famous phrase in the subtitle of his book. It is worth quoting at length a passage that demonstrates Gilroy's belief in the importance of this concept for diasporic blacks:

> Double consciousness was initially used to convey the special difficulties arising from black internalization of an American identity: "One ever feels his twoness—an American, a Negro; two souls, two thoughts, two unreconciled strivings, two warring ideals in one dark body whose dogged strength alone keeps it from being torn asunder." However, I want to suggest that DuBois produced this concept . . . not just to express the distinctive standpoint of black Ameri-

cans but also to illuminate the experience of post-slave populations in general. (Gilroy 1993: 126)

Along with the double consciousness, the other shared characteristic Gilroy proposes is the "memory of slavery" (Gilroy 1993: 39). As I discussed in chapter 1, for Gilroy, the memory of slavery is not dormant but an active resource for the cultural, political, and ideological struggles that breathe life into the global black community. Yet I show in that chapter how certain conditions can render the memory of slavery unimportant, thereby casting into question the extent to which diasporic blacks share a common experience.

The fact that Peru has a Pacific coast leads authors such as ethnomusicologist Heidi Feldman (2006) to place Afro-Peruvian cultural production within the realm of the "Black Pacific" (7), distinct from the Black Atlantic. Feldman contends that the Black Pacific is distinct insofar as black Peruvians must negotiate with local criollo culture, indigenous cultural forms, and the Black Atlantic itself. She further asserts that "Afro-Peruvians identify with the transnational Black Atlantic but also are deeply engaged in an identity project that responds to Peruvian national discourses" (9). Feldman concentrates on Afro-Peruvian artists in Lima and Chincha who are in fact engaged in an identity project. This project of the revival and creation of Afro-Peruvian cultural production is far removed from Ingenio. Many of my interviewees were aware of Susana Baca and Victoria Santa Cruz, subjects of Feldman's study, but did not see themselves as sharing a common Afro-Peruvian culture with these or other Afro-Peruvian artists. Even if they self-identified as black and identified Afro-Peruvian music as black, many of my interviewees did not experience a cultural connection to this music. This disjuncture points to the importance of questioning what it means to be black, and to be part of a Black Pacific or Black Atlantic, rather than assuming that the African diaspora is "merely a logical manifestation of dispersion" (Patterson and Kelley 2000: 65). Patterson and Kelley, for example, argue that

> diaspora is both a process and a condition. As a process it is constantly being remade through movement, migration, and travel, as well as imagined through thought, cultural production, and political struggle. Yet, as a condition, it is directly tied to the process by which it is being made and remade. In other words, the African diaspora

itself exists within the context of global race and gender hierarchies. (Patterson and Kelley 2000: 20)

If we think of the diaspora as something that just is, we are unable to think about how it was formed and how it is changing. In contrast, thinking of the diaspora as a process and a condition allows us some flexibility in conceptualizing the black experience. Whereas Gilroy implies a shared experience among diasporic blacks, and Feldman suggests that there is cultural commonality among Afro-Peruvians, to understand blackness in Ingenio it is more useful to take into account the condition of being black, then to examine the processes through which blackness is endowed with meaning in this locality.

Conceptualizing the diaspora as a process and a condition allows us to heed Herman Bennett's (2000: 112) suggestion to ask "how, when, why and under what circumstances slavery and racial oppression produced a black consciousness." Plus, it may permit us to avoid thinking of "the primary link uniting Diasporic studies" as "exclusively one of color," which Ben Vinson (2006: 4) equates with "a sort of reductionist, racial essentialism." I do not pretend in this chapter to be able to move us completely away from the essentialization of blackness, but I do suggest that, by questioning the limits of global discourse and focusing on the processes and condition of being black, we can better understand the diversity within the diasporic experience.

To this end, I draw on recent scholarship that describes the diaspora as a process and a condition (Patterson and Kelley 2000; Zeleza 2005) to understand black Peruvian subjectivity. My analysis relies on tropes set forth by Gilroy (1993) that highlight the importance of the condition of blackness but is enhanced through insights from more recent scholarship that argues for the importance of process and meaning making for understanding diasporic identity (Patterson and Kelley 2000; Zeleza 2005; Vinson 2006; Bennett 2000). The African diaspora as a condition cannot be separated from its brutal past and present, yet as a process it continues to be produced and imagined in different ways. By recognizing the importance of the diaspora as a condition, we continue to invoke global blackness as an inescapable force in shaping contemporary black communities. I perceive global blackness, as distinct from local blackness, to encompass those people who see themselves as descendants of African slaves, derive inspiration from that experience, and feel that being both citizens of the nation they live in and members of the black community creates a divided sense of self.

Both the condition and process of being a diasporic subject are shaped by gender. Many contributors to the debate have not given sufficient consideration to the importance of gender for the experiences of diasporic subjects. As Yogita Goyal (2006: 411) points out, "the normative diasporic subject remains masculine, mobile, and Western." In Ingenio, residents vary considerably in their mobility and masculinity, and have different levels of access to Westernization—understood here as modernization. The gendered differences in access to diasporic discourses raise questions about how the diaspora is produced and experienced in different ways by men and by women.

The people of Ingenio share with other diasporic blacks the condition of oppression. Some people in Ingenio draw on diasporic experiences to contend with this oppression. Others do not, because discourses, diasporic and otherwise, are produced through communication, and there are gendered divisions in access to these conversations. This chapter builds on the work of scholars who explore "the gendering of diasporic space" (Brown 1998: 291) to examine how men versus women in Ingenio have different levels of access to diasporic discourses.

Local Blackness

My interviews reveal that understandings of blackness in Ingenio are sometimes but not always based on global discourses of blackness. Discourses on blackness in Ingenio are heterogeneous and often qualitatively different from global discourses. The following analyses of the local discourses of blackness aid in understanding how the local and global interact. These analyses also provide insight into the difference between diaspora as a condition and as a process, as they reveal that the condition of being a diasporic black person does not always entail having developed a diasporic consciousness, and that people draw from different discourses to make sense of themselves as black. Finally, they point to the gendered nature of access to global discourses of blackness.

When I asked people in Ingenio what it meant to be black, almost everyone told me that being black meant having a black skin color. Rosa, a dark-skinned woman in her fifties with kinky hair, told me in conversation that others called her morena. When I asked her why, she responded, "Me dicen morena porque soy negrita . . . por la color" (they call me morena because I am negrita . . . because of my color. I asked her if people called her negra; she affirmed that they sometimes did in an affectionate way, adding "casi es igual el moreno con el negro" (moreno and negro are almost the same thing). Her responses were very similar to John's. John was in his late twenties, and had very dark skin with coarse hair. When I asked him what black meant, he shrugged his shoulders. I asked him why people called him negro. He responded, "por la color, pues" (because of my color).

In my interview with Roberta, a brown-skinned woman with kinky hair, she equated both blackness and whiteness with skin color:

TGB: Why do people call me white?

Roberta: Because you are white . . . they call you white (laughs).

TGB: My color?

Roberta: When you first came, don't you remember, people took notice of you, when you first came, to see you so white (laughs), because we are all morenos here.

TGB: Okay, and what does *moreno* mean?

Roberta: Moreno is a person who is a little; well, negro is very black, [moreno] is a little lighter. . . .

TGB: . . . when people say "negro," what does *negro* mean?

Roberta: Negrito, negro (laughs)

Roberta contrasted my white color with the moreno color of people in Ingenio. When I asked her what *moreno* meant, she said that morenos were somewhat lighter than negros. When I asked her what *negro* meant, she said it meant "negro." Like several other interviewees, Roberta laughed when talking about skin color. Notably, she laughed when talking about my color as well as the color of others. Nevertheless, she did not associate any value-laden descriptors with blackness or whiteness in this interview. Roberta's laughter when talking about my whiteness and her blackness was likely due to the status differential between us. Although it was common in Ingenio to use color terms to describe others, people were less likely to use color terms to describe those people perceived to be of higher status. For example, Fiorela told me that her boss called her negrita, yet Fiorela never called her boss, who was of Asian descent, *chinita*. Calling a person negro/a or negrito/a is not necessarily an insult, yet it does imply that the person is of equal or lower status. This is evident in my conversation with Gertrudis.

Gertrudis was in her early fifties, was quite dark-skinned, and had straight, thick black hair. She told me that people called her negra or morena, and that sometimes the label was offensive, other times affectionate. She recounted a story of a time when someone called her "negra" loudly, which she did not appreciate:

If someone calls out to you, "hey, negrita," that can be affectionate, but if they say "NEGRA," not so much. . . . Once this guy screamed "NEGRA" at me. It was in Morropón that this happened. "Negra, negra," and I just kept walking. I did not pay him any attention. He kept saying "negra," and I kept on going. We were going to the same place. When I got where I was going, I sat down. He said, "Hey, negra, I was calling you so you would wait for me." I told him, "I have my name, just like you have yours. We are in another town. Why are you screaming 'negra' at me?" . . . He responded, "Oh, sorry, I didn't know you would be upset." I responded, "I am not upset, I am just correcting you. How you gonna be calling me negra like that? Just because I am morena doesn't mean you have to scream 'negra' at me from far away." That's what I told him (laughs). . . . Now, when he sees me, he doesn't scream "negra" at me, he calls me by my name.

In contrast, Minerva ("Señora Negra") told me that she did not like being called by her given name.

TGB: Here in Ingenio, people refer to me as white. How would they refer to you?

Minerva: People call me negra; they mostly call me negra, hardly ever by my name. . . . When they call me by my name, I don't like it. I like it when people call me negra. My name is Minerva, but I don't like it. Once, Señora Carmen called me "Señora Minerva." I didn't hear her at first. Then, I went back, and I told her, "Call me by the name I go by. Don't call me by any other name . . . I don't like it." I like it when they call me negra.

TGB: And why do people call you negra?

Minerva: Perhaps because of my color; perhaps people are just used to it. I have a son, too, Luis. But everyone calls him negro.

Whereas Gertrudis didn't like being called negra, that was the name Minerva preferred to go by. Most Ingenieros usually did not mind being called negra, but preferred that people use their name. Gertrudis wouldn't mind someone calling her negra in an affectionate way, but objected to having "negra" yelled at her in public and especially outside of Ingenio.

These interview excerpts also point to the primacy of skin color in local discourses of blackness in Ingenio. When I asked my interviewees to explain what it meant to be black, their response was that being black was about having dark skin. They did not indicate that blackness was connected to Africa or to slavery, or that blackness stood in opposition to Peruvianness. From these excerpts it might seem as though diasporic discourses were not present in Ingenio. As I will show, however, these discourses did come through in other ways. Digging deeper into the interviews and asking more questions led some of my respondents to engage in a more diasporic discourse. In the next section, I compare the responses of three interviewees who engaged with diasporic discourses in fundamentally different ways, in order to develop an understanding of how local and global discourses of blackness can coexist, and how access to these discourses is gendered.

Armando: My Ancestors Were African Slaves

Armando was in his late forties, had skin the color of caramel, and had coarse black hair. He had two teenaged children, and owned a small plot of land where he cultivated rice. Armando loved to read books and newspapers and enjoyed talking about local history as well as current events. He told me that most of his knowledge about Ingenio, Piura, Peru, and the world came from books; he developed a love for reading as a small child and read every book he could get his hands on.

His understanding of the regional history of slavery was much deeper than that of anyone else I interviewed in Ingenio. In an interview, he described the experiences of African slaves, and directly connected his family history to that experience:

Here, the labor force was blacks, people brought from Africa, or, slaves, to work in the fields. So, in this region, Alto Piura, there was a place where the majority of blacks settled, Yapatera. . . . This black race that arrived there, these slaves . . . stayed there. They no longer moved, and with freedom, they had access to . . . land, and began to move to other places and other towns. In this way, the race spread out. My grandfather met my grandmother in Chulucanas, in an annex close to Yapatera. My grandfather was moreno, negro, and they got married.

Unlike most of my interviewees, Armando not only was aware that Africans had been enslaved, he also knew that there had been slavery in the Hacienda Yapatera, which was a few miles by footpath from Ingenio. Knowing that his grandparents were black and from Yapatera, he concluded that his ancestors must have been slaves. This is likely true, although Armando is many generations removed from slavery. Apart from invoking this diasporic experience of slavery, Armando is also aware of institutionalized racism today and of the position of blacks in the Peruvian racial hierarchy.

> Generally, in terms of owning land, it has almost always been the case that the white person has control over the other levels. . . . The plantation owner was, as they say, the manager, and lived in Lima. Thus, he would leave an administrator here. This administrator would be white, not as white as the owner, but at least wheat-colored. But he wasn't moreno or zambo. He, in turn, would have control over an overseer, or a personnel chief, you could say. And, as such, it seems that as the color lessens, one could achieve a certain level. The lowest level that everyone had control over was that which was negro.

Armando saw a relationship between race and the class hierarchy in Peru. According to him, in the hacienda era prior to the agrarian reform (a time he was too young to remember personally), the hacendados tended to be Spaniards or the Peruvian-born descendants of Spaniards. They frequently lived in Lima and would leave the hacienda under the charge of an administrator who was usually a mestizo. The administrator would have several overseers working for him. Armando described the overseers as lighter in skin tone than the field hands.

Few people in Ingenio drew such a direct relationship between skin color and the class hierarchy, either in the present or in the past. For example, when I asked an elderly Ingeniero, Don Ramón, to describe life during the time of the hacienda, he did not report a direct relationship between skin color and social position. He actually told me that people had come down from the sierra to work in the fields, and that they were white.[1] In light of the lack of historical documentation on the skin color or racial status of the field hands, it is hard to know what an accurate depiction of hacienda life would be in color or racial terms. What is clear is that Armando is drawing from diasporic discourses that posit a relationship between skin color and class position, because his analysis does not form part of the local discourse.

In the interview, I realized that Armando was familiar not only with the history of blacks in Peru, but also with renowned blacks in the local community. For example, he recounted the story of Alberto Ramírez, a black person from La Pilca, a neighboring town, who despite his lack of formal schooling, was at the forefront of the struggle for agrarian reform in the community. In addition, he told me about Ramón Domínguez, a black poet also from La Pilca. When Armando recounted these stories, he highlighted that these men were black, signaling that he believed their blackness was important and relevant. This indicated that blackness was more than a skin color to Armando. By invoking the memory of slavery and pride in the contributions of blacks to the nation, Armando was engaging in diasporic discourses and connecting himself with the global black community.

In a follow-up interview, I told Armando that he was almost the only person in Ingenio who told me that his ancestors had been brought from Africa to the port of Paita, and then to Yapatera. I asked him why he thought he was one of the few to know that history. He replied that he had always been curious, and that this curiosity instilled a desire in him to know where he was from. He explained that he knew more than others because of his inquisitiveness and his love for reading. Notably, he did not say that his parents had told him the story or that he had garnered it from listening to his elders. He learned it by reading books written by people outside of Ingenio. Thus, Armando did not limit himself to the local discourses, but rather sought outside information. His understanding of his ancestry, then, was not based solely on local conceptions, but was heavily influenced by diasporic discourses that placed importance on Africa and slavery.

Fabio: *Nosotros Somos Negros*

Fabio did not engage as fully as Armando in diasporic discourses. Don Fabio, my host in Ingenio, was a fifty-year-old agricultural worker who had been involved sporadically in a black social movement. In the late 1980s, the Movimiento Negro Francisco Congo led a few workshops in Ingenio. Fabio was involved in some of the local organizing for these workshops, and had attended workshops in other communities led by this and similar groups.

Fabio often welcomed me into his home to talk about the history of Ingenio, his family, and his experiences outside of Ingenio as a professional soccer player, in the military, and attending workshops. On many occasions, Fabio told me that he never forgave his father for not allowing him to get a secondary education. Nevertheless, Fabio served as a provider of information for the townspeople, especially on matters related to maneuvering the complex Peruvian state bureaucracy in order, for example, to obtain a national ID card or a copy of a birth or death certificate.

Given Fabio's extensive exposure to the outside community and his participation in black social movement workshops, I was taken aback in our initial interview when he told me that he did not have any African ancestry or ancestors that came from Africa. When I asked Fabio what his roots were, he said, "Nosotros somos negros." (We are blacks.) Upon further probing, he told me that blacks came from Yapatera, where they were bought as slaves by different plantation owners. He also told me that Africans were brought to Peru as slaves. Given his contradictory responses— first telling me that he did not have African ancestry, and subsequently telling me that he was black and that blacks came from Africa—I asked him for a re-interview. Here is an excerpt from my field notes, written just after the re-interview:

> This afternoon, I went to talk to Fabio, to ask him about his responses to the interview. I first asked him if it was correct that when I asked him if he had African ancestry, that he said no. He said that that was correct. Then, I pointed out to him that he also said that Africans had been brought to Peru on boats. He agreed that Africans had been brought to Peru, and that they had been brought to Yapatera. He also agreed that Africans were negros. So, I asked him again if he had African ancestry. He said that he might, but that he wasn't sure, because his parents had never told him what his roots were. So, then, I said that before Pizarro came, there were no blacks in Peru, and he agreed that that was true. Then, he said that he most likely does have African ancestry, but that his parents or grandparents had never told him.

Fabio strongly identified as black, but did not associate his blackness with Africa. He also did not draw as heavily from a diasporic discourse as Armando did. Although both had learned outside Ingenio that Africans had been brought to Yapatera, only Armando related this information to his family history. Fabio learned the history, but did not connect himself or all blacks to it. Instead, he continued to see himself as black, but not necessarily African. This was similar to the case of Diana, a young woman who told me that she had learned about the enslavement of Africans in school. Yet, she did not associate her family's history with that history, even though she identified her family as black.

I should point out that neither of these cases should be construed as an attempt to deny African ancestry in order to distance oneself from Africa. In her 1998 book *Racism in a Racial Democracy*, France Winddance Twine argues that her Afro-Brazilian respondents intentionally forgot their African ancestry. Twine attributes this denial of Africanness to her respondents' desire to distance themselves from their blackness. This is not the dynamic I found in Ingenio. Twine's interviewees would claim Portuguese or Indian ancestry while denying African ancestry. In contrast, Fabio insisted that his ancestry was black, and did not claim Spanish or indigenous ancestry, although he most likely had indigenous antecedents in his family tree. His sister, for example, had strongly indigenous features. Like many of my interviewees, Fabio and Diana denied not only African but also Spanish and indigenous roots. Unlike Twine's informants, who whitened their family trees, my informants' family trees seemed to have no roots. There was a failure of transmission of oral history across generations in Ingenio, but it is not clear that this occurred because of either a denial of African roots or a desire to be whitened. Neither Fabio nor Diana connected the history of Africans in Peru to their personal family histories and thus did not engage in diasporic discourses that connect blackness to Africa. This leaves open the question of what meaning Fabio attaches to blackness.

To try to get an idea of what blackness meant to Fabio, I asked him what it meant to him that he, his wife, and his children were black. At that point he corrected me, saying that two of his seven children were not black. He identified his two children who were lighter in skin tone than him and his wife as "trigueños," not "negros." His assertions indicated that, despite Fabio's consciousness of his roots, he still saw blackness as, above all, a skin color. This distinction between skin color and descent is worth emphasizing. People in Ingenio understand that blackness *can* be, but do not believe that it *must* be, transmitted intergenerationally. For example, one day while walking across town, Mariana, Fabio's daughter, told me that she did not want to marry a black man (un negro) because her children would come out black (negros). She said, "Yo negra y él negro, los niños saldrán negros." (Me black and him black; the children would come out black.) The flip side of this was that if she were to marry a non-black man, she could have non-black children, thereby avoiding the transmission of her blackness.

Fabio's perception of blackness as being primarily a skin color did not preclude him from telling me, in the first interview, that he was proud to be black. In the follow-up interview, I asked him why he had said that he was proud to be black. In response, Fabio told me that sometimes whites tried to marginalize blacks, to discriminate against them, but that he did not let this get to him, because he was proud to be black. In fights, people might call him "negro mogoso" (filthy black) or similar insults, but this name-calling did not bother him, because he was proud to be black. For Fabio, therefore, his black identity served as a defense mechanism against verbal abuse. Fabio claimed to be proud of being black, but did not cite reasons for that pride, such as because his ancestors survived slavery or were African kings and queens. He did not actually say what he was proud of, only that his being proud protected him from insults.

I asked Fabio if it meant anything to him to be black, in light of the fact that there were other black people in Peru. There, he smiled and said yes. For example, when he went to an unfamiliar place, if he saw another black person, he and the stranger would greet each other "hola, familia" (hello, family). This custom is similar what occurs in some parts of the United States, where blacks typically greet one another, even if they are strangers. It also can be likened to the use of "brother" and "sister" in the U.S. black community, with its implications of kinship.

This sort of solidarity based on skin color is indicative of a collective black identity in Peru, which raises the question of the basis for this collective identity. As Helms (1990) points out, in the United States a collective identity as black relates to a common experience of historical and present-day oppression. In Peru the collective identity as black, to the extent that it does exist, is clearly not based on an overt recognition of historical oppression, although it can be used to counter present-day racial oppression. Fabio's self-identification as black is primarily based on his skin color, not on his recognition of a common historical experience. He does however identify as black and has the awareness that there are others who also identify as black and who face racial oppression as he does. Reminiscent of Wade's (1993) description of blacks in Colombia, Fabio's identification as black makes him part of a larger community of people who engage in similar political struggles. Fabio's insistence on skin color as the defining feature of blackness, however, is an indication that he rejects the diasporic discourse that insists on African ancestry as the defining feature of blackness.

Perla: I Have No Idea Where My Ancestors Are From

Perla, Fabio's wife, is an example of someone who is very removed from global discourses of blackness. Perla is a fifty-year-old mother of seven with skin the color of dark-roasted coffee and coarse, wavy hair. In conversations, Perla often referred to herself and her children as negro or negra. Perla was born in the neighboring village of Morropón, but had spent all of her married life in Ingenio, with the exception of a few visits to her daughter, Fiorela, who lived and worked in Lima. While sitting at Perla's dining room table—an aging slab table with metal legs, covered with an elaborately woven white lace tablecloth—I asked her about her ancestors. She told me that her family was all from Ingenio and the surrounding towns:

> TGB: So your great-great-grandparents also were born here?
> Perla: All of them.
> TGB: Ah, all of them. And do you know how they got here, to Ingenio?
> Perla: No, I don't know, no.
> TGB: You don't know if you have African ancestry or ancestors who came from Africa?
> Perla: No.

I then asked Perla if she had any indigenous, Spanish, or Asian ancestry, and she replied no to each one. She told me she did not know anything about her ancestors beyond the fact that they were from Ingenio. I inquired if she had ever heard how Africans had come to Peru, and she replied that she had not. Perla's conception of her ancestry was an example of a general pattern in Ingenio: people knew information about the ancestors they had personally met, but no more. This is similar to what Gow (1991) found in the Peruvian Amazon. However, whereas Gow treats this finding as an indication that, for native people, knowledge is a reflection of personal experience, this would not be a complete explanation in Ingenio: some of the villagers are able to give more extensive recountings of their ancestry, indicating that it is not simply a part of "native" culture to discount ancestry beyond a couple of generations back. Perla differs from Fabio and Armando insofar as she is unaware of the history of the African slave trade in Peru and, specifically, of the history of slavery in nearby Yapatera.

Although Perla did not see herself as African-descended, she referred to herself as black (negra) in my presence on various occasions. For example, one afternoon Perla, Isabela, and I were discussing how the daughters of one of our neighbors had been arguing, and that one had said "dirty" things to the other. Perla said it was a shame that the young woman was so pretty but had such a "dirty mouth." Perla continued, "I may be black and poor, but I would never permit such dirty things to come out of my mouth." This assertion of blackness is the closest Perla came to correlating moral traits to blackness. By saying that even though she was black she maintained her respectability, she implied that blacks in general were less than respectable. Another interpretation is that Perla was associating blackness with physical unattractiveness and saying that her neighbor's daughters were light-skinned (and hence pretty), and their behavior should be as pretty as their appearance. This was not the only time that Perla associated blackness with ugliness. I discuss conceptions of beauty in more detail in chapter 5 but, for now, it is important to point out that these associations draw on both local and global discourses. There is a local discourse of beauty that gives preference to light skin, and there is also a pattern across the African diaspora to associate light skin with beauty (Hobson 2005; Hunter 2002).

Blackness in the diaspora is very much associated with not only the history of racial oppression, but also present-day manifestations of it. Nevertheless, Perla did not see herself as a victim of racism. When I asked her if there was any racism in Ingenio, she replied that there was not. She stated that there were no racial or color preferences in Ingenio, and that everyone was treated as an equal. She further said that she had never been discriminated against and that no one had ever insulted her on account of her skin color. Perla's responses to my questions about discrimination indicated that she did not recognize a shared subjection to racial oppression among Peruvian blacks. Still, I decided to ask Perla for a follow-up interview to probe these issues further. Over the six months I spent in Ingenio, Perla and I got to know each other quite well, and I thought that perhaps I could get her to be more forthcoming in a second interview. In the hope that she would feel more at ease, and more like we were having a conversation, I did not record the follow-up interview. I first told her that I would explain to her my analysis of the initial interview. I told her that one part of my study was to figure out what it meant to people in Ingenio when they described themselves as black. I said that, based on her responses in her interview, it seemed that being black did not have very much meaning for her, that it was just a color. She reiterated that her blackness was indeed just a color.

I decided to point out a case of what I perceived to be discrimination, in order to see how Perla viewed the event. I chose an incident that had occurred just a few days before the re-interview. Natalia, a five-year-old girl who lived in the house next to mine and across from Perla, was at my house, swinging on our hammock. I asked her if she liked her brother's girlfriend. Natalia replied no, because she was negra. I asked Natalia if she herself was negra, and she said, "No, yo soy blanca" (No, I am white). Then, Natalia continued that she liked blancos, not negros. I recounted this event to Perla, who had babysat Natalia for most of her infancy. Following is an excerpt from my field notes, recorded just after my follow-up interview with Perla:

> I told Perla that I had asked Natalia what she thought of Jason's girlfriend, and Natalia said that she didn't like her, because she was "negra." Perla finished that sentence for me. It seemed as though she had heard Isabela [Natalia's mother] say that, because she nodded knowingly, and said that Natalia had heard it from her mother. Perla then told me that Natalia must hear when her mother says that Jason "anda con esas negras de mierda" (runs around with those black pieces of shit).[2] Then Perla told me that when Isabela fights with her sister, she calls her a "negra de mierda," even though they are the same [brown] color.

I asked Perla why, in the interview, she had said that she had never experienced discrimination. She responded that she had never been directly insulted. I then asked her if she had seen other cases of discrimination, and she agreed that she had. She said that, in fights, she had heard people call each other negro de mierda. I asked her if she felt bad when that happened, and she said that she did.

It turns out that Perla told me that there is no racism in Ingenio or in Peru because she interprets racism to mean direct acts of bigotry. Ironically, this is how many white Americans interpret racism today (Feagin 2000). Perla is clearly aware of antiblack rhetoric in her community, but she does not see this rhetoric as being tied to a prevailing system of black oppression. She sees these events as isolated cases of people doing unpleasant things, not as part of a system of racial oppression.

On the other hand, Perla did have a positive view of blacks. In the re-interview, I asked Perla if she felt any sort of camaraderie with other blacks. She said that she did, that they shared affection (*cariño*). Her eyes lit up as she told me that, when she was in Lima and she saw other morenas, she always felt a connection to them. When I asked her why, she said that she did not know, that perhaps it was just because morenas were affectionate people. Thus, it did mean something to Perla to be black. It meant she was affectionate. It also meant that some people might see her as unattractive. Perla not only identified with the label *black*, she also attributed meaning to it, even though she did not seem to be drawing from diasporic discourses.

Black Identity, Gender Roles, and a Globalized Discourse of Blackness

When we compare the ways that Armando, Fabio, and Perla talk about their blackness, a number of differences come to light (in addition to the commonality that they all see blackness as being related to color). Armando is most consciously aware of his ancestry, whereas Fabio is more aware of discrimination, and for Perla, an identification with other blacks is most salient. When we examine why they think of their blackness in such distinct ways, it becomes apparent that this is related to the extent to which they draw from diasporic discourses of blackness. Moreover, their access to these diasporic discourses is affected by the gendered division of social roles and social spaces in Ingenio, their access to the world outside Ingenio through reading and traveling, and their experiences of racism. In the next section, I discuss these factors and how they affect Ingenieros' conceptions of blackness.

Gender Matters

To address gender differences, it will be useful to examine more closely why, despite the fact that Perla and Fabio are husband and wife, Fabio invokes a relatively rich discourse of racial oppression, while Perla does not seem to have access to this discourse. The reason is the gendered division of social roles and social spaces in Ingenio, which results in unequal access to discursive tools and diasporic knowledge. Fabio and Perla are both very active in the local community, but in different ways. Fabio is active in the local radio station, in a political party, and in the black social movement. Perla, on the other hand, is active in the soup kitchen, in the religious association, and at charitable social events. Thus, whereas Fabio's activism is in the public sphere, Perla's is an extension of her household activities. Furthermore, Fabio and Perla do not talk about public issues to each other. When Fabio has friends over the house, Perla may be present, but she is primarily backstage, preparing and serving food and drinks for her husband's guests. In fact, men in Ingenio participate regularly in politicized discussions in male spaces—their living rooms, the benches in the plaza, the cantina, the chichería, the riverbank where men gamble and drink cane liquor, and the cockfights. The topics they discuss are influenced by the places where their conversations occur. Men inebriated by chicha and cane liquor at the cantina after the cockfight are apt to converse about the history of the town and the oppression of the farmworkers.

In his discussions in male spaces, Fabio disseminates the knowledge and way of speaking that he has garnered from his participation in workshops outside his community. Moreover, he has the opportunity to discuss issues with others who have had similar outside exposure in public spaces. The times that I chose to breach these gendered roles and join the men drinking at the chichería, I learned an immense amount about the history of the town, the local politics and development policies, the economic intricacies of the rice market, and the local freedom fighters and poets.

In contrast, my conversations with women rarely were about such politicized topics and took place primarily in female spaces. Although women did not participate in many conversations with men, they did converse with other women. Women discussed household-related topics in female spaces—on the front porch, in the kitchen, at the river where they washed clothes, and at the school gate where they waited for their children. The topics women discussed were influenced by the places where these conversations occurred. In contrast to my politicized discussions with men, my conversations with women revolved around pregnancy, childbirth, child care, caring for small animals, cooking, and the onerous nature of domestic work in the countryside.

Because of her gender, Perla did not have the same access to politicized discourses as Fabio did. Whereas Fabio frequently traveled out of town to the mayor's office and attended workshops in the area, Perla almost never left town. Her father and sister lived in Morropón, only seven kilometers from Ingenio, yet Perla was lucky if she saw them once a year. Fabio, on the other hand, traveled to Morropón on his bicycle several times a week. Fabio once proudly showed me a folder full of certificates from workshops he had attended in Morropón, Buenos Aires, Piura, Trujillo, Lima, and other places in Peru. Some of these had been organized by black social movements, while others had been organized by NGOs such as Plan International or by the local radio station.

The limitations on Perla's mobility and her restricted access to the public sphere were compounded by the collective limitations on the other women with whom she conversed. Whereas Fabio's discursive ability was enhanced by his access to male public spaces, Perla's was limited by her access to primarily female spaces. This point was made most clearly by the exception to this rule. Cecilia, who was in her early forties, was the only person I met in Ingenio who was actively involved in a black social movement. (Fabio had previously been involved, but had not been active in any black social movement for nearly a decade at the time of my research.) Cecilia regularly participated in meetings in Lima, Morropón, and other places. In her interview, she told me, "I have been participating since 1978, since I was very young; my husband has always supported this." On this and other occasions, Cecilia made it clear to me that her husband did not prevent her from attending events. Her constant affirmation of his acceptance of her travels and active participation indicated that this was not the norm. It is also worth noting that one woman told me other women did not like Cecilia because she had been known to steal husbands. Possibly Cecilia's violation of traditional gender roles through her participation in social movement activities contributed to this depiction of her as a sexually transgressive woman.

Fabio, in contrast, had a reputation for being quite virile, but his male counterparts did not denigrate him for this. In addition to rumors that he had a lover in another town, Fabio was known to be very outspoken and forthright. He had a politicized black identity due to his exposure to black social movements and his conversations with fellow villagers. Fabio, as a man, was permitted to take trips out of town to attend meetings and discuss black politics in a way that Perla was not. When the workshops came to Ingenio, she could go, but there has only ever been one workshop on black identity in Ingenio, about fifteen years ago.

Perla has had minimal exposure to the ways that transnational social movements have defined black identity as a diasporic experience of racial oppression. Thus, although Perla may point out that the local schools are of poor quality or that her employment options in Ingenio are practically nonexistent or that there is no water in her tap this morning, she does not invoke a rhetoric of racial marginalization and exclusion in these contexts. Nevertheless, Perla is aware of what I would label racial oppression. When she hears her neighbor call a young woman a black piece of shit, Perla knows that this statement denigrates her as well because she is black. Perla also understands that whiteness is valued and blackness devalued in Peruvian society, as can be seen in her self-deprecating statements about her blackness and her laudatory statements with regard to whiteness. In the re-interview, I found out that Perla also knows that blacks were slaves and that they were mistreated—she overheard her uncles talking about it when she was younger. However, nobody has shown Perla how to put all of this information together and call it racial oppression. Nobody has told Perla that this racial oppression should be the basis of her black identity. This is very different from the situation in other parts of the diaspora, where blackness is closely tied to a history of oppression (McPherson and Shelby 2004; D. Thomas 2004; Twine 1998). Because Perla is a woman, she is too busy cooking, cleaning, and serving men to sit down at the table with them to discuss politicized issues such as race and oppression. Just because racial oppression exists, and Perla sees it and feels it, does not mean she will name it, internalize it, and react to it in the same way that Fabio does.

Nevertheless, it does mean something to Perla to be black. Perla's blackness consists in her recognition of the denigration of blacks, her awareness of historical oppression, and the affection she feels for other blacks. Perla does not connect these three factors herself. Her own black identity is disjointed. Shelby (2002) suggests that a black identity is based on common experiences of racial oppression; Helms (1990) argues that it is based on a shared racial heritage; and Wade (1995) asserts that self-identification as black is a choice made in the light of common interests. Perla's case does not fit with any of these generalizations, since she attributes her self-identification as black to her skin color and does not use a language of oppression or of common heritage to describe her blackness. In fact, a woman in

Ingenio would have to violate gender norms in order to develop the kind of politicized racial consciousness that Shelby (2002) suggests is necessary to develop a black identity, or to have access to the diasporic knowledge requisite for the understanding of a common racial heritage.

This discussion of segregated spaces is useful insofar as it sheds light on how heterogeneous localized knowledge production can be. Global and diasporic discourses of blackness do exist in Ingenio, but not everyone has access to them. Next, I will discuss another way villagers gain access to diasporic discourses: by leaving the village.

Community Matters

In Ingenio, people referred to one another as black regularly, and this usually was not seen as offensive. Some villagers did however point out that calling someone black could be insulting in certain situations. People told me that to say "esa negra" was impolite, because *esa* is used to refer to objects or animals, not people. Others did not like to be called negro instead of by their name. Alan, a newly married agricultural worker in his twenties, explained to me why he objected when people called him black. Alan told me that he was offended when non-blacks called him negro. When I asked him why, he said that the person who calls him negro "se quiere creer más mejor que uno" (likes to think of himself as better than others). Alan had been to Piura to work for a while, and reported that people there shouted offensive racial slurs at him, such as "chupete de brea" (roughly translated as "tar baby") and "bisú del burro" (donkey's dick); those experiences caused him to change how he thought of himself as a black person. Similarly, Cecilia recounted to me that her daughter's uncle would always call her daughter "negra," and the daughter didn't like it. So, she told her daughter to tell her uncle, "Thank you. You don't offend me, because I am not a gringa." And the next time the uncle called the daughter "negra," the daughter didn't respond until he shouted her name. At that point, she said, "Yes, Uncle, that is my name. You can call me black, and I won't get upset because my race is black; I am not white."

Most people in Ingenio feel that being called negro or negra is not offensive, yet Alan and Cecilia feel quite differently. This difference can largely be explained by the fact that these discourses about blackness come from outside of their community: Alan's from his sojourn in Piura, and Cecilia's from her involvement with a variety of black social movements and her frequent trips to Lima and other urban areas in Peru.

Many of the young women in Ingenio went to Lima to work as domestics, and some came back with new ways of thinking and talking about their blackness. For example, I asked Doris, a housewife in her late fifties, if she had ever been insulted by someone because of the color of her skin. Her immediate response was "no, no, never." At this point, her daughter, who had just returned from Lima where she had been involved in a social movement that promoted domestic workers' rights, challenged her mother's response, asking her, "Has anyone ever said to you 'negra,' 'that negra'? You have been offended, right?"

Her mother responded, "Yes, I think so. But not like that. Just, 'black,' but no one has yelled at me."

Her daughter retorted, "What? How is that possible? Never, never, in all these years, and you are black? No one has ever insulted you for being black?"

This exchange demonstrates that people who travel outside of the community have access to different understandings of blackness and discourses of racial oppression. Doris and her daughter, Lorena, have witnessed similar situations where people refer to Doris as "esa negra." For Lorena, this is discrimination against her mother, whereas, for Doris, this is not necessarily discrimination. Lorena's politicization in Lima has led her to believe that these sorts of comments constitute discrimination. Lorena can thus draw strength from her understanding of blackness and its politicized nature in order to contest what she sees as verbal assaults. Doris, on the other hand, sees things differently; she does not need to defend herself against such remarks, since she does not perceive them to be insults. I am pointing out this distinction not to suggest that Lorena has a more accurate understanding of the situation, but merely to argue that access to larger discourses is likely to influence how people interpret local particularities.[3]

It is not that women have no access whatsoever to discourses of black oppression: Cecilia, her daughter, and Doris's daughter clearly demonstrate otherwise. However, the gendered nature of social spaces in Ingenio helps to explain why women such as Perla and Doris who have little access to outside knowledge will develop a distinct understanding of their blackness and what it means to them. This, in turn, sheds light on the complex relationship between the local and the global.

Local Blackness, Global Discourses

At the beginning of the chapter, I posited that global blackness encompasses the memory of slavery, racism, the place of blacks in the global racial hierarchy, and double consciousness. In Ingenio, blackness is a skin color that, at times, holds deeper meaning. Thus, when an Ingeniero identifies with his or her blackness, there are a number of layers of meaning in this declaration. Yet the individual's access to global discourses fundamentally affects how he or she perceives blackness, whether diasporic or local or somewhere in between.

Perla, for example, does not see herself as possessing a fundamental twoness as both a black and a Peruvian. She also does not draw her strength from a memory of slavery, nor does she see herself as holding a particular position within a global racial hierarchy. She does not invoke global discourses of blackness and thus does not appear to be part of the black diaspora. On the other hand, others see Perla through a veil of blackness, her life is greatly affected by the legacy of slavery, and she holds a particular position within the global racial hierarchy. In this sense, it seems folly to deny her entry into the black diaspora because, as Patterson and Kelley (2000) point out, the diaspora is both a process and a condition. Perla's condition is diasporic, and she is part of diasporic processes. She does not draw from diasporic discourses to understand her situation, but some of these discourses could resonate with her. For example, when I asked Perla if she felt a connection with other blacks, her eyes lit up when she said that she did. And when I asked her if she found insults directed at blacks to be offensive, she said that she did. In addition, when I probed deeper into the question of slavery, Perla began to remember snippets of conversation where her elders had talked about slavery.

Armando uses discourses that have a diasporic element to them, in that he refers to the experiences of slavery and institutionalized racism, two themes common to diasporic blacks. Even in this case, however, he draws only indirectly from global discourses. Armando does not explicitly associate himself with black Americans or black Jamaicans, for example. This is distinct from what scholars have found in Jamaica (D. Thomas 2004), Nicaragua (Pineda 2006), and Brazil (Sansone 2003), where people who self-identify as black use their blackness as an assertion of modernity or cosmopolitanism. In Ingenio, in contrast, blackness is not seen as indicative of cosmopolitanism. Blacks do not, for example, gain prestige from knowing about the latest global black cultural production. I never once heard any music produced by African Americans or blacks from the English-speaking Caribbean played in Ingenio. Toward the end of my stay, reggaeton began to gain popularity in Peru, and quickly found its way to Ingenio, although it was popular only among the youth. In Peru, however, reggaeton is not associated with blackness of the local, national, regional, or global varieties.

Local and global discourses of blackness share common threads yet do not always work in tandem. An example of this is the stereotype that blacks are good dancers. During my fieldwork in Ingenio, I never heard anyone suggest that blacks were better dancers than non-blacks. At parties, the most popular music was *cumbia* and the most notable difference in movement was that older people moved their hips quite a bit less than the younger ones did. Older people would often distance themselves from younger people on the basis of musical preferences or even dance styles, but there was no racial undertone to this separation. When blacks from Ingenio left the village and found themselves in Lima or other parts of Peru, the expectation that they knew how to dance would however become apparent. For example, Milagros, Fabio and Perla's eighteen-year-old daughter, accompanied us to Cuzco, Peru—a region with very few black Peruvians. One evening, we went out to a dance in the town square. When the DJ put on *música negra* (Afro-Peruvian music), Milagros began to dance and people began to cheer her on, with the expectation that she was black and therefore knew how to dance to that music. This particular music form was not a part of local culture in Ingenio. Milagros did know how to dance, however, and seemed quite comfortable doing so. I later asked her how she learned to dance, and she said that it just came naturally.

Milagros was dancing *festejo*, an Afro-Peruvian cultural form that originated in southern Peru. In northern Peru, where Ingenio lies, local cultural production was not generally referred to as black or Afro-Peruvian. The villagers in Ingenio usually did not characterize local cultural production as black, although they were aware of black cultural production in Peru. For example, when I asked Alexandra, a homemaker in her forties, if there was any black cultural production in Ingenio, she responded that the only black culture she was aware of was what she saw on television. When I asked her if this sort of black culture also existed in Ingenio, she denied it, although she pointed out that there were blacks in Ingenio. When I asked

Esteban if there were any black cultural forms in Ingenio, he first said no, but after a pause, indicated that there could be. Since there were blacks in Ingenio and some of them could dance, they could form a dance troupe, and he said that he would think about doing that, as it might do the village some good. Esteban, like other villagers, had seen black Peruvians perform on television, which inspired his idea that blacks from Ingenio could do the same. Alexandra, however, did not reach the same conclusion.

Now we can return to the question posed at the beginning of this chapter: What does it mean when someone in Ingenio says, "Yo soy negro"? The answer depends on the life experiences, social location, and especially the gender of the person asserting his or her blackness. Villagers who have limited access to diasporic discourses, who are more likely to be women than men, see their blackness very differently from those (typically men) who have more access. In this way, global discourses of blackness can and do affect local conceptions of blackness. It is however also true that local cultures are resilient and that local conceptions of blackness can and do exist apart from global discourses. Access to these discourses affects how individuals identify with their blackness and the larger black community. Nevertheless, those people for whom the condition of blackness is inescapable draw from the local and global discourses that make the most sense to them in their daily lives.

Thinking of the diaspora as both a process and a condition helps us to understand better the multiplicity of black identities that exist, and the extent to which global and local discourses interact to produce new conditions and processes. The condition of being part of the black diaspora is not enough to produce a double consciousness, a sense of commonality with other blacks, and an elaborate understanding of historical and present-day racial oppression. Nevertheless, the fact that being black in Peru has meant being marginalized affects how blacks are treated in Peru. These experiences of marginalization sow the seeds for the creation of a diasporic consciousness, if and when diasporic discourses are accessible.

The voices of the people in Ingenio also allow us to understand how meanings are ascribed to blackness at the local level. First of all, we can see that flows of knowledge and meaning, such as migration, the media, the written word, and political movements, work in different ways to imbue blackness with meaning. As a result, the significance of blackness is always changing. The voices from Ingenio can also help us in creating new understandings of blackness that are not necessarily based on the Black Atlantic model. To be sure, representations of blackness from the United States, United Kingdom, and Caribbean influence how blackness is understood everywhere, but it is important also to take into consideration what Ingenio brings to blackness on its own terms. Thinking about the interaction between the local and the global helps us to remember how the complex web of meanings surrounding blackness is produced and reproduced while also keeping in mind that localities matter a great deal. Blackness in Ingenio would likely have a very different meaning were there not a global discourse of blackness, yet the multiplicity of meanings at the local level shows the limitations of thinking on only the global level.

In Peru, the local and the global work together to produce meaning around blackness. This is nothing new: the production of meaning with regard to blackness has been the product of transnational conversations and local social interactions since the start of the Atlantic slave trade, and likely before that. European thinkers wrote about what it meant to be black, or what qualities a black person had, based on travel accounts of other Europeans. These reports were then disseminated across Europe and the Americas. Some of these ideas were adopted in the Americas, and others were rejected. Linnaeus's *Systema Naturae* is an early example of this. His categorization of humans into four races, each with particular physical and moral traits, still influences how people around the globe think about blackness in particular and race in general. Nevertheless, our daily experiences also affect our ideas on race and blackness, and these are constantly changing as we continuously receive new information and have new interactions. This interaction between the global and the local is given further consideration in the next chapter, which addresses beauty norms in Ingenio.

chapter 5

Black Is Beautiful or White Is Right?

> *Ellas son morenas, pero bonitas. (They are brown-skinned, but pretty.)*
> Ricardo, Ingenio resident in his fifties, describing two women

> *Puede que seas blanca, pero picuda. (You may be white, but [you are] big-lipped.)*
> Carlos, a boy from Ingenio, arguing with his sister

From time to time during my fieldwork in Ingenio, I would go to Señora Zulema's house in the afternoons and watch *telenovelas* with her and Señora Gertrudis, her sister. Both women were in their fifties and lived relatively comfortably, although not nearly as luxuriously as the wealthy people portrayed in the telenovelas they watched. Señora Zulema's daughter worked in Lima as a household domestic and regularly sent her mother money. She bought Señora Zulema a television for her birthday one year, and subsequently installed a solar panel on her house so that she could watch television all afternoon, even though there was no electricity in Ingenio at the time. Señora Gertrudis ran a small but relatively lucrative restaurant out of her living room. The profitability of this enterprise caused some women in town to accuse her of doing witchcraft to ensure her financial success. Nevertheless, both of these women would self-identify and be seen by development agencies as poor, on the basis of the adobe brick walls and dirt floors of their homes.

One afternoon, I tried to get Señoras Zulema and Gertrudis to give their opinions as to why the stars of the telenovelas they watched were always white and blond, and the kitchen staff was always darker-skinned. In the telenovela we were watching at the time, the brown-skinned maid was frantic about relationship problems that the blonde, white-skinned lady of the house was having. I thought to myself that the lady of the house would be unlikely to be so worked up about the maid's personal life. During the commercial break, which was the only time I could expect the engrossed women to respond to me, I asked, "Why is it that the stars are always blond and the maids brown?" Señora Zulema said, "¿Porqué será?" (Why is it so?), and Señora Gertrudis shrugged her shoulders and gestured her chin in agreement. They had no further comment on the subject. I then asked whether it bothered them that this was always the case. Both women responded no, and that was the end of the conversation.

That conversation was part of my attempt, through ethnography, to understand how media portrayals of blacks and whites affect the ways that African-descended villagers in Ingenio talk about race and racism. In Peru white models predominate not only in telenovelas, but also in advertisements for beer, retail stores, grocery items, and beauty products. Ingenio is relatively isolated, and villagers are largely unable to afford the consumer items advertised by white models. Nevertheless, the walls of stores in Ingenio are frequently decorated with images of scantily clad, light-skinned models promoting the consumption of one or another brand of Peruvian beer. Villagers are inundated with images of white heroes, white beauty queens, and brown- or black-skinned people in servile positions. On the other hand, they also they have access to images of beautiful black women, such as Alek Wek, Naomi Campbell, and Rosa Elvira Cartagena, Miss Peru in 1999, as these representations also come to the small screen in Ingenio. The question is how villagers interpret these images and what their interpretation means for how they think about themselves and their fellow villagers in racial and color terms.

Both Señoras Gertrudis and Zulema are the color of dark-roasted coffee, and thus potentially could have been offended by the small number of people who look like them in starring roles in telenovelas. Alternatively, they could see that telenovelas reflect a certain reality in Peru, in that they know personally quite a few brown-skinned women who work in the homes of wealthy white Limeños, including Señora Zulema's own daughter, Yraida. Their nonchalance could lead us to believe that they are victims of negative portrayals of blacks and have internalized these images to the extent that they see depictions of black subservience as completely normal. This explanation is however at best incomplete because at times these women make statements that value blackness and denigrate whiteness. It also leaves unanswered the question of why other villagers do not express similar nonchalance. Eighteen-year-old Milagros, whom I met in Ingenio and later saw in Lima, told me that the reason behind the representations of whites as rich and beautiful in telenovelas was racism. She informed me very matter-of-factly that casting companies did not give blacks a chance to play leading roles.

In the previous chapter I focused on how diasporic discourses influence the meanings given to blackness in Ingenio; here, I focus on how global and national representations of blacks and whites influence local beauty norms and valorizations of blackness and whiteness. The influence of global discourses of beauty and blackness is clear; yet the salience of local discourses is also evident in a variety of ways. Thus far, we have seen that as a result of the history of Ingenio, slavery and Africa are not important facets of the local discourse of blackness, and that some villagers engage in diasporic discourses of blackness but others largely do not. An examination of beauty, blackness, and whiteness will make clear the extent to which local racial geography and history mediate the impact of globalization on local discourses of race, beauty, and sexuality.

Local and Global Discourses

An analysis of local understandings of beauty and race requires a theoretical elaboration of the interaction between local and global processes. This analysis will provide insight into how people in Ingenio experience the purportedly homogenizing forces of globalization. This study builds on the work of a host of ethnographers who have looked at the local-level effects of globalization. In these endeavors, ethnographers generally choose research sites where the effects of transnational processes and actors are ubiquitous, ranging from sex tourism destinations, such as Sosúa in the Dominican Republic (Brennan 2004), and incursions of multinational banks in Honduras (J. Jackson 2005) to places that have a little of both, such as Boca Chica, also in the Dominican Republic (Gregory 2006). These ethnographic studies provide us with rich insight into the human face of globalization, including who is effecting it and who it is affecting.

In Ingenio, global forces are not so rampant. Thus, the changes have been slow and the metamorphosis incomplete.

Ingenio only recently has begun to experience some of the consequences of globalization, and in some ways more than others. Globalization has affected Ingenio primarily through the rapid spread of technology, which has increased the spread of global discourses through the media, facilitated internal migration, and changed the way rice is harvested. Whereas a few years ago, rice farmers would hire several helpers to work for seven days during the rice harvest, it is now easier and even a bit cheaper to rent a harvester that gets the job done in a few hours. An added advantage is that people no longer have to sleep in the fields for several nights to protect their harvest. In another example, older villagers recounted to me that having a party used to entail contracting a musical group to play the *cajón* and guitar for entertainment. Now a social event often requires bringing in a disk jockey with powerful speakers and an up-to-date collection of CDs and other forms of digital music. This new access to music from all over the world has transformed people's musical tastes. When I did the bulk of my fieldwork there was no Internet in Ingenio, although there was one rarely used Internet café in nearby Morropón. Yet when I went back in 2006, there were four Internet cafés in Morropón, as well as an increasing number of call centers, connecting people to the rest of the world.

Ingenio may have increased access to global communications, but there are no sweatshops owned by multinational corporations, the World Bank has not financed the building of any hydroelectric plants along the Río Piura, and very few people from Ingenio migrate outside of Peru. There is also no cable television or Internet in Ingenio itself, and none of the national cell phone companies had built towers to provide service there at the time I last visited in 2006.[1] So, why study globalization in a place that is so *not* global? The answer is that doing so provides us with a unique opportunity to understand how communities resist, accommodate, and incorporate global trends and discourses. Despite its relative isolation, Ingenio is not completely outside the global economy and its residents are not entirely without ties to the rest of the world. Even though there was no electricity in Ingenio during the bulk of my fieldwork, nearly every house had a television antenna perched on its roof. Through these black-and-white television sets, powered by rechargeable car batteries, residents could have the rest of the world in their living rooms with them, and at least be aware of what there was to purchase, experience, and see in the world, even if those things were out of their reach. In addition, although international migration was infrequent, migration to the cosmopolitan capital city of Lima was common, and these migrants provided an important link to the rest of the world.

This spread of cultural knowledge and representations is part of cultural globalization, where, through technology, ways of seeing the world are shared across borders. This sharing of cultural discourses is the primary way that people in Ingenio participate in globalization. Ingenieros exist on the edge of the global economy; nevertheless, even here on the edge, they have access to cash and consumer items. One of the first items new families purchase or acquire is a television. These televisions must be black and white and small, since that is all a car battery can power. Still, through these televisions, people in Ingenio have access to a world of images and to worlds very different from their small, isolated village.

The landscapes of media images, or "mediascapes" as Appadurai (1996) has labeled them, contain a wide variety of messages that can be interpreted in many different ways. People use the discursive strategies made available to them through these mediascapes to make sense of the world they live in. These mediascapes present people in Ingenio with various representations of blackness, whiteness, beauty norms, and racism. Ingenieros do not simply adopt these representations as their own, but rather adapt them to the local context. The mediascapes to which Ingenieros have access present images that reaffirm their blackness by portraying beautiful, cosmopolitan, wealthy blacks. They also present images sending the message that whites are better than blacks and are more likely to be successful.

A variety of researchers have pointed out that we are living in a globalizing world, but that local and national cultures are resilient, and we are not likely ever to live in a world that is completely globalized (e.g., Appadurai 1996; Besnier 2002; P. Jackson 2004; Steger 2004). Ingenio provides an example of this insofar as people adapt global discourses in ways that make sense to them. People in Ingenio have access to and strategically make use of a "multiplicity of discursive elements" (Foucault 1990: 100). Rather than simply adopting the global discourses on blackness and whiteness wholesale, people in Ingenio select elements from these discourses that are most relevant to them, and leave behind those that are less useful. Before I provide examples of how villagers pick and choose their discursive strategies, it will be useful to discuss the media representations available in Ingenio.

Seeing the World in Black and White

When villagers in Ingenio turn on their televisions, they have few options in terms of channels. Nevertheless, television provides them with a wide variety of representations. They generally have access to programs and advertisements produced in the United States, in Lima, and in other Latin American countries. The representations of blacks and whites on Peruvian television are influenced by national understandings of race, Latin American racial norms, and global discourses of blackness and whiteness. Media representations in Peru primarily send the message "white is right" by portraying white stars as the epitome of beauty, goodness, and success. Despite the fact that most people in Latin America are black or brown, white faces predominate in televised Latin American entertainment and news shows. At the same time, Peruvian television broadcasts shows produced in the United States and Brazil that highlight black cultural production. And, as Sansone (2003) points out, black cultural production often invokes transnational themes and representations of blackness that are likely to resonate to some extent with blacks across the diaspora, including black Peruvians.

The "black is beautiful" discourse derives from black pride movements and pan-African struggles, especially in the 1960s, that reaffirmed blackness or Africanness as a desirable and valuable quality. This discourse has changed the way people in the United States think about race. For example, studies of self-esteem among black children prior to the 1960s uncovered high levels of self-hatred, whereas studies after the 1960s began to show that black children were learning to value blackness (Porter and Washington 1979). These U.S.-based discourses become globalized as songs such as James Brown's "Say It Loud, I'm Black and I'm Proud" are played on transnational television and radio networks, along with television shows and movies that contain positive portrayals of black people. These counterhegemonic discourses also reach people in Ingenio and widen the realm of discourses to which they have access.

Telenovelas provide an ideal site for the consideration of the interaction between the global and the local in Ingenio for two main reasons. First of all, telenovelas are eminently transnational in themselves, often financed in one country, set in another, featuring actors from various countries, and globally marketed. Second, they are immensely popular in Ingenio. Every evening in Ingenio, men, women, and children crowd around twelve-inch black-and-white televisions to watch telenovelas. The evening shows nearly always end with cliffhangers that work to get viewers hooked and anxiously awaiting the next episode. Some of the telenovelas are Peruvian, but others are Mexican, Colombian, Venezuelan, or Brazilian. A good number of them are produced in Miami.

Telenovelas are popular across Latin America and among U.S. Latinos/as, and have been a transnational phenomenon for several decades (Mato 2005). They are even making inroads into the English-speaking U.S. market with the adaptation of the popular Colombian telenovela "Betty la Fea." "Ugly Betty" began airing in the United States in 2006 with unexpected success. Increasing media consolidation has meant that many of the telenovelas people watch in both the United States and Latin America are produced in Miami, and many Peruvian television stations are owned by or are subsidiaries of transnational media corporations. In addition, in many cases, the telenovela stars are imported from other countries. Latin American telenovelas are different from U.S. soap operas in that they end after 180 to 200 episodes, and they are shown daily during prime time. They are designed to appeal to women, men, and children; generally focus on romantic relationships, class conflict, and social mobility; and are typically quite melodramatic (La Pastina, Rego, and Straubhaar 2003).

Across Latin America, telenovelas reinforce Western beauty norms insofar as European-looking characters are usually portrayed as beautiful and successful, whereas non-European characters are portrayed as unattractive and poor (Urrieta 2003). In Peru, telenovelas work to reaffirm the racial hierarchy by nearly always portraying whites as wealthy and people of color as subservient. Peruvians can see that this racial hierarchy is prevalent not only in Peru, but across Latin America, which further naturalizes white dominance in Peru. In this way, the Peruvian media, like most media outlets, construct the Peruvian reality through the lens of the elite who control the media (Gamson et al. 1992). Although Peru is a primarily nonwhite country, one study showed that 70 percent of commercials used exclusively people with European features. Moreover, those commercials that used nonwhites portrayed them in low-status occupations—as slaves, servers, maids, or cooks (Estupiñán 2006). Given that telenovelas are the most popular television genre in Ingenio and that they portray people who look similar to most Ingenieros as undesirable and low status, it is reasonable to expect that these images influence conceptions of beauty and status in Ingenio.

Discourses of Race and Beauty in Ingenio

In many of the homes and small stores I visited in Ingenio, I saw calendars prominently displayed that featured a skimpily dressed white woman in a provocative pose. In many more homes and stores, I saw calendars adorned with pictures of blond children with angelic expressions on their faces. Black children or babies did not figure in any of the calendars or other wall decorations that I saw in people's homes, despite the fact that the majority of villagers saw themselves as black. These pictures and pinups, as well as media representations of whites, worked to reinforce "White European standards of beauty" as well as the "marginalization of certain types of beauty that deviate from" these standards (Patton 2006: 24).

Despite the widespread presence of positive portrayals of whites, most of my interviewees vehemently denied that locals had internalized Western beauty norms. I asked people if they thought that other villagers took skin color into account when choosing romantic partners, and the overwhelming answer was no. "In love, there is no color," I was told time and again. Some people even told me that, if there was any preference in Ingenio, it was for brown-skinned people. Other interviewees told me that the ideal of beauty in Ingenio was *café-con-leche* (coffee with milk) skin color and dark, wavy hair. An interview with Rocío provided an excellent example. Rocío was a young woman who grew up in Ingenio but had worked in Lima for a couple of years. In the interview, Rocío told me that there was a preference for brownness in Ingenio, so I probed her a bit further:

> TGB: For example, when I watch telenovelas here, I notice that the star is always blond.
> Rocío: Yes
> TGB: And, I would say that it seems as though, in Peru, there is generally a preference for blonds. But here in Ingenio, you say that this does not exist?
> Rocío: Here, generally, well, there is little of this. But at the national level, yes, there is preference for whites, right?
> TGB: Yes.
> Rocío: But here there is little of that.

Rocío was willing to admit that the telenovelas reflected a national fondness for whiteness, but insisted that this preference did not carry over to Ingenio.

These interview responses did not resonate with my findings from my fieldwork in Ingenio. Although Rocío denied that a preference for whiteness existed, I saw that preference play out on many occasions. For example, one afternoon after teaching English at the local high school, I chatted with a few girls outside the classroom. I had brought my camera that day, and asked the girls if I could photograph them. They readily agreed and began to pose for the picture. While I was shooting photographs, a boy yelled that I should be careful, as the camera was likely to break because the girls were black. This association of blackness with ugliness might be dismissed as children teasing one another except that it happened on several occasions.

The most poignant example of the association of blackness with ugliness occurred when my brother and family came to visit us in Ingenio. My brother is blond, with blue eyes, and so are his two children. They arrived in Ingenio in the evening, and my neighbors came over to welcome them. The men and women alike were very keen on holding the nine-month-old baby, and many people commented that he looked just like a doll or an angel. Everyone loves babies, so I was not surprised by this attention. However, I was taken aback when I heard Señora Perla say, "¿Qué pensará el bebito de esos negros feos?" (What must the baby think of these ugly blacks?) Señora Perla, who was dark-skinned, said this in front of three of her similarly dark-skinned children, who seemed unfazed by her comment. It is worth pointing out that Perla and her children are not by most standards ugly. In fact, people in the village often referred to them as good-looking, and one of Perla's daughters was elected the town queen in the annual beauty contest.

The following afternoon, I took my brother and his family to Don Armando's house to introduce them to him. I often visited Don Armando to chat, and he was always able to provide me with a story about Ingenio or the neighboring village, La Pilca, as well as give me useful information about what was going on in the world. Don Armando was a farmer and his wife a schoolteacher, but he seemed the more avid reader of the two, and was always up-to-date on the latest national and world news. When we arrived, Don Armando was in the living room with his family. There were a number of small children at the door who had been following us around to get a peek at my brother and his family. Don Armando made the same comment as Doña Perla in reference to all the attention my brother's children were getting: "Qué pensaron de esos negritos feos?" (What must

they [my niece and nephew] think of these ugly blacks?) I had not expected Don Armando to vocalize such a devaluation of blacks, since he
had exhibited to me on other occasions substantial knowledge about black
history and black culture, and had told me that he was proud of his racial
origins and felt that he was equal to whites.

In a subsequent formal interview, I asked Don Armando why people
in Ingenio sometimes referred to "ugly blacks" and specifically mentioned
the incident with my niece and nephew. I did not remind him that he
himself had used those words because I did not feel comfortable doing so.
Don Armando responded that the comment was just a joke, that blacks
had turned around jokes made on them and now made such jokes about
themselves. Donna Goldstein (2003) found that blacks in a Rio shantytown would also make denigrating jokes about one another. She argued
that such jokes got their "punch precisely by expressing a perspective that
would otherwise be inexpressible. Statements made in the process of 'only
joking' can often provide a window into deeply held and troubling feelings,
such as those that deal with race" (129).

Calling children, especially your own, ugly is something that seems inexpressible. However, I am reminded of a time when Perla told her daughter Milagros that she was fat and ugly, since she had gone away to school
in the capital city and come back about twenty pounds heavier. Milagros
responded to her mother, "¡Ay! Mamá, I can lose the weight anytime."
When Perla told Milagros that she had gained weight and that it was not
attractive, her tone was critical, not joking. Her tone was different from
the one she used when she asked what my niece and nephew must think
of the "negritos feos." Whereas her children had laughed at the "negritos
feos" remark, Milagros did not find her mother's comments on her weight
to be funny. Perla felt it was appropriate to comment directly on Milagros'
weight, as that might induce Milagros to lose some weight. However, calling her daughter an ugly black in a serious tone would have been inexpressible insofar as her blackness was something she could not change.

When I asked Rocío why my brother's children had gotten so much attention, she admitted that there was some fascination with this particular
brand of whiteness, that is, with white foreigners. She added that she had
heard blacks say on other occasions that a white baby might get scared
when being held by a black person. When I asked her whether that statement reflected an overall preference for whiteness she reiterated that, in
Ingenio, the ideal of beauty was a brown-skinned woman. To back up her

argument, she pointed out that when white-skinned people moved to Ingenio from the mountain areas, they were not seen as desirable. People said that they smelled funny and walked and talked differently.

Serranos

Rocío was referring to serranos. *Serrano* can be translated directly as mountain-person, and the term bears some resemblance to the English word *hillbilly* in terms of its slightly negative and mocking connotations in reference to people who live in mountainous regions. Although in southern Peru most Andean people are of primarily indigenous descent, the northern Andes are characterized by a much larger presence of people of European descent. According to residents of Ingenio, which lies at the foot of the northern Andes, this is because Spaniards arrived first in northern Peru, and many Spanish soldiers took indigenous wives and settled in northern Andean villages. This legend holds some truth: the Spanish presence is largely a result of Spaniards setting up towns in the Andes that required a Spanish administrative presence (Huertas Vallejo 2001). Many of the people who live in the highlands today are the descendants of these colonial authorities. In Ingenio, *serrano* is often equated with whiteness, although it is a particular brand of whiteness. Serranos have been migrating from the northern Andes down into the valley where Ingenio is located for most of the twentieth century. However, they only began to settle in this valley in the latter part of the twentieth century, particularly in the last two decades. Older people in Ingenio told me that serranas used to come to Ingenio to work as domestic servants, and that serranos came at harvesttime to help pick the crops. As I discussed in chapter 1, the presence of fair-skinned serrano field hands precluded a strict racial hierarchy in the hacienda era. Serranos, many of whom were lighter-skinned than the hacienda owners or managers, worked alongside negros from Ingenio. These days, young women from the Andes are more likely to go directly to Lima to work as domestics, and there are fewer jobs for temporary farmworkers with the introduction of rice-harvesting machines.

During a trip to Ingenio in the summer of 2006, my family and I made a brief visit to a few highland towns to get a better idea of their ethnic composition. The first town we visited, Silahuá, was primarily indigenous, and it was the only town we visited that had a Quechua name. One of the schoolteachers told us that due to Silahuá's relatively hidden location, the

Spanish conquistadores did not see it, and it escaped pillage. The historian Alejandro Diez Hurtado (1998) explains that the residents of Silahuá were ordered to relocate to Frías but refused to do so and were able to avoid Spanish domination for several centuries.

The other villages we visited shared a different fate and were marked by a strong European presence. Although some people were quite indigenous in appearance, others were blond-haired and blue-eyed, and the majority were quite light-skinned with brown hair. People in Ingenio had told me that in the highlands "son puros zarcos" (there are only light-eyed people). This turned out to be an exaggeration, but the ethnic composition of the highlands was markedly different from that of Ingenio. As the late Octavio Céspedes[2] pointed out to me, Piura has three distinct ethnic groups— serranos, cholos, and negros, and they generally live in distinct locations. Serranos tend to live in the highlands, to be lighter-skinned, and to have brown hair and light eyes. Cholos live on the coast and often have black hair and brown skin. Negros live in between these two groups on the flat lowlands where the plantations are, and are generally dark-skinned with curly hair. This is a generalization, and the regions are certainly not racially segregated in a strict sense. Nevertheless, negros who live in Ingenio often perceive the serranos who live there to be outsiders. Specifically, negros consider themselves to be criollos (meaning "of this place") and serranos to be the quintessential outsiders.[3] In addition to skin color, criollos distinguish themselves from serranos because of their way of speaking, their gait, their dress, and according to Rocío, even their smell.

The label *serrano* denotes a geographical origin, but Ingenio is the last town before the sierra. A twenty-minute walk up the hill from Ingenio is a small town called Pampa Flores, considered to be part of the sierra, as is the next town up the hill, Pueblo Libre. One day, Perla and I decided to walk up to Pueblo Libre, about an hour by foot from Ingenio. I had expected it to be much farther, as people often characterized Pueblo Libre as being very far away.

On the way up the hill, we talked quite a bit about the differences between serranos and criollos, and I came to realize that Perla primarily defines herself in opposition to serranos. She sees herself as a criolla and as everything serranos are not. In her mind, serranos are white; she is black. Serranos speak a somewhat stilted Spanish; she speaks a more sing-song Spanish. Serranos like to drink and fight; criollos are less likely to get violent. Serranos are more likely than criollos to abuse their wives (although both do). Serranos are more likely than criollos to save money. Perla said she admired serranos' ability to save, but spoke disparagingly about their unwillingness to buy food for their families, something that would never occur in her house. Serranos are, in many ways, the closest "other" to Ingenio. Although residents of Ingenio see images on television of people very different from themselves, Perla and other Ingenieros are more likely to define themselves in opposition to serranos than to wealthy whites on television.

As Perla indicated, serranos were generally viewed to be less refined than criollos, as well as more frugal with their money. The most salient representation of serranos was however their presumed predisposition to violence and drunkenness. People often would say that serranos were quick to pull out their knives. In June 2006, there were parties and cockfights almost every weekend in Ingenio, as there are every June, since it is harvest season. One afternoon, Señora Perla and I were talking about the upcoming cockfights. She mentioned that she hoped that the cockfights would be on the upper side of town, not on the lower side. She explained that a serrano organized the cockfights on the lower side, and she did not like those cockfights as much, because "vienen hartos serranos" (lots of serranos come to them). I asked Perla why she did not like it when a lot of serranos came, and she replied because they fought a lot. They drank *cañazo* (cane liquor), got drunk, and then took out their knives. The negative reputation of serranos in Ingenio has some parallels with the stereotypes of white Costa Ricans held by blacks in Limón, Costa Rica, who view whites as "dangerous, violent, alcoholic savages" Bourgois (1986: 159).

The general distaste for serranos among criollo residents of Ingenio was evident in my conversations with villagers after my family's 2006 trip up to the sierra. To get to the sierra, we took a moto-taxi from Ingenio to Morropón, a truck up to Silahuá, two donkeys from there up to Naranjo, and three mules from Naranjo to Chalaco. From Chalaco, we took a bus down the other road to Santo Domingo and a station wagon from there all the way back to Ingenio. Ingenio is a relatively small town, so when we got back from our three-day excursion to the sierra, most people seemed to have heard that we had gone to the mountains for a few days. The first thing people wanted to know was whether we were able to eat the food. When Isabela saw me, she smugly asked me if I liked the food in the sierra. Perla then pointed out that "serranas son bien cochinas para cocinar" (serranas are unhygienic in their cooking), and that "serranas cocinan en el suelo" (serranas cook on the floor [meaning they squat, as opposed to standing up, to cook]). Francisca was surprised that we were willing to eat the food in the sierra, since she did not think much of the cuisine. She also told me that she had never gone to the sierra because of her fear of serranos' tendency to violence. And when I saw Brenda, she asked me if we had been bitten by fleas while we were in the sierra (which we had). The fact that we had traveled by donkey and mule, as opposed to horse or motorcycle, was also a source of great amusement for the villagers, serving as further confirmation of the presumed backwardness of serranos. This reaction was also in part related to the fact that the few people who rode donkeys around Ingenio tended to be serranos. Criollo men often rode horses but rarely rode donkeys or mules, and very few criolla women rode any pack animal. The people in the sierra explained to me that they used mules because they were stronger than horses, and donkeys because they were less expensive.

Another common stereotype of serranos is that the men are *machistas,* and that the women have too many children. This goes along with the general view that serranos are not as modernized as criollos. Several women told me that serranos believe that so long as there is a man in the house, a woman has to oblige him sexually, and that they don't believe in birth control. Alaya told me a couple of stories about serranos that are worth discussing. Alaya, a young mother of two, runs a small shop where she sells a limited stock of over-the-counter medicines. Alaya told me that serranos believe that "habiendo gallina en casa, tiene que poner huevos" ("when there is a hen in the house, she has to lay eggs," meaning that the women's role is to have babies). I heard a couple of other sayings with reference to roosters and serranos. This equation of serranos with animals, again, is an indication that they are not generally seen as very eloquent or sophisticated people.

Alaya's second story was also in line with the idea that serranos were machistas. She, like many people in Ingenio, criticized them not only for having too many children, but also for making them work in the fields at a very young age. Villagers would often recount to me stories of serranos making their children work too much or too hard. One afternoon, when I was visiting Alaya at her house, she told me a story that provided additional insight into how people in Ingenio viewed serranos. Alaya told me that her father occasionally would walk up to the sierra to purchase livestock. On one such trip, he came across a little boy who was calling for help. The boy, who appeared to be about five years old, was out taking care of the cows. Her father ran over to see what the boy was screaming about and discovered that a lion was stalking him. Her father helped the boy escape by attracting the lion's attention. The father then spent a few hours in a tree until the lion got bored and left. In Alaya's account, she made it clear that she thought serranos had so many children so that they could use them for labor, and that they sent them out to work at a very tender age. This story of the boy alone with the cows being chased by a lion exemplified the danger to which serranos subjected their children.

Alaya also told me that, not only did serranos make their young children work hard, they did the same to their wives. A young woman from the sierra came into Alaya's shop while we were talking. After she left, I asked Alaya what had happened to the woman, because although she was only thirty-two, she had severe varicose veins all over her legs. Alaya told me that her husband wouldn't give her the money to go to the doctor nor would he let her take birth control. Thus, the woman was pregnant again and already had four small children. In recounting these two cases, Alaya showed clear disdain for serranos and their lack of education and what she referred to as "civilization."

In general, there is a sense of disdain for people from the Andes among villagers in Ingenio. Yet, this disdain is complemented by an aesthetic appreciation for serranos, at least once they get cleaned up. For example, on our journey up to the sierra, our driver commented that, although serranos might look ugly because of the way they dress, once you put a pair of jeans and a clean shirt on them, many are actually quite good-looking. And Señora Adriana told me that people from the sierra are generally good-looking, as they have light skin and blue or green eyes.

Perla spoke negatively about serranos in general, yet on one occasion, she told me that some serranos were quite attractive. She followed that up by saying that others were not, because they were undernourished and yellowish, but that some of the serranas went to Lima to work and came back good-looking, and that some of them married very well.

Rocío also told me in an interview about a friend of hers from the sierra who went to work in Lima and was given the opportunity to study. Rocío was of the opinion that this young woman's luck could be attributed, at least in part, to her white skin and good looks:

I have a friend from here who is white, white, white. And, she worked as a domestic. She is white; she is pretty, my friend. . . . Her boss [*patrona*] would say to her: "look, you have [a nice] appearance; you are not fit for domestic work." She enabled her to study so that she would not have to work as a domestic, because she would say, "No, you have the looks for another type of work."

In this case, this young woman's whiteness made her seem unfit for domestic labor. Thus, although serranos might be devalued in Ingenio, some of them were able to benefit from their whiteness in Lima, if they were able to downplay their mountain origins. Rocío was well aware that in Lima she would be seen as an ideal candidate for domestic service, and that it was unlikely anyone would tell her she had the looks for another line of work. Nevertheless, Rocío remained unshaken in her belief that brown skin was appreciated in Ingenio.

Mejorando la Raza/Improving the Race

Serranos are seen as potentially good-looking without being of mixed race. Blacks, on the other hand, have the potential to be attractive only if they are not too black; that is, if they have white or Indian blood. Mixed blacks have hair that is less kinky and skin that is less black, and thus are seen as more desirable. Despite the disdain many villagers hold for serranos, in some cases serranos can be seen as appropriate romantic partners, or at least as preferable to negros, in that interracial unions serve to "improve the race."

Many villagers in Ingenio indicated to me in one fashion or another that it is preferable for a dark-skinned person to marry a lighter-skinned person. For example, Perla and Fabio are both quite dark-skinned. On numerous occasions, other villagers commented that the reason why all of the couple's children are dark-skinned is that she is black and so is he. They would use this as an example of what happens when two dark people get together. Some would then add that, since love has no color, they couldn't criticize them, but I was left with the general impression that they did not necessarily approve of the match. And, although many people expressed the opinion that morenos are good-looking, most admitted that they would not find someone who was too black attractive. An interview with Rocío clarifies this issue:

TGB: Is there a preference for a morena over a negra in terms of beauty?

Rocío: Yes, yes, more so the morenas.

TGB: Ah, a person who is quite black with very kinky hair would not be seen as pretty?

Rocío: No . . . in that sense, there is a little bit of discrimination up until today.

TGB: Do they directly insult them? Or, is it that they do not want to marry them?

Rocío: Yes, sometimes, they laugh at them.

TGB: Yes, how?

Rocío: Well, they start to, how should I say this? They make fun of them. . . . In La Pilca, there is a morena, a well, she is mo . . . she is negra, negra, the girl. . . . She is brown in color and has short nappy hair. For example, when she walks by and is dressed up in bright colors. . . . She walks by and everyone is already laughing at her. Or saying, "Look! What's up with that? Look at that negra. Those clothes don't even look right on her and she is wearing them." Yeah, that happens.

According to Rocío, alongside the appreciation for morenas exists a lack of appreciation for negras. As Goldstein (2003: 121) points out with regard to Brazil, "purely African characteristics with no mixture of white characteristics are considered ugly . . . whiteness, unsurprisingly, has a high value by itself." Sansone (2003: 54), in his research in northern Brazil, reports, "This hegemonic somatic norm, however, does not imply that people would always, for example, like to marry a person with blonde, straight hair and blue eyes. What people in general do not desire is *o preto mesmo* (real black) or *aquele preto preto* (that black black). The great majority of my informants claim that the ideal man or women is *moreno*." For Ingenio, I would add that whiteness is valued so long as it is not serrano whiteness. The general preference for mixture, however, was evident in my interviews and participant observation.

For example, in an interview Armando first stated that love had no color, then commented, "Si yo soy moreno, soy negro, entonces, sería bonito que la mujer que yo ame sea blanca, porque, mejoraríamos el color, la apariencia, ¿no?" (If I am moreno, I am black, then it would be nice if the woman that I love is white, because we would improve the color, the appearance, right?) I asked Armando if he thought that the color of the white or the black parent would be bettered, and he responded, "Ese hijo saldría mestizo, ya más claro, pues ¿no?" (This child would come out mestizo, lighter, right?) Nevertheless, he also recognized that "estaríamos un poquito como nosotros mismos, un poquito auto discriminándonos, ¿no?" (We would be sort of discriminating against ourselves, though, wouldn't we?)

Liliana was less apologetic in her insistence that blacks should marry whites. She argued that "los negros debemos de perdernos la raza negra . . . porque ya mucho negro . . . la persona que es negra debe de buscarse su mujer que sea blanca. Si él es negro, debe de buscar su mujer blanca. . . . Porque sea negro con negro salen tintos." (We blacks should lose our black race . . . because there are so many blacks . . . the person who is black should look for a white woman. If he is black, he should look for a white woman. . . . Because black with black, they come out soot black.) At the end, she admitted that people called her racist for holding such views, but repeated "si mi familia ha sido bien negra, ¿para qué yo iba a buscar marido negro?" (If my family were very black, why would I look for a black husband?) Although most people were not so forthcoming, there was a general acceptance of the idea that lighter was often better.

The opinion of many people in Ingenio that it is better to be brown than black reveals the extent to which light skin is valorized there. Just as Lavalle wrote in an 1893 story that a quadroon character was "a refined product of the mixture of the black and white races" (cited in Velázquez Castro 2005: 163), people in Ingenio usually find lighter-skinned people of African descent to be more attractive than darker-skinned ones. This preference highlights the importance of color for blacks in Ingenio at the same time it reminds us that color distinctions, just like race distinctions, often carry value judgments. As I discuss next, *white* was often a synonym for good-looking.

Negro pero Bonito

In an interview with Diana, a young single woman who lived with her parents, I asked her if people sometimes referred to very dark-skinned babies as cute. She responded, "Cuando son bonitos. Porque hay bebitos morenitos pero bonitos." (When they are nice-looking. Because there are babies that are morenos but cute.) She also told me that when black babies were not attractive, people would call them "negro feo" (ugly black). When

I asked her if parents were pleased when their babies were light-skinned, she responded, yes, sometimes, because they thought that the baby "será el mejor" (will be the best); she added that the parents would notice if the baby was "más blanco, más bonito que sus hermanos" (whiter, better-looking than his brothers), although she was quick to point out that the parents would still treat all of their children equally.

What was particularly noteworthy in this exchange was the way Diana said "más blanco, más bonito" (whiter, prettier) in reference to a light baby, but "morenitos pero bonitos" (morenos but pretty) in reference to dark babies. This was a common pattern in my interviews. Marita, for example, described one of the villager's children as "bien blanquitos, bien bonitos" (very white, very pretty), whereas Ricardo described Perla's daughters as "morenas pero bonitas" (morenas but pretty). In most cases, when someone from Ingenio referred to a good-looking black person, they would describe him or her as black but beautiful. They would never refer to a good-looking white person in the same way, as white but beautiful. They would simply say white and beautiful or white, beautiful. This indicated villagers did not generally expect blacks to be beautiful. Señora Segunda, a widow in her fifties, for example, when talking about a former local priest, told me that he had been "bien simpático, con ojos verdes" (good-looking, with green eyes). His green eyes added to his good looks, whereas black eyes would be less likely to have done so. Segunda also told me that there were some U.S. nuns in Santo Domingo, a town in the mountains where "la gente es bien simpática; son zarcas" (the people are good-looking; they have light eyes). Again, the light eyes amplify their good looks. This contrasts with the saying "negra pero bonita," where blackness is apparently at odds with good looks.

Roberta, a married woman in her forties, said in conversation that her children often fought and used racial slurs to insult each other. Her lighter-skinned daughter would call her darker son "negro," and he would respond, "Puede que seas blanca, pero picuda." (You may be white, but big-lipped.) This exchange was revealing because the son clearly recognized that it was better to be white, and highlighted the daughter's African features as being unattractive and as taking away from her whiteness. When people pointed out unattractive features on a black person, they did not use the word *but*. For example, Perla and I were gossiping one afternoon about people's infidelities. She told me that Mariela, a woman who made chicha for a living, had been cheating on her husband with a man who was "negro y parece como un gorila" (black and looks like a gorilla). Notably, she did not say "black *but* looks like a gorilla." His unattractiveness did not take away from his blackness; it just made it worse.

Someone who was black and good-looking was almost always characterized as "black but beautiful." Two more examples come to mind, although there are many more I could share. My daughters had two brown-skinned dolls that we had brought from the United States with us. On one occasion, a young woman picked up the dolls and said, "Son morenitas, pero bien bonitas" (They are brown, but cute little things). In an interview, Eva, a married woman in her fifties, told me that sometimes she would ask her mother, "¿Porqué no se ha casado usted con un blanco?" (Why didn't you marry a white?) Her mother would answer, "Calla mierda aunque sea negro pero bien buen mozo mi viejo." (Shut the fuck up, he might be black but he is handsome, my old man.) Even in defending her husband (and his blackness), Eva's mother invoked the language of "black but beautiful."

Another subtlety arose in my interview with Armando, when I asked him why people often equated blackness with ugliness. He explained to me that people sometimes did not realize what they were saying when they said that blacks were ugly. "Porque, muchas son personas de la misma raza que dicen así, dicen, este, 'Ay, ese es tu hijito' y le comentan a la que está al costado, dicen, 'que negrito para feo,' dicen. Pero ella no sabe de que ella, también es morena y que, también es fea." (Because many are people of the same race who say, 'ah, this is your son,' and then say to the person next to them, 'What an ugly black child.' But she doesn't know that she also is morena, and also is ugly.) In these remarks, Armando equated being moreno with ugliness in responding to my question as to why people did this. Ironically, he suggested that people made this equation without realizing it, and then proceeded to do so himself. Later in the interview, however, I asked Armando if "aquí en el Ingenio ¿no es que la gente prefiere, en términos de belleza, el blanco al moreno?" (Here, in Ingenio, isn't it the case that people prefer, in terms of looks, whites to morenos?) He responded quickly, "No, here, no." Despite his recognition of this issue, Armando still insisted that morenos were not devalued.

Not only was blackness often placed in opposition to good looks, it was even at times contrasted with intelligence. While I was in Lima, Perla came to town to visit her daughter Fiorela. One evening I invited Perla to accompany me to a seminar at the Spanish Cultural Center. A number of Afro-Peruvian NGOs were organizing the seminar, and I thought

Perla would enjoy the experience and might like hearing about the topic, which was experiences of discrimination among Afro-Peruvian women. We listened attentively throughout the presentations, and afterwards I introduced Perla to a few people I knew. Once we were outside and as I was getting ready to hail a cab, Perla commented that the speakers, who had all been African-descended women, had been "feas pero inteligentes" (ugly but intelligent). With these three words, Perla not only equated the women's blackness with ugliness, but opposed it to intelligence. Perla seemed surprised that black women would be in professional positions in Peru, and further would be capable of giving public presentations. The predominance of black women in servile roles in telenovelas certainly could have played a role in these notions, and so would the absence of black professionals in Ingenio or any of the surrounding towns.

Here, we can reflect again on Armando's insistence that blackness is valued in Ingenio. This suggests that he at least sees it as important to value blackness, even if at times he denigrates it. He does not simply embrace the idea that "white is right," but draws from it at times in ways that resonate with his experience. At other times, he draws from the "black is beautiful" discourse to describe how blackness is esteemed in Ingenio.

Michel Foucault (1990: 102) suggests that we think of discourses as strategies for maintaining power, but that "there can exist different and even contradictory discourses within the same strategy" and that it is important to ask "what reciprocal effects of power and knowledge they ensure." It is also important to think about which discursive strategies are subtle and which are relatively overt because their interactions with power are distinct. In Ingenio, we see the subtle ways in which the value of whiteness is reinforced through expressions such as "negro pero bonito." We also see more direct insults such as "negro feo." It is worth noting that the direct insult "negro feo" has a counterpart: "serrano cochino" (dirty hillbilly). Subtle discourse, it turns out, is more difficult to counter than overt discourse, by nature of its subtlety and the way it forms part of local parlance. Thus, when thinking about how people use discourses, it is crucial to think about not only how discourses are effects of power, but which kinds of discourses are at play and what strategies one can use to counter them. Although the dominant discourse of "white is right" is to a certain extent ingrained in Ingenieros' minds, they can contest it through denigrations of serranos. They are much less likely to contest it through subtle linguistic maneuvers that valorize blackness.

One example of the devaluation of serranos is a commonly heard insult "con el papel blanco se limpia el culo" (with white paper we clean our asses). This can be understood as a discursive strategy that denigrates whiteness and thereby uplifts blackness. As another example, in an interview Roberta said to me, "¿Por si acaso ves papel negro tirado en el suelo? Yo solo veo papeles blancos, porque el papel negro es valioso." (Do you ever see any black papers thrown on the floor? I only see white papers, because black paper is valuable.) These equations of whiteness with trash can be understood as responses to discourses that devalue blackness compared to whiteness. Nevertheless, they are heard less frequently than the more subtle phrase "negro pero bonito."

Black Is Beautiful

Despite a general tendency to express a subtle preference for whiteness, in many instances people expressed an overt preference for brownness, if not blackness. Both Rocío and Diana reported to me in interviews that people generally preferred brown-skinned people with wavy hair. They also both admitted that a very dark-skinned person with kinky hair would not be seen as attractive.

Positive portrayals of blackness on television are somewhat rare in Ingenio, but they do occur. Some examples are blacks who dominate soccer teams in Latin America, Europe, and Africa; some of the women in the Miss Universe contest; African American superstars; and actors on television shows produced in the United States and to some extent in other countries. These representations may be problematic, but as Hobson (2005: 8–9) points out, it does make some difference that Alek Wek and other women of African descent now appear as models. Since women with African features have long been considered "antitheses to beauty," the appearance of Wek and other black women on the fashion scene will have some influence on beauty norms, even if it is ephemeral. Although I agree with Hobson that the inclusion of blacks does not alter "the dominant culture's beauty paradigm," my fieldwork in Ingenio does indicate that it has some impact on how blacks perceive themselves.

One afternoon when I was watching television with Perla, an African American actress appeared on the screen, and Perla commented, "Bien bonita la negrita." (What a pretty little black woman.) Right after that, an advertisement for the Miss Universe broadcast came on, and Perla said that the women in the Miss Universe contest were beautiful, and she enjoyed watching it. I pointed out that a former Miss Peru, Rosa Elvira Cartegena, had been morena. Perla said that she had been a pretty morena. I asked her what the people here thought about that, and Perla said, "La gente estaba alegresissíma, por lo que siempre las blancas ganan y ese año ganó una morena." (People were very happy, because the whites always win, and that year a morena won.) With these comments, Perla not only said that this black woman was beautiful but identified herself and her community with this woman's blackness.

Rosa Elvira Cartagena, a light-skinned woman of African descent who self-identifies as black, was dethroned as Miss Peru 1999 after it was revealed that she had lied about having won a modeling contest in order to qualify for the competition. Nevertheless, she remains a beautiful black Peruvian. Her winning the contest serves as an affirmation in Ingenio that black Peruvians (sometimes) are beautiful. Her disqualification has caused some critics to claim that Peruvian society is not willing to accept an Afro-descendant as the symbol of national beauty (Ramírez Reyna 2003), while others insist racism did not factor in this case (Ramos 2002).

That debate aside, it meant something to Perla that a contestant who self-identified as black won the contest. On one occasion, Perla and I were looking at photos and came across the photo of a brown-skinned woman in the village. Perla commented that she was "muy simpática" (very pretty). I asked her if the woman had been good-looking in her youth, and Perla said she had been "una morena bonita." This description of the woman as a beautiful morena resonated with Perla's description of Rosa Elvira Cartagena.

On another occasion, I was watching the World Cup on television with Fabio. An African team was playing and Fabio commented that they were really black, even blacker than he was. In some ways, this remark could be interpreted as Fabio attempting to associate himself with whiteness, but it also could be read as Fabio aligning himself with the blackness of the players. Fabio could have construed positively this appearance of people darker than himself on international television in positions of prominence, albeit as sports stars, especially since he had a history as a soccer player himself.

These last few examples show that people in Ingenio do have an appreciation for certain kinds of blackness. People often refer to the whole town as being black and to the residents as being ugly, but they will also point out that some blacks are beautiful. For example, Ricardo told me that, although it generally is better for blacks to marry whites, Fabio and Perla's children are good-looking, even though they and both of their parents are black. Thus, despite the history of black subordination in Ingenio and the increasing permeation of media images that promote whiteness as an ideal, villagers still appreciate blackness in some forms.

Local and Global Discourses of Blackness, Whiteness, and Beauty

Blacks are often portrayed on Peruvian television as subservient, unintelligent, and exotic, yet black Peruvians do have access to images of successful and beautiful blacks such as Oprah Winfrey, Michael Jordan, and Rosa Elvira Cartagena. These positive representations of blackness appearing on television provide an alternative to the dominant discourse that only white is right. These representations of blacks allow for an affirmation of certain kinds of blackness. The dark-skinned women who participate in the Miss Universe competition have high status because of their cosmopolitanism and the glitz and glamour surrounding them. On stage, black is beautiful. However, given the paucity of representations of very dark-skinned women with kinky hair as beautiful, and the way dark-skinned people are talked about in Ingenio, it would perhaps be more accurate to say "brown is beautiful." Similarly, although whites are generally portrayed on television as more modernized than other races, in Ingenio the serranos' perceived lack of participation in modern cultural forms allows people to disassociate serranos from the whites they see on television. Blacks' relative modernity in Ingenio is reinforced by the (ultra)modern cosmopolitanism of blacks portrayed on television. The local reality that blacks are, in many ways, more modern than local whites creates a space in which the global "black is beautiful" discourse makes sense.

In present-day Ingenio, not all whites have high status, which means that whites are not always interpreted as representing preferred notions of beauty and status. Light skin, light eyes, and light hair are not enough for serranos to be read as good-looking. They must also be modernized— meaning they have to speak Spanish without a mountain accent and wear Western clothes—in order to be perceived as attractive. By the same token, not all blacks are interpreted as unattractive. Blacks who have attained fame in the national or global arena can be seen as good-looking. And local blacks with brown skin and curly hair are also considered attractive, even preferable to serranos with white skin and blue eyes. Thus, although Mariana told me she did not want a black husband, her mother told me that she did not want her daughter to marry a serrano, because "you know how they are," meaning that he would likely be machista. In Ingenio, disdain for certain forms of blackness is accompanied by disdain for certain kinds of whiteness, and these two countervailing discourses provide us with useful insight into how global, regional, and national mediascapes with a variety of images give rise to heterogeneous ideascapes, even in relatively homogenous localities (Appadurai 1996).

What is at work in Ingenio is the intersection of local, national, and global discourses. Although the global discourse on blackness contains elements of "black is beautiful," in Ingenio, it is translated as "black is beautiful, so long as it isn't *too* black." This discourse nevertheless contrasts with the national and Latin American discourses of "blacks are exotic" or "blacks are subservient" or "there are no blacks." In a similar fashion, the global and national discourses of "white is right" mean that white skin is more valued and, in Peru, that whites are wealthier, better-looking, and smarter. In Ingenio, however, this is often translated as "white is right, so long as it isn't serrano" and "foreign whites are better."

People in Ingenio employ different discursive strategies and draw from a variety of discourses to engage with and understand the world in which they live. The discourse that whites are better than blacks should be expected to give rise to a counter-discourse that blacks are better than whites, since a discourse is often a "starting point for an opposing strategy" a "point of resistance" and "an effect of power" (Foucault 1990: 100–1). The discourse that white is right and the discourse that black is beautiful should not however be understood as contradictory, but as containing discursive elements that people can use in strategic ways to gain or manipulate power. In Ingenio, the serrano's lowly position in the social hierarchy puts him in a position where his whiteness can be denigrated. Thus, villagers are inundated with images of whites as successful, beautiful, and happy, yet are aware that local whites are often poor, unattractive, and not particularly happy. Because of this reality, local whites are denigrated and negative stereotypes are attached to them, whereas foreign whites are viewed as attractive and successful. This case demonstrates how local discourses can be affected by but not determined by global discourses.

Conclusion

Throughout this book, I have argued that color is at the core of discourses of blackness in Ingenio. In this chapter, I have made it clear that color is not "just" about skin tone. Color is valorized: lighter skin generally is preferred. Color also is associated with culture: when people from the sierra, who generally are defined as white, come to Ingenio, residents make a wide range of assumptions about their lack of hygiene and morality. In Ingenio, *serrano*—a reference to mountain origins—is contrasted with *criollo*—a reference to coastal origins. Both are closely associated with ideas of whiteness and blackness insofar as serranos are often, but not always, white, and criollos are often, but not always, brown or black. People in Ingenio distinguish serranos from negros in part through skin color. Thus, although color is at the core of racial discourses in Ingenio, color is more than meets the eye. Perla may say "negro is just a color, that's it," yet she makes value judgments on the basis of skin color. Those value judgments are heavily influenced by local discourses of blackness and whiteness in Ingenio but also are related to a global discourse of blackness and of white supremacy.

Patton (2006: 38) argues that, in the United States, there is a color caste system that entails the "belief that the lighter one's skin color, the better one is and that straighter hair is better than kinky hair." Patton attributes this "hierarchy of skin color and beauty" to the slave system, in which house slaves tended to be lighter and field slaves darker. Hunter (2002: 177) posits that the association of light skin with higher status is a reflection of internal colonialism and that people of color have adopted the values of the dominant group. She further argues that "beauty is highly racialized and informed by ideals of white supremacy established during slavery and colonialism," and thus that "beauty operates as a tool of white supremacy and a tool of patriarchy by elevating men and whites in importance and status." The ideology of white supremacy encompasses the notion that white is always better than black, and that lighter is always better than darker. This ideology plays a role in Ingenio and is propagated by the media. It is not however adopted wholesale, in that locals denigrate serranos while associating them with whiteness, and they claim that the ideal beauty is a brown-skinned woman with curly hair. In Ingenio, like in the United States, light skin and curly hair are often seen as more attractive than very dark skin or very kinky hair. It would however be a mistake to conclude that this preference means the people of Ingenio have simply adopted hegemonic beauty standards. Rather, it makes more sense to say that they have *adapted* hegemonic beauty standards to make sense in their locality. Ingenieros have not simply internalized the idea that white is always better than black; the denigration of serranos is evidence of this. Their adaptation of white supremacist ideology comes about in part because people adapt global discourses to local realities and in part because global discourses themselves are multilayered.

When we look at the evidence in this chapter, we see three themes: (1) blacks in Ingenio range from light- to dark-skinned; (2) brown-skinned blacks are seen as more attractive than dark-skinned blacks; and (3) the differences between blacks and serranos are racialized. The first point manifests when Armando refers to the "negritos" looking into his house at my brother's children. The "negritos" peering into his house were of a variety of hues. The second point is made explicit when Rocío explains in an interview the preference for brown skin. The third point comes out of my conversations with Perla about serranos when she makes moral and cultural judgments about serranos and contrasts them with criollos (local blacks).

In previous chapters, I have argued for the particularity of the local discourse on blackness in Ingenio and emphasized the importance of color as a defining feature of blackness. This chapter shows that color is crucial, yet that color distinctions are dependent on racial distinctions and are related to a global ideology of white supremacy. The valorization of light skin in Ingenio is part of the global racial hierarchy, even though people in Ingenio do not use a language of race and they apply a particular local flavor to this hierarchy. The color hierarchy in Ingenio gives preference to local brownness, a feature that is reinforced by media images portraying light-skinned blacks as more beautiful and desirable than dark-skinned blacks. This local hierarchy is informed by global white supremacy even as it denigrates white serranos for their backwardness—for white serranos are perceived as desirable once they "clean up."

In the next chapter, I consider the possibilities for multicultural reforms in Peru, in light of the specific discourses of blackness in Ingenio and the prevalence of structural racism in Peru.

chapter 6

The Politics of Difference in Peru

*Peruvian blacks avoid speaking about the condition of blacks
as an ethnic group, which confirms their option for assimilation
in the official culture through miscegenation and/or cultural
integration. Only blacks associated with revival or specific artistic
groups seem conscious of their ethnic origins.*

Raúl Romero

*National elites in Latin America have tended to perceive
Indians as a distinct cultural group in a way that has not been
true for blacks.*

Juliet Hooker

In this book, I have made the case that there is a local discourse of blackness in Ingenio that is connected to Latin American discourses of racial
difference as well as to diasporic discourses of blackness, yet is unique
in the primacy it gives to color as the defining feature of blackness. The
unique nature of the local discourse of blackness in Ingenio raises questions about the implementation of multicultural reforms in Peru. For example, if blacks in Peru see themselves as different in skin tone, but not
as distinct in culture from non-blacks, what is the role of multicultural
reforms?

Blacks in Ingenio do not usually differentiate themselves culturally
from non-black Peruvians. Most Ingenieros identify with the dominant
coastal (criollo) culture in Peru. Throughout the history of the Peruvian
nation, Peruvian elites have defined blackness primarily based on skin

color, whereas they nearly always have defined indigeneity based on culture. Nevertheless, distinct Afro-Peruvian cultural forms have survived in Peru. And, although blackness is defined in terms of color, these color identifications are imbued with cultural significations.

In this chapter, I argue that Ingenieros generally do not see themselves as partakers in black culture because of the limited way that black culture has been defined in Peru—as consisting solely of cultural forms that emanate from communities in southern Peru such as Chincha and Lima. These cultural forms have little to do with the local experience in Ingenio. Nevertheless, the possibility exists for blackness to be uplifted and celebrated in Ingenio insofar as blacks there are connected to the black diaspora through their self-identification as black and their history and present-day experience of exclusion and oppression. Moreover, a multicultural reform that took on structural racism and individual bigotry would no doubt be of benefit in Ingenio.

Blacks and Indians, Separate and Unequal: Multicultural Reforms in Latin America

Multicultural reforms are well under way in Peru. A recent set of multicultural reforms took place with a $5 million loan from, and under the auspices of, the World Bank. This project, called the Indigenous and Afro-Peruvian People's Development Project, undertaken between January 2000 and June 2004, is part of a larger World Bank initiative to promote a multicultural agenda in Latin America.

Although these multicultural reforms had an external influence (the World Bank) we can trace the roots of Peruvian discussions of multiculturalism to President Juan Velasco Alvarado's efforts at inclusion. On June 24, 1969, President Velasco renamed June 24, which had been the Day of the Indian, the Day of the Peasant, "symbolizing the administration's presumed commitment to move away from divisive ethnic categories and towards a more inclusive and unified Peruvian nation" (Yashar 2005: 230). A politics of sameness—"We are all Peruvians"—held center stage in Peruvian nationalist discourse throughout the 1970s and 1980s, although there were certain gestures toward Andean indigenous groups (but rarely to Amazonians or Afro-Peruvians). During the 1970s, agrarian reform took center stage, with Velasco promising to give land to those who tilled it. The official discourse centered on the rights of peasants as peasants, not as members of any particular ethnic group. Most of Velasco's measures directed at indigenous people were designed to make the nation more inclusive. Velasco instituted the Educational Reform of 1972, which was targeted at indigenous communities, and a 1975 law made Quechua co-equal with Spanish. This law required the usage of Quechua in courts and schools and provoked an outcry among middle- and upper-class people in Lima (García 2004). The decade of the 1980s was overshadowed by Peru's dirty war—the struggle between Sendero Luminoso (Shining Path) and Peruvian military forces. The violence of this period made it difficult to gain support for any demands for indigenous rights (García 2004). Presidents Fernando Belaúnde and Alan García were unsuccessful in their attempts to stop the terror that pervaded Peru. In addition, García's policies brought economic turmoil to the country.

In this context, Alberto Fujimori, the son of Japanese immigrants, ran for election against Mario Vargas Llosa, a novelist from the Peruvian oligarchy. Fujimori's candidacy brought issues of racial and class differences to the fore. Surprisingly, Fujimori was able to create a sort of ethnic unity with Peru's large indigenous population by claiming that he, as a hardworking Japanese Peruvian, had more in common with the Peruvian masses than the aristocratic Vargas Llosa. Fujimori's tactic of declaring solidarity with *cholitos* and distance from *blanquitos* proved successful, and he won the election with 57 percent of the vote (García 2005). The discussion of difference in Peru that was developed in the context of Fujimori's campaign carried over into his presidency. In 1993, Fujimori revised the constitution to pay lip service to multiculturalism in that it "recognizes and protects the ethnic and cultural plurality of the nation" (Article 2) and "respects the cultural identity of rural and native communities" (Article 89). In 2000, when Fujimori had served his limit of two terms, he was able to amend the constitution to enable him to run again. This time, his most remarkable opponent was Alejandro Toledo.

Alejandro Toledo's candidacy in the hotly contested election of 2000 again brought racial issues to the surface. Toledo was born in the Andes, but had spent many years in the United States, both studying at Stanford and working at the World Bank. In Toledo's campaign for the presidency, he drew on indigenous symbolism to paint himself as more authentically Peruvian than Japanese-descended Alberto Fujimori. Fujimori had won the 1990 election by wearing ponchos and dancing *huaynos* (Andean dances). In 2000, Toledo used the same symbols to bolster his own legitimacy. Fujimori ostensibly won the 2000 election, amidst outcries of electoral fraud. Shortly after he took power for a third term, videos of Fujimori's spy chief, Vladimiro Montesinos, bribing politicians with bags of money were widely televised across Peru. In the wake of this scandal, Fujimori was ousted and new elections were called.

In the interim, Valentín Paniagua, the president of the Congress, became acting president of Peru. Although short-lived, Paniagua's transition government opened up important possibilities for indigenous people in Peru. Patricia Oliart (2008) argues that, whereas Fujimori took steps toward multiculturalism primarily because of pressure from the World Bank, Paniagua's efforts were more heartfelt and directed toward real reform. This move towards multiculturalism carried over into the government of Alejandro Toledo. Under Toledo's administration, the Peruvian government instituted a series of multicultural reforms and, most notably, passed antidiscrimination legislation. Prior to this, most gestures towards the indigenous communities in Peru were done in the context of agrarian reform or help directed towards peasant communities. Still, Afro-Peruvians and Amazonians were notably absent from nearly all of these measures, continuing a long tradition of excluding them from cultural reforms in Peru (Garcia 2005; Greene 2007).

The final World Bank report indicates that the Indigenous and Afro-Peruvian People's Development Project was largely ineffective, but it did put issues on the table that had not previously been considered important in Peru. The most flagrant failure was that of the Comisión Nacional de los Pueblos Andinos y Amazónicos (CONAPA), which Eliane Karp, the Belgian wife of President Alejandro Toledo, was largely responsible for establishing. Although the creation of CONAPA was made possible by World Bank funds and the first lady's initiative, it was also a response to considerable pressure from indigenous and Afro-descendant groups for more governmental recognition, both in Peru and in Latin America more generally. In 2004, Toledo disbanded CONAPA due to corruption charges against Karp. Later that year, the Peruvian Congress passed legislation that created the Instituto Nacional de Desarrollo de Pueblos Andinos, Amazónicos y Afroperuanos (INDEPA). One major distinction between CONAPA and INDEPA is that CONAPA was led by Karp, a white foreigner, whereas the two leaders of INDEPA, Juan Manuel Figueroa

Quintana and Luis Huarcaya Alzamora, have been Andean. In addition, INDEPA has, by congressional mandate, four Andean, three Amazonian, and two Afro-Peruvian delegates (Greene 2006; INDEPA website).[1]

Despite the inclusion of Afro-Peruvians in the official title of the World Bank project, and in the names of both of the governmental commissions in Peru, Afro-Peruvians were not invited to the preliminary discussions about the formation of CONAPA, and it seems likely that their inclusion was largely due to World Bank insistence that the funds be used to benefit both Afro-descended and indigenous groups (see Greene 2007 for a discussion of Afro-Peruvian exclusion).

The majority of the funding for Afro-Peruvian NGOs derives from international rather than Peruvian organizations (J. Thomas 2008). Given the international influence on multicultural reforms, it is important to ask if the formula promulgated by the World Bank makes sense in the Peruvian case. Should Afro-Peruvians be banding together for cultural recognition? Or, as Hooker (2005) suggests, would it be more appropriate for Afro-Peruvians to focus their efforts on antiracism struggles?

In this chapter, I discuss what a multicultural reform could look like for blacks in Peru by examining the distinct roles that blacks and Indians have played in nation-making projects. I also hold up to question the claim that Afro-Peruvians are culturally indistinguishable from criollos by examining discourses of Afro-Peruvian cultural difference and providing evidence that Afro-Peruvians are marked as different in Peru. Finally, I argue that since Afro-Peruvian culture has been exoticized and folklorized, multicultural reforms are necessary in that all Peruvians could use some re-education about the contribution of Afro-Peruvians to the Peruvian nation. Nevertheless, my support for multicultural reforms comes with some qualifications, as it is important to ensure that multicultural reforms do not work to essentialize blackness or give the state power to define who is black and what black culture is.

Politics of Recognition, Mestizaje, and Cultural Citizenship

Advocates of multicultural citizenship reforms like those included in the World Bank initiative use a "politics of recognition" (Taylor 1994) to make their claims. Proponents of the politics of recognition emphasize the importance of recognizing difference (as opposed to aiming for homogeneity) for maintaining a healthy democracy. An important component of this framework is that "assimilation to majority culture or dominant cultural norms" should not be necessary for full citizenship (Fraser and Honneth 2003: 6). Instead of advocating assimilation, a politics of recognition proposes that the recognition of difference is essential for full citizenship rights, or for the "equal capacity to exercise the three dimensions of citizenship"; namely, rights and responsibilities, access, and feelings of belonging Jenson (2001: 5). The third dimension—that of "being empowered" and "sharing a sense of belonging to the political community" (5)—is at the root of cultural citizenship. Cultural citizenship requires having a symbolic presence in a cultural space that is seen as an integral part of the nation (Richardson 1998; Pakulski 1997).

Cultural citizenship requires that people not be obliged to conform to dominant cultural norms and that all cultures which exist within a state be valued by the state. This framework extends the idea of citizenship into the domain of the politics of recognition. As Pakulski (1997: 77) argues, "The claims for cultural citizenship involve not only tolerance of diverse identities but also—and increasingly—claims to dignifying representation, normative accommodation, and active cultivation of these identities." To a greater extent than ever before, discourses of democracy and citizenship in the West are focusing on the importance of cultural rights—the right to cultivate distinct cultural identities—for the deepening of democracy. The question thus becomes, Do Afro-Peruvians need the right to cultivate a distinct cultural identity to be full citizens of Peru?

Should the Peruvian state take action to ensure that Afro-Peruvians have the right to cultivate a distinct identity? If current practices and policies in Peru do require conformity to the majority culture, proponents of a politics of difference would argue that Afro-Peruvians are denied the right to cultivate their distinct identities. Alternatively, if Afro-Peruvians do not have a distinct culture, then a politics of recognition would be misplaced. Thus, one of the aims of this chapter is to discuss the extent to which Afro-Peruvians are possessors of a unique culture that is in need of state protection and promotion.

Racial Democracy and Mestizaje in Peru

In a discussion of Latin American multiculturalism, it is important to point out that a politics of *difference* is in fact the opposite of the traditional politics of *sameness* that dominated national discourses in Latin America for most of the twentieth century. Across Latin America, debates have centered on the extent to which a racial democracy exists—a situation where people "regard each other as fellow citizens . . . without regard to color or ethnic differences" (Freyre 1959: 7, quoted in Bailey 2002). Discourses of racial democracy de-emphasize color or ethnic differences, whereas the politics of recognition emphasize their importance.

As noted, racial democracy requires color blindness and even the cultivation of *sameness* (as opposed to difference), which many scholars view as problematic. In addition, claims that Brazil or Peru or Mexico or any other Latin American country is a racial democracy hold little acclaim among the vast majority of academics who conduct research in Latin America. Nevertheless, some scholars have recently suggested that racial democracy is still an ideal for Latin American nations. Robin Sheriff (2001: 57), for example, points out that her informants in Rio de Janeiro argue that "neither race nor color *should* matter because we are all members of the (miscegenated) Brazilian family." And, Alejandro de la Fuente (2001: 326) contends that, in Cuba, "government propaganda, which has claimed since the 1960s that all Cubans are equal and deserve full access to all sectors of national life," created "an ideal of egalitarianism that was shared by vast sectors of the population." Sheriff and de la Fuente, along with Stanley Bailey (2009), point to the importance of racial democracy as an ideal, even if it does not describe the reality of race relations in Latin America.

Holding up racial democracy as an ideal is, however, distinct from what Stanley Bailey (2009: 25) calls "antiracialism," where scholars celebrate mixture and claim that any discussion of racial polarity is out of place in Latin America. Antiracialism is evident among some Peruvian intellectuals. For example, the Peruvian scholar Edgar Montiel (1995) contends that any solution to the marginalization of blacks in Peru must be in the context of mestizaje and national identity, not in terms of ethnicity and racial identity, for "si ubicamos el problema en términos de etnia y raza y no en términos de mestizaje y nación, estaremos creando un problema artificial, pues el mestizaje ha sido la dinámica central del comportamiento de las razas en el Perú" (if we locate the problem in terms of ethnicity and race and not in terms of mestizaje and nation, we are creating an artificial problem, since mestizaje has been the central dynamic in racial behaviors in Peru) (265). In addition, the Peruvian ethnomusicologist Raúl Romero (1994: 311) argues that black Peruvians do not constitute an ethnic group, and that blacks "have traditionally identified themselves as Creoles and have historically avoided considering themselves as a separate and independent group." Romero further posits that "Peruvian blacks avoid speaking about the condition of blacks as an ethnic group, which confirms their option for assimilation in the official culture through miscegenation and/or cultural integration. Only blacks associated with revival or specific artistic groups seem conscious of their ethnic origins" (322). These statements about Afro-Peruvians and mestizaje provide support for Juliet Hooker's (2005: 299) claim that "national elites in Latin America have tended to perceive Indians as a distinct cultural group in a way that has not been true for blacks." Hooker's proposition resonates both in terms of the preceding quotations and in light of the history of mestizaje in Peru. As I have argued in previous chapters, Peruvian elites have defined indigeneity culturally, whereas they have defined blackness in terms of skin color.

Antiracialism has its critics within Latin American studies. Whereas Montiel sees mestizaje as the solution to racial exclusion in Peru, Cuche (1975) argues that mestizaje has produced racial exclusion in Peru. "En realidad, la ideología del mestizaje era una sutil maniobra para marginar a las masas de color y eliminarlas del proceso de construcción nacional." (In reality, the ideology of mestizaje was a subtle maneuver used to marginalize people of color and to eliminate them from the nation-building process) (108–9). These contrasting discourses of color blindness versus color recognition present us with a pressing question: Is a politics of recognition framework useful for understanding racial exclusion in a country where the traditional ideal society has been a racial democracy? More specifically, if blacks identify themselves as criollos, then are claims of cultural rights and cultural citizenship inappropriate in the Peruvian context?

Race and Mestizaje in Peru

The first step in this analysis is to examine how Afro-Peruvians have been included and excluded from discourses of mestizaje in Peru. In Peru, the idea of racial democracy cannot be disentangled from that of mestizaje—loosely defined as racial and cultural mixing. Racial democracy in Peru incorporates the ideal that all Peruvians are or can become mestizos, and thus equals, through participation in miscegenation and cultural mixing. Peru is a racial democracy in that any Peruvian can in theory become a mestizo, and therefore a full-fledged citizen of Peru, even its president. Bourricaud (1975) explains that Indians can become mestizos by abandoning their indigenous roots and integrating themselves into the Peruvian nation. However, the idea that Indians must abandon their indigenous roots to become Peruvian contains the inherent assumptions that indigenous culture is inferior and that Indians should do their best to become more like whites. In addition, this process of incorporation through mestizaje is difficult to apply to blacks because blacks already possess many of the cultural features of *costeños*, including music, food, and language. Whereas an Indian can become a mestizo by speaking Spanish instead of Quechua, eating rice instead of quinoa, and dancing cumbia instead of *huayno*,[2] black Peruvians already speak Spanish, eat rice, dance cumbia, and generally participate fully in costeño cultural forms. As I argued in chapter 2, mestizaje is not the same for blacks and Indians.

Scholars have argued that mestizaje in Peru "reinforces the identification of Indians and blacks as inferior" (Aguirre 2000: 21) and masks racial inequalities (Cuche 1981). Mestizaje has a history not of celebrating difference, but of aiming to eradicate it in order to replace it with whiteness. In terms of blacks, not only have they been marked as inferior, but they have been made invisible in discourses of the ethnic makeup of Peru. Marisol de la Cadena (2000), for example, argues that Peruvian racial understandings correspond to the geographically distinct regions of Peru—the coast, the sierra, and the jungle, and that blacks have no place in this geography.

> To the image of the coast as the historical site of colonial culture corresponded the idea that it was the natural environment of Spaniards or their *criollo* descendants. Since the nineteenth century, they have been labeled as "whites," regardless of their color.... Indians were the natural inhabitants of the sierra ... the jungle was associated with 'primitive,' 'savage' tribes.... *Mestizos,* those ambiguous individuals of all kinds, could live anywhere in the highlands or on the coast. Blacks were considered a foreign race, and therefore lacked a specific place of origin in the national geography; yet as a 'tropical people' they were deemed to adapt to the hot coastal areas. (de la Cadena 2000: 21)

According to this understanding, although blacks inhabited the coast, and coastal inhabitants were seen as higher in social status than highlanders, blacks were viewed as foreigners, thus distinct from whites and not accorded this status.

De la Cadena further argues that black Peruvians are seen as a race not an ethnicity, and that blacks are seen as "dispensable in most Peruvian nationalist projects" (29). The idea that black Peruvians are a race rather than an ethnicity implies that Afro-Peruvians are not culturally unique, but simply have a different skin color and ancestry from most Peruvians. This view is supported by Romero's (1994) claims that "blacks in Peru do not constitute an ethnic group" and that "blacks have traditionally identified themselves as Creoles" (322). Thus, unlike Indians, blacks cannot shed their ethnic traits to become Peruvian. How, then, do they become Peruvians? What of Romero's claim that blacks are in fact criollos?

Afro-Peruvian versus Criollo

Criollo is the term originally used to refer to Spaniards born in Latin America, but in Peru it has evolved to refer to people from the coast, and there are differing perspectives on whether or not this term is inclusive of blacks. Javier León Quirós (2003) associates criollo with a European or Spanish sense of identity. For example, he argues,

> Today, music is the most prominent marker of the endurance of Afroperuvian culture in the midst of a society that has historically pressured members of various marginalized groups to self-identify only as members of an imagined community generically identified as criollo. . . . [T]he use of the term criollo . . . points toward the subordination of these other ethnic and cultural influences to a predominantly European-based sense of cultural identity. (8)

León further makes the case that Afro-Peruvian musicians must actively work to develop a cultural identity that is distinct from criollo identity and to distinguish themselves from criollos, although he acknowledges that not all Afro-Peruvians see criollo identity as oppositional to black identity. Aldo Panfichi, a sociologist, argues that being criollo "no anulaba el hecho de ser negro, zambo o mestizo, significaba ser alegre y jaranera" (does not annul the fact that one is black, zambo, or mestizo; it means one is happy and festive) (2000: 153). Thus, whereas León argues that Afro-Peruvian culture is effaced by criollo culture, Panfichi makes the case that one can be criollo and also black, brown, or mestizo. This is similar to Romero's claim that blacks are criollos. Does the categorization of blacks and black culture as criollo deny Afro-Peruvians access to cultural citizenship? Or, alternatively, is criollo an inclusive discourse that integrates Afro-Peruvians into the national identity? To answer this, it is useful to consider what Afro-Peruvians have to say about their being criollos.

As I discussed in the previous chapter, I found that criollo was a category with which Afro-Peruvians identified. For example, one day when I was speaking with Perla, she used *criolla* to mean "down-to-earth." In talking about a middle-class woman who was from another town but was able to adapt to life in Ingenio, Perla said that she was "bien criolla." In Ingenio, *criollo* was also used to refer to chickens raised in one's own corral, as opposed to in large chicken factories. In an interview with Marita and her husband, Juan, Marita contrasted criollos with cholos, telling me that criollos were people from Ingenio, whereas cholos were Indians from the coast and serranos were people from the mountains.

Many people also listen to criollo music during the lunch hour, when it is played on the local radio station, or watch "Medio-día Criollo," which comes on television at noon. Notably, *tondero*—a barefoot dance similar to *marinera,* accompanied by the cajón, that most people in Ingenio agree is part of local culture—is also part of the criollo genre of music, and all criollo music, including tondero, incorporates the Afro-Peruvian cajón, a box drum. In addition, many of the musicians are Afro-Peruvians. The close association of criollo music with blackness indicates that criollo-ness is not oppositional to blackness.

My informants saw the labels *criollo* and *negro* as complementary, and many self-identified with both. For example, Perla and Marita identified themselves as both criolla and negra, and they both told me that tondero and *cumanana* (a kind of call-and-response poetry) are not black cultural forms, but local, Morropano cultural elements. As León suggests, Perla and Marita see themselves as part of an imaginary criollo community and, in this sense, are connected to the larger Peruvian nation. León also points out that "during the early part of the twentieth century, nation-building narratives were firmly polarized along regional lines. This was the result of deeply ingrained political, cultural, and ethnic differences between the predominantly criollo coast and the largely indigenous and *mestizo* highlands" (2003: 21). Since Afro-Peruvians are concentrated on the coast, their inclusion in the nation-building process would have to be in terms of cultivating a common criollo identity, not a mestizo one. Given Perla and Marita's self-identification as criollas and blacks, and the association of the Afro-Peruvian town of Ingenio with things criollo, it is fair to say that criollo-ness does incorporate blackness. Perhaps, then, Montiel is correct and the problem is not Afro-Peruvian *difference* but the failure to recognize Afro-Peruvian *sameness*. After all, from the cultural citizenship perspective, Afro-Peruvians should not be forced to assimilate. If, however, they have chosen to do so, this can hardly be problematic. Think, for example, of the Italian immigrants to the United States who, along with pizza and spaghetti, have become American. What about blackness? Has it become Peruvian?

Blackness in Peru Today

There is a dearth of scholarly discussions of blackness in contemporary Peru. One exception is Heidi Feldman's excellent book *Black Rhythms of Peru* (2006). Feldman's book discusses the revival of Afro-Peruvian music in Lima and in towns south of Lima, mainly in Chincha. Although her work is an examination of "Black Peru," Feldman's findings have little to do with the people of Ingenio, in that there has not been a revival of Afro-Peruvian cultural production there. Nevertheless, her scholarship sheds light on the contentious nature of defining Afro-Peruvian cultural forms, which does have relevance for Ingenio. Recall that Feldman places Afro-Peruvian cultural production within the realm of the "Black Pacific" (7), contending that the Black Pacific is distinct from the Black Atlantic because Black Peruvians must negotiate with local criollo culture, with indigenous cultural forms, and with the Black Atlantic itself. She further asserts that "Afro-Peruvians identify with the transnational Black Atlantic but also are deeply engaged in an identity project that responds to Peruvian national discourses" (9). This engagement with Peruvian national discourses, indigeneity, and global blackness is evident in the cultural production I discuss next.

To gain insight into the contemporary national discourse on blackness, I draw from popular media: two films, one from 1988 and the other from 2003, and a newspaper special report on race in Peru, published in 1999. These three examples open a window into representations of blackness in Peru, where there are relatively few depictions of blackness in the cinema and newspaper. The two films were produced by Afro-Peruvians, whereas the newspaper special was written by non-blacks.

The internationally recognized Peruvian film *Juliana* (1988), codirected by the late Afro-Peruvian cineaste Fernando Espinoza features two black boys who make their living by performing typical Afro-Peruvian music on the streets. They go by the street names of Arañita (Spider) and Pelé. Both nicknames hint at transnational blackness, in that the Spider may refer to a trickster figure, and Pelé is undoubtedly a reference to the black Brazilian soccer star. Arañita and Pelé are orphans, and live collectively with a group of other boys who fend for themselves through street performances in Lima.

One afternoon, after their boss and surrogate father yells at them and beats them for not bringing home enough tips, the boys sit in their bare room with the other street performers and begin talking about their troubled lives. When it is one of the two black boys' turn to speak, he says,

> A mí, cuando, cuando pasan, me dicen, negro, negro. Y, a mí, no me gusta que me digan negro. Y, los gringos están picones, porque los negros saben bailar, tocar, y los gringos solamente saben rock, rock. Y, pitukeando, y está con su chica cada rato. Y, a mí no me gusta que me digan negro porque dicen negro con asco, y me caliento.
>
> When I pass by, they say to me black, black. And, I don't like it when they call me black. And, the gringos are fired up because blacks know how to dance, to play [music], and the gringos only know about rock, rock. And, they walk around like they are something, and always with a chick by their side. And, I don't like it when they call me black, because they say disgusting black, and I get worked up.

Then the other black boy chimes in,

> Esos gringos, son un par de huevones, oye. Nosotros, los negros, sabemos sembrar las plantas, sabemos, este, sembrar toda clase de, de plantas. Los gringos pitukeando con su grabadora acá en el hombro, con su chica agarrada de la cintura, así, para todo panudo por la calle así. Esos gringos son un par de huevones porque ellos ni chambean, paran, paran vagueando no más. Los negros somos trabajadores porque nosotros sabemos trabajar bien. Y, negros, cholos, zambos, entre todos nos jodemos.
>
> Those gringos are a bunch of assholes, you hear. We, the blacks, know how to plant things; we know how to plant all kinds of things. The gringos be walking around like they are all that with their boom box up on their shoulder, with their chick's arm around their waist like that. They walk around all decked out on the streets like that.

Those gringos are a bunch of assholes because they don't even work, and they just hang out. We blacks are workers because we know how to work well. And, blacks, cholos, zambos, among ourselves we can talk jive.

From these monologues, we can gather quite a bit of what it means to be black in Peru. Being black means having knowledge of certain cultural forms, namely music and dance. It also has a negative connotation and creates a certain feeling of disgust in other Peruvians. Being black also evokes rural origins, having agricultural knowledge that is useful for growing food, and being no stranger to hard work.

What is equally interesting in these short monologues is what being black does *not* mean. It means not being wealthy, not being very well dressed, and not being vagrants. It also means not being a gringo. These boys are juxtaposing themselves to wealthy Peruvian whites in a dialectical fashion—they are everything the whites are not. By calling whites "gringos," the boys are implying that whites are foreign to Peru, whereas they, in contrast, are of the land. This could be construed as challenging the implication that blacks are foreigners, as Marisol de la Cadena (2000) has argued that blacks have been excluded from nation making on the basis of their presumed foreignness.

Notably, the second boy's claim that blacks are hardworking could also be interpreted as a defiant response to the stereotype that blacks are lazy. A well-known joke in Peru is that blacks are useless after midday, meaning they do not work all day long. By the same token, the first boy's affirmation of blacks' musical endowments is a recognition of the stereotype that blacks are musically and rhythmically adept. As Milagros Carazas (2006) points out, blacks in Peru are still presumed to be good lovers, athletes, cooks, musicians, dancers, servants, pallbearers, and delinquents. Blacks are notably underrepresented in the Peruvian oligarchy that runs the country but overrepresented in the doormen who open the doors to the luxury hotels that accommodate them, in the cooks who prepare their fine meals, in the musicians that entertain them, and in the pallbearers who take them to their final resting places.

Next, we will turn our attention to the documentary *El Quinto Suyo* (2003), also directed by Fernando Espinoza. This twenty-six-minute documentary, written and produced by Afro-Peruvians, uses no voiceover and allows the participants, most of whom are Afro-Peruvian, to express what being black means to them. The title translates as "The Fifth Suyo." The other four suyos are a reference to the "four corners" of the Incan Empire, and thus to indigenous peoples, and the title creatively adds blacks as the "fifth suyo" in Peru. The title itself is thus an engagement with Peruvian national discourses that give primacy to indigeneity. One of the producers, Carlos López Schmidt, told me in conversation that he and his colleagues made the movie in order to make blacks more visible and to instill pride in black Peruvians.

El Quinto Suyo uses segments from interviews with well-known Afro-Peruvians, including Victoria Santa Cruz and José Campos, in addition to scenes of Afro-Peruvian youth dancing and making music, and clips from rural areas with strong Afro-Peruvian presences. A few scenes from Ingenio appear in the documentary, most notably the local *cumananero* (poet) reciting a few verses. The inclusion of Ingenio in this documentary signals that Ingenio is a black space in the minds of Afro-Peruvian leaders in Lima. The scenes of daily life in Ingenio show viewers how rural blacks live.

This film correlates blackness in Peru with an agricultural lifestyle, slavery, Africa, and discrimination. It also addresses Afro-Peruvian cultural production, specifically *festejo* (a dance and musical form that is a vestige of slave songs) and cumanana, as representative of black culture in Peru. Two other major themes are Señor de los Milagros (the black patron saint), and Alianza Lima, the Limeño soccer team that has historically been identified with black Peruvians. The film draws from diasporic discourses of cultural and political struggles, and also invokes slavery as part of blacks' past. Nevertheless, the primary focus of this film, written by and for Afro-Peruvians, is on the uniqueness of being black and Peruvian.

El Dominical, a weekly magazine included in the Sunday edition of the prestigious Limeño newspaper *El Comercio*, printed a four-page segment on race in Peru in its August 29, 1999, issue. The title of the segment, "¡Qué tal raza!," was followed by a brief headline indicating that race in Peru was about culture, not skin color. The introductory piece mentioned that race was being discussed quite a bit in Peru at that time. This was likely in part due to the August 19, 1999, dethroning of Rosa Elvira Cartagena, the first Afro-Peruvian Miss Peru, which some black leaders claimed was racially motivated. Nevertheless, the former Miss Peru was never actually mentioned in the segment. In addition, most of the pieces, none written by Afro-Peruvians, focused on indigenous people in Peru, with peripheral attention to blacks. Juan Ossio, an anthropologist, did briefly point out that the stereotypes associated with blacks—that they were happy, faithful, and funny—were cultural not racial stereotypes. This was the only time he mentioned blacks in the six paragraphs he wrote, compared to some eight references to indigenous people

Nelson Manrique, the next contributor, does not refer to blacks at all. Alejandro Ortiz does, with reference to Ricardo Palma, a canonical figure in Peruvian literature, most famous for his collection *Tradiciones peruanas* (1872). Ortiz points out that Ricardo Palma's mother had been a black slave but that, nevertheless, "nadie alude a él como zambo, sino todos lo reconocen como el gran escritor que siempre fue" (no one refers to him as a zambo; instead, they all recognize him as the great writer that he always has been). Ortiz argues that the fact that Palma is such a great writer allows us to forget about his race. Subsequently, he asserts that, in the United States, one who is born black, dies black, whereas in Peru, one's social status can change one's racial classification. From his perspective, the fact that you can change your race in Peru but cannot do so in the United States indicates that Peru is more racially progressive. The overall message here is that Peruvians do not mind if you are black, so long as you do not do anything that might remind them of your blackness.

The last contributor, Marco Aurelio Denegri, is much less subtle in his expressions of racism. Denegri argues that racism is "natural in human beings," although he does not consider himself to be a racist. He (uncritically) argues that the Fujimori administration will never have a black minister, not because of blacks' capabilities, but because Peruvians would make fun of any black official on the basis of his or her race. He then goes on to insist that blacks have something in their skin that makes it difficult for them to swim well. Whatever it takes to be a good swimmer, blacks, he assures us, "do not have in their genetic program." The fact that the most esteemed Limeño newspaper would publish the last comment can be taken as indicative of the sorts of discourses that are acceptable to Peruvians. It is hard to gauge the public response to Denegri's remarks from this distance, but there is currently nothing on the Internet suggesting a public outcry over the *El Dominical* special report, although there is controversy over the dethroning of Cartagena.

We thus have before us the perspectives of both Afro-Peruvians and non-blacks. The films produced by Afro-Peruvians highlight black cultural production, blacks' rural origins, the history of oppression, and discrimination. Notably, the films purposefully include black bodies and faces, thereby calling attention to the black presence in Peru, whereas the newspaper articles, all written by non-blacks, insist on the lack of importance of skin color in Peru. The newspaper feature starts off with the notion that race in Peru is about culture, not color, and Ortiz supplements this with his statements regarding the inconsequentiality of Ricardo Palma's black ancestry, which is trumped by his literary genius. Black cultural production is mentioned, yet minimized, in keeping with the neglect of the black presence in Peru. By calling attention to blackness, the films invoke diasporic discourses, whereas the newspaper feature, by downplaying the importance of race, invokes Latin American exceptionalism.

These national discourses on blackness engage with diasporic discourses on blackness as well as with the criollo narrative within Peru. *Juliana* highlights blacks' musical abilities and rural origins. *El Quinto Suyo* underscores blacks' cultural contributions to the nation, history of oppression, and rural and urban presence. The contributors to *El Dominical* downplay the importance of race, color, and blacks in Peruvian society, and reveal their implicit preference for whiteness. As Feldman (2006) argues, Afro-Peruvians find themselves engaging both with national narratives that highlight criollo and indigenous facets of the nation as well as with diasporic discourses to assert their particularities.

Afro-Peruvians and Mestizaje

These competing narratives about blackness point to the importance of considering blacks' roles in mestizaje in Peru. For the non-black columnists, blacks play an active role in mestizaje. By highlighting mestizaje, these writers downplay the importance of blackness in Peru. In contrast, the black Peruvian films focus on the uniqueness and visibility of blacks, and could be read as a counter-discourse to mestizaje.

Although the bulk of the work on mestizaje in Peru ignores Afro-Peruvians (de la Cadena 2000), my research reveals that Afro-Peruvians participate in both cultural mixing and miscegenation in Peru, as individual actors and as a collective. As individual actors, the progeny of Afro-Peruvians can become mestizos through miscegenation. Neither cultural amalgamation nor migration can however make mestizos out of Afro-Peruvians, unlike the case for indigenous Peruvians. On a collective level, Afro-Peruvian cultural forms have been incorporated into Peruvian culture through mestizaje. Later I take a closer look at this cultural incorporation, but first I discuss individual participation in mestizaje.

One common type of mestizaje in Ingenio is cultural mixture, a prime example of which is chicha consumption patterns. Chicha is a mildly alcoholic beverage that dates back to the Incan era but has become part of daily life for Afro-descendants as well. Chicha consumption is racialized to the extent that cholos are reputed to drink more chicha than others, and even to give it in baby bottles to their very young children. Nearly all villagers drink chicha, however, and its consumption does not make anyone less black or more Indian. Another kind of mestizaje is the intermarriage among blacks, whites, and Indians that is prevalent in Ingenio. The offspring of these unions are usually labeled negros or morenos, but not mestizos or whites. Migration to Lima is another form of mestizaje, since moving to Lima implies modernization, which has been described as mestizaje by Varallanos (1962) and others. Finally, people that move to Lima often marry people who are not from Ingenio, and this sort of racial mixture produces children who could be labeled as white, mestizo, moreno, or negro in the Limeño context. Yet Ingenieros themselves do not view migration to Lima or increased financial resources as altering individuals' fundamental blackness. These findings indicate that the adoption of Indian cultural forms by blacks does not render them Indians, nor does migration to Lima whiten them. The finding that the Afro-Peruvian experience of mestizaje is distinct from the Indian one is not surprising, but it does suggest that perhaps the solution to black exclusion is also distinct from the solution to indigenous exclusion.

From Afro-Peruvian to Peruvian

Individual Afro-Peruvians cannot become mestizos; in some cases, however, their cultural forms have been appropriated into national culture. The traditional art forms my informants identify as their own are tondero, cumanana, and cumbia. Notably, most villagers do not see these art forms as part of black culture, despite abundant evidence that they have Afro-Latin roots (Baca, Basili, and Pereira 1992). These cultural forms are a product of cultural amalgamation and have become Peruvian, or at least norteño. The African roots of tondero, cumanana, and cumbia have been rendered unimportant, as have the African roots of the Ingenieros. They and their music are norteño, criollo, or peruano, but not African or even Afro-Peruvian.

In stark contrast, other forms of Afro-Peruvian music and dance, such as festejo, have not been appropriated through mestizaje but exoticized as distinct from other Peruvian cultural forms. Festejo is derived from slave songs, uses the prototypical Afro-Peruvian cajón, and incorporates the guitar and the *djimbe*, a sort of conga drum. Dancing festejo involves pronounced hip and chest gyrations. This music, unlike cumbia, is identified as Afro-Peruvian rather than Peruvian. The modifier *Afro-*, or black, always precedes *Peruvian* in describing festejo, indicating that it has not been fully incorporated into Peruvian national identity as cumbia has. In the same way that Andean music such as huayno or *san juanito* is not Peruvian music, but Andean music, festejo and *alcatraz* are not Peruvian music, but Afro-Peruvian music or *música negra*.

When Afro-Peruvian forms are incorporated into criollo culture, the African elements are erased and the form becomes Peruvian, part of national identity. For example, when I asked my interviewees whether or not the cumanana is part of black culture, many responded yes, because black people are the ones who recite cumananas. There is more divergence on the question of tondero. For example, Reina, an interviewee in her early twenties, asserts that blacks are not the only ones to dance tondero, and therefore it is not part of black culture. This is intriguing because it means that as soon as non-blacks start to engage in black cultural forms, they become de-blackened.

Whereas most of my interviewees referred to the music from southern Peru, such as festejo or alcatraz, as black music, only some considered tondero and cumanana to be black cultural forms. A few of my interviewees recounted that Don Ramón Domínguez, an Afro-Peruvian from neighboring La Pilca, had invented cumanana, and that, therefore, cumanana was a black cultural form. Morropón, which is a few kilometers from Ingenio, claims its fame as "La Cuna y Capital del Tondero y de la Cumanana." My interviewees challenged this claim, asserting that cumanana was in fact from La Pilca. In contrast, other interviewees told me that these cultural forms were from Morropón and were Morropano not specifically black. Overall, the majority of my informants in Ingenio did not see themselves as partakers in black culture, although most of them did think that black cultural forms existed in Peru.

Thus, what we have is a group of people, many of whom self-identify as black, recognize that black cultural production exists in Peru, and yet do not see themselves as partakers in that black culture. (This is not the case with all of the villagers.) So, does this subset of individuals need the right to be different? Perhaps more important, would they potentially be harmed by state policies dictating who is black and what cultural production they should have the right to cultivate? As legal theorist Richard Ford (2004) points out, any politics of recognition potentially gives power to the state to define and enforce who belongs to which culture.

Some villagers do see themselves as partakers in black cultural production, lending some support to the research of Cuche and Vásquez Rodríguez, who both argue that Afro-Peruvians do have a distinct culture. Cuche (1981: 141), for example, argues that although larger Peruvian society does not recognize Afro-Peruvians as "agents de culture," Afro-Peruvians have created a culture that is a fusion of their African traditions with those of the New World, and that this culture continues to be nourished and to develop. Vásquez Rodríguez (1982) also contends that black Peruvians have created a cultural community in Peru that is a synthesis of African and Spanish elements. Cuche (1981: 179) brings up another pertinent point: "Les Noirs sont donc pris dans un double mouvement externe: de négation de leur identité ethnique (pour mieux les intégrer) d'une part et de curiosité pour leurs coutumes et traditions culturelles d'autre part." (Blacks [in Peru] are therefore between two external pressures: the negation of their ethnic identity [to better integrate them] on the one hand and a curiosity about their cultural traditions on the other hand.) This, Cuche argues, has led to a "folklorization" of Afro-Peruvian culture. Most important, Cuche's and Vásquez Rodríguez's ethnographic research in Afro-Peruvian communities does not lead them to believe that Afro-Peruvians are culturally indistinguishable from criollos.

In sum, my research supports the claim that Afro-Peruvian culture does exist, but also the claim that black culture in Peru has very different meanings for different people, which again points to the danger of enforcing a politics of difference that could serve to homogenize black culture. It is useful at this juncture to discuss the evidence of Afro-Peruvian culture I gathered in Ingenio, alongside the finding that not all Afro-Peruvians see themselves as participants in that culture.

Afro-Peruvian Culture in Ingenio

In many Afro-Peruvian towns in southern Peru, one finds traditional Afro-Peruvian music accompanied by a cajón played at parties and other public events. While I was living in Ingenio, I never heard a cajón being played. I did hear of one young man, Juan, who played cajón, but he had moved from Ingenio. Juan learned to play cajón from his late father. In another case, Edmundo, a retired baker in his eighties, told me that when he was younger, he would go to parties where musicians played the cajón. "El hombre manejaba agachado el arpa y el otro tocaba el cajón y el otro tocaba la guitarra. Tres hombres hacían bailar cien hombres. Cien cristianos. A golpe de cajón como dice la cumanana, como dice la marinera, a golpe de cajón baila mi chino y bien bailado nosotros." (One man played the harp hunched over and the other played the cajón and the other played the guitar. Three men made one hundred men dance. One hundred Christians. To the beat of the cajón, the cumanana as they call it, the marinera, as they call it, to the beat of the cajón, one danced and, oh, how we danced.) He lamented that this musical tradition had faded and people now listened only to recorded music, "cosas modernas" (modern things).

Although the cajón had faded from Ingenio, I did meet people who told me that they danced tondero, and I had the opportunity to hear three older villagers recite cumananas. All of my interviewees had heard of cumananas and tonderos and knew that these arts were practiced in Ingenio, yet many did not consider them to be part of black culture. Take, for example, a conversation I had with Miguel, a villager in his forties:

TGB: Tondero and cumanana are part of black culture or Morropano culture?

Miguel: That culture is Morropana, but the tondero has practically no relation with the dances, as they say, of the black community . . . or of African origin. They are different. Tondero isn't, well, . . . the cumanana and the tondero, originate directly from La Pilca. . . . This gentleman's name was Ramón Domínguez. Mr. Ramón Domínguez was born here, but afterwards, he left that place, and everyone came to know him in Morropón and he, sang or told his décimas in cumananas. . . . Since he lived in Morropón, they say that he was born there in Morropón. . . .

TGB: Does this music have roots in African culture?

Miguel: No. . . . The dances are completely different. . . . Nothing to do with it, no sort of relationship. Because, tondero is tap dancing, flirting, playfulness, I don't know how else you would refer to it, but, and the other dancing is different.

Here, Miguel insists that tondero has no black or African roots. He sees Afro-Peruvian, or black, music as being something completely different. Nevertheless, Miguel is proud that the cumanana comes from his village, and makes a point of clarifying its source as La Pilca, not Morropón. Given that Miguel does not see the cumanana and tondero as part of black culture, what effect does this have on his inclusion in Peru's democracy and his status as a full citizen of Peru? To what extent does Miguel have a sense of belonging to Peru in a cultural sense? More broadly, is a cultural-rights framework appropriate for understanding Afro-Peruvians' citizenship status?

Let us consider an interviewee who does associate these art forms with black people, and see if a politics-of-recognition framework could serve as a mechanism of inclusion and of creating a sense of belonging for Afro-Peruvians.

TGB: Do you think that here in Ingenio there exists a black culture or a culture of morenos, any black dances or black music that come from here?

Rocío: That come from here? For example, those sorts of dances, right, folkloric, were born in La Pilca, right? Cumanana was born in La Pilca. . . . Tondero, which is a dance, also was born in La Pilca.

TGB: Yes, but, for you, is this something that was born of moreno people?

Rocío: Yes.

TGB: Yes.

Rocío: Yes, yes, yes. . . . Earlier, there was a gentleman, Ramón Domínguez . . . who was born in La Pilca. He was born, he was the first cumananero, and one could say that, from there, from La Pilca, authentically from La Pilca. Ah, cumanana is like a verse, right, which is like, for example, you say one thing and the other person responds with something else, right. It is like responding verses [counterpoint].

TGB: Ah, both are singing.

Rocío: Like singing, but everything is improvised. Nothing is studied, nothing like that. And, there are still people today. Yes, in La
Pilca, there are several people; among them, there is a woman
who is quite dark-skinned.

Rocío sees cumanana and tondero as local forms of black cultural production and appreciates their ingenuity. What does it mean, in terms of
cultural rights, that she, unlike Miguel, identifies them as black? In a subsequent interview, I asked Rocío why other villagers might not see tondero
and cumanana as black cultural productions. She responded that perhaps
others see these cultural forms as coming from somewhere else but, "No
sé porque no lo consideran que es de la gente morena. Será porque, ahor-
ita ya se baila a nivel nacional." (I don't know why they don't think of it
as being something that belongs to black people. Perhaps this is because
now it is something that is danced across the country.) In these comments,
Rocío is saying two important things: (1) that something from her town is
something "de la gente morena" (of black people), and (2) that something
that is practiced nationwide (a nivel nacional) may well not be perceived
as black. Again, this shows that black culture is something performed in
black spaces, by black people. Anything with a wider audience is no longer
black. This raises interesting questions regarding how difference is recognized and negotiated in Peru. What does this sort of recognition of
difference mean for Afro-Peruvians' citizenship status and the Peruvian
racial democracy? What would it mean for the state to cultivate black cultural production if, by definition, it can be performed only by blacks? Who
would have the power to decide who is black and who is not, or what is
black culture and what is not?

In order to have his cultural rights fulfilled, Miguel would either have to
feel empowered as a member of the dominant group or feel as though he
belongs to the nation because his cultural identity is integral to the national
identity. In Miguel's view, cumanana and tondero are cultural forms that
are part of his cultural identity and of northern Peruvian coastal criollo
culture; therefore, he too is part of this culture. Rocío, on the other hand,
feels empowered to develop her cultural identity, yet she sees her cultural
identity as particular to black people. Her cultural identity is also threatened because as soon as non-blacks start to perform black cultural forms,
they become de-blackened. Rocío herself, in contrast, cannot become de-
blackened by participating in non-black cultural forms. Whether or not

Rocío or Miguel see themselves as culturally different from the dominant culture, they are marked as black.

Miguel identifies with tondero and cumanana and sees them as local cultural productions with no African roots. Despite evidence that mestizaje works very differently for Indians and blacks in Peru, this situation is strikingly similar to what Indians face. In order to become Peruvians, Indians must shed their cultural affiliations. In this case, Miguel sees tondero and cumanana as Peruvian not African in origin. The cultural forms have shed their Africanness and become Peruvian. Miguel, however, cannot shed his blackness and become Peruvian, precisely because he is marked racially *and* ethnically as black.

Racial Exclusion and Stereotypes in Peru

Not only are my interviewees marked as black, they also self-identify as black (negro or moreno) and are cognizant that others see them as negros or morenos. These color-based identifications are far from neutral. As Carlos Aguirre points out with regard to Peru:

> La identificación del color de la piel con una condición inferior ... todavía la arrastramos hoy día. Se trata de un racismo que es alimentado por conductas cotidianas a veces imperceptibles y con frecuencia consideradas inofensivas (chistes, expresiones de mal gusto, valoraciones estéticas, estereotipos y otros), pero que también responde a ciertos componentes estructurales (pobreza y marginalización de las poblaciones negras, falta de representación en los niveles directivos del país, bajos índices de movilidad social). (The identification of skin color with an inferior condition ... is something we still carry with us today. We are dealing with a racism that is fueled by everyday behaviors that are sometimes imperceptible and frequently considered inoffensive [jokes, expressions in bad taste, aesthetic judgments, stereotypes, and others], but that also correspond to certain structural components [poverty and marginalization of black peoples, lack of representation in the governance of the country, and low rates of social mobility]). (Aguirre 2000: 73)

Blacks in Peru experience both individual and structural racism. In terms of individual racism, they are stereotypically displayed on television, in the newspaper, and on billboards as cooks, as primitive, as hypersexual, and as unintelligent. In addition, there are common jokes that associate blacks with criminality. For example, "Si tú ves un blanco corriendo, sabes que está haciendo deporte, pero si tú ves un negro corriendo, ya sabes que es un ladrón." (If you see a white person running, you know he is running for sport, but if you see a black person running, you know he is a thief.) I previously cited another common joke claiming that blacks are useless after noon. These jokes and advertisements carry cultural meaning, indicating that blacks are seen as culturally different from non-black Peruvians. Afro-Peruvians' racial differences lead to assumptions about their cultural differences—even though not all Afro-Peruvians see themselves as participants in Afro-Peruvian culture. Peruvian society is clearly not color-blind, but should it be? Is color blindness the solution to the inclusion of blacks as Peruvian citizens? In addition, how do we interpret the situation of black Peruvians who claim that they are not culturally different, that their cultural forms are the same as national cultural forms, and that they do not participate in black cultural forms? Are they being denied their cultural rights? Or are they insisting on their cultural belonging by invoking a discourse of sameness?

Politics of Difference and Sameness in Peru

At this juncture, it is useful to revisit the idea of cultural citizenship. Cultural citizenship entails both the right to belong and the right to be different. The fulfillment of cultural citizenship is a prerequisite to being a full citizen, or what Rosaldo (1994) calls a "first-class citizen," as opposed to a "second-class citizen." Democracies have long existed with first-, second-, and third-class citizens—Wallerstein (2003) even argues that the very concept of citizen requires the creation of a hierarchy of citizens. Nevertheless, current theorists of citizenship propose that political, social, and cultural inequalities are detrimental to the realization of a truly democratic society (Jenson 2001; Richardson 1998; Pakulski 1997). This democratic society is understood as one in which all people (or at least all adult citizens) have equal access to the rights and responsibilities that go along with being a full member of the society. In the case of Afro-Peruvians, the question we must answer is, Can Afro-Peruvians have access to cultural citizenship, to a sense of being an integral part of Peru, through a politics of sameness, or is it necessary to invoke a politics of difference?

The evidence presented in this chapter indicates that to be black in Peru is to be different from the unmarked Peruvian. Afro-Peruvian cultural forms can be incorporated into national culture, but only if they are no longer performed primarily or exclusively by Afro-Peruvians and are no longer called Afro-Peruvian, but Peruvian. The African element is effaced. For Afro-Peruvian people to be referred to as simply Peruvians, their African ancestry must no longer be evident, their blackness invisible. Insofar as cultural forms retain their African element, they are folklorized. Insofar as Peruvians are visibly African-descended, they are marginalized. To be black in Peru is to be different, to be exotic, to not be simply Peruvian. Thus, Afro-Peruvians do not have both the right to belong and the right to be different. They have only the right, and in many cases, the obligation, to be different. The folklorization of black culture and marginalization of black people are remnants of a long history of structural and individual racism in Peru.

Because Afro-Peruvians are treated as different, many have come to see themselves as different. Afro-Peruvians are labeled as blacks, are treated as blacks, and know that they are blacks. This labeling is not a neutral act because the label *black* in Peru carries a number of cultural assumptions. Blackness in Peru is associated with a certain way of speaking Spanish, with sensual dancing, with good cooking, and with physical and sexual prowess. This labeling invokes a discourse of cultural difference and creates a situation where black Peruvians see themselves as distinct. For example, Fabio reported to me that he was proud to be black. When I asked him why, he said that sometimes whites try to marginalize blacks or discriminate against them, but that he does not let this get to him, because he is proud to be black. In fights, people might call him "negro mogoso" (filthy black) or similarly insult him, but these insults do not bother him, because he is proud to be black. Whether or not Fabio sees himself as culturally different from criollos or mestizos, he knows that other Peruvians label him as black and make assumptions about him because of his blackness. This other-izing has given meaning to Fabio's blackness.

It would be unreasonable to suggest to Fabio that he abandon his celebration of his blackness, precisely because this assertion of blackness is the direct result of his having been treated as different based on his skin color. The reason that Fabio does not embrace an ideology of sameness is because he has been treated as an other, as ethnically and racially different from other Peruvians. Thus, Fabio claims his blackness. Juliet Hooker (2005) argues that it is potentially problematic for Indians and blacks in

Latin America to base their claims for inclusion on demands for cultural recognition as opposed to a discourse against racial discrimination. Fabio's case indicates that cultural recognition is often inseparable from racial discrimination. As Hooker points out, "not all Afro-Latinos are perceived by national elites and publics as having a distinct 'ethnic identity' worthy of being protected by special group rights" (301). The fact that Afro-Latino culture is not seen as "worthy of protection" is a form of racial discrimination. For this reason, an essential part of ending racial discrimination in Peru is the enactment of a multicultural reform that re-educates Peruvians about Afro-Peruvian culture and Afro-Peruvian cultural contributions to the nation. Any multicultural reform that fails to address widespread racism in Peruvian society is not worth undertaking.

As Aguirre (2000) points out, blacks in Peru are subject to denigration and are structurally disadvantaged in the society. Many Peruvians have no qualms about expressing racist opinions of blacks. In a recent study of racial discourses in Lima, I found that Limeños frequently describe blacks as unintelligent and criminally inclined (Golash-Boza 2011). The need for racial justice and antiracist activism in Peru is clear. What is less clear is how multicultural reforms in Peru could work to ensure the cultural citizenship of black Peruvians.

Black Peruvians and Cultural Citizenship

Should the goal of multicultural reform in Peru be the full integration of Afro-Peruvians into the nation or the creation of a cultural community of Afro-Peruvians? Either situation would meet the criteria of cultural citizenship. To decide, it is useful to think about this in practical terms of what a multicultural reform would look like.

Africans and their descendants have made substantial contributions to Peru's cultural landscape. Unfortunately, other Peruvians either do not recognize these contributions or do not see them in a positive light, and those Afro-Peruvian cultural forms that have not been incorporated into national culture have been folklorized and exoticized. Thus, one important element of a multicultural reform would be a change in the school curriculum such that textbooks and classroom discussions would be designed to teach students (and teachers) about the cultural and social contributions of African-descended Peruvians. In the current school curriculum, African-descended Peruvians figure most prominently as slaves brought from

Africa who were granted their freedom by Ramón Castilla in 1854. Renowned African-descended historical figures are also presented, but their African ancestry is not usually mentioned. For example, in a widely used high-school textbook, the African-descended community leader María Elena Moyano is lauded for her courage and community activism in Villa El Salvador, Lima, yet neither her African ancestry nor her blackness is mentioned. Given prevailing stereotypes that Afro-Peruvian women are much more likely to be excellent cooks or sensual lovers than community leaders, it might help to break down stereotypes if the textbook identified Moyano as Afro-Peruvian.

This depiction of Afro-Peruvians as historically but not presently important gives students the idea that once there were blacks in Peru, but they are not currently an integral part of the nation. A change in the school curriculum to teach students about the contemporary and historical contributions of Afro-Peruvians, accompanied by government-sponsored events and research on Afro-Peruvians, would work to teach all Peruvians that African-descended Peruvians have made and continue to make important contributions to Peru. This sort of multicultural reform would be appropriate and useful.

In contrast, it would not be suitable to implement a multicultural reform that homogenizes black culture. For example, it would be inappropriate to implement a multicultural reform requiring that festejo be taught in all schools, along with huayno and the marinera, in order to represent different aspects of national culture. This sort of reform could actually work to reinforce stereotypes—for example, that Indians dance huayno, whites dance the marinera, and blacks the festejo—whereas the reality is that the marinera, given its great similarity to the tondero, is more predominant in Ingenio and the surrounding villages than is the festejo, which is exclusive to southern Peru. Although it is imperative to recognize the existence and importance of Afro-Peruvian cultural forms, it is equally important to avoid essentializing them.

Were the Afro-Peruvian contributions to Peruvian culture and society to be recognized by all Peruvians, it is likely that discrimination against Afro-Peruvians would decline. At present, discrimination against Afro-Peruvians is one aspect of the black experience that creates a cultural community. The absence of discrimination, thus, could contribute to the integration of Afro-Peruvians into the Peruvian nation. Individual Afro-Peruvians who desire to integrate socially could choose to do so; however, those Afro-Peruvians who desire to maintain a separate cultural community should also have the right to do so. Black Peruvians should not have to reinvent themselves as culturally different in order to become full citizens any more than they should have to hide or abandon their culture. People of African descent in Peru participate to varying degrees in cultural forms that are part of "black culture." Their participation or lack thereof in these cultural forms should have no bearing on their citizenship status. A democracy entails that all people have the right to cultural citizenship, but it does not entail that people have the responsibility or obligation to participate in certain cultural forms.

The Afro-Peruvian experience reminds us of the danger of multicultural reforms that would serve to reify or essentialize black culture. Whereas someone like Rocío might be comfortable with a reform that promotes a black cultural community, Miguel and Perla would likely prefer a reform that promotes their integration into Peruvian society, and might not agree with a reform that exclusively defines them as black and that defines their blackness for them. These two sorts of reforms do not have to be mutually exclusive, however. Any reform whose primary purpose is to reinforce the dignity of Afro-Peruvians must simultaneously underscore the value of Afro-Peruvian cultural contributions to the nation and the common dignity of all Peruvians. Thus, although Rocío should be able to take pride in the cultural contributions of her ancestors and contemporaries, Miguel should not be restricted to identifying with only those cultural forms that have been labeled as belonging to him.

Conclusion: Multicultural Reforms and Racial Justice in Peru

As I described in chapter 1, many Afro-Peruvians are unaware of the history of enslavement of Africans in Peru. This is due in part to the lack of oral transmission of local histories but is also a reflection of the low quality of public schooling in Peru, especially in rural areas. It is crucial that all Peruvians, and especially Afro-Peruvians, have an accurate understanding of the history of people of African descent in Peru. A key component of a multicultural reform in Peru should include investment in primary and secondary education—not just to teach about "black culture" and "black history," but to provide all Peruvians with an adequate education. When I visited Ingenio in 2006, the educational facilities were poor. The school had new books, but no place to store them. There was not a single computer in the school. The teachers frequently did not show up, in part because almost none of them lived in Ingenio. Even students who graduated at the top of their class had almost no chance of attending university. The lack of opportunities for higher education was one reason none of the teachers were from Ingenio.

Inadequate education in places like Ingenio, combined with the lack of opportunities for attaining higher education, means that people from such places are very unlikely to be able to participate in designing or implementing multicultural reforms. Programs that improve education overall and offer more opportunities to students from towns such as Ingenio must be part of any multicultural reform. In short, narrowly defined multicultural reforms that do not take a holistic approach to societal change will likely be of little benefit to people in places such as Ingenio. By the same token, efforts at multicultural reform that do not address the structural racism in Peruvian society that is responsible for the poor education in rural areas will do little good either.

State-sponsored education of all Peruvians about the Afro-Peruvian contribution to the nation is required in order for Afro-Peruvians to become full citizens of the nation. This sort of reform would require the active participation of Afro-Peruvian intellectuals and students, and would result in the increased visibility of prominent Afro-Peruvians who are not singers or soccer players. These reforms, along with their implications, would lead Peru closer to a society in which Afro-Peruvians are not seen as proficient only at entertainment, sports, and cooking. This new perception would make it easier for Afro-Peruvians to perform well in school and university, gain professional employment, and achieve prominence in politics. Multicultural reforms in Peru, to be successful, must be holistic because they need to address widespread bigotry and structural racism. The educational system provides one avenue for these reforms.

Epilogue

In this book, I have explored why generalizations about the black experience in the diaspora, in Latin America, and even in Peru are not always useful for describing blacks in Ingenio. I also have considered why generalizations about racial categorizations and processes of racialization in Latin America have limited utility for the case of Ingenio. In approaching these issues, I have demonstrated that localities matter a great deal. Despite the importance of localities, however, global processes continue to be important. Global representations of blacks and whites do influence ideas of racial difference in Ingenio, even though local realities continue to be significant and the global influences uneven.

I set out to write this book in large part because there are no books that explore Afro-Peruvian identity. As I wrote, I realized that this is not exactly a book about Afro-Peruvian identity either. It is an exploration of how people in Ingenio engage with the label *black*, which is used to describe them and which they use to describe themselves. In Ingenio, the label *black* is not tied to a history of slavery; it does not refer to ancestral roots in Africa; and it does not denote a common experience of oppression. Instead of being an identity, *black* is a label used to describe the skin color of most people in Ingenio. As an identifier, *black* carries with it plenty of social significations.

In Ingenio, being black is normal, but being mixed with white or Indian makes you more attractive. Your family's history as the descendants of African slaves makes it likely that your family lives in poverty. The history of slavery and tenant farming in Peru makes it unlikely that you have much understanding of the lives of your African ancestors. When you go to school, you may learn that blacks were enslaved, but you are not likely learn anything about African civilizations or the history of prominent Afro-Peruvians. As a black person from Ingenio, you differentiate yourself from serranos, who are white and not as modern as you. You also see yourselves as different from cholos, who eat a lot of fish and drink a lot of chicha. In looking for a romantic partner, you may consider it preferable to marry someone with lighter skin, but will not reject a suitor solely because of his or her color.

When you leave Ingenio, your blackness will take on new meaning. People will call you "negro/a" or "moreno/a" on the street, at the same time they claim that your color has no influence on their perception of you. People will presume you know how to dance, to cook if you are a woman, and to play soccer if you are a man. You will have difficulty securing front-office positions in wealthy neighborhoods. You will be reminded frequently of your blackness, as you will be likely to have a nickname like "negra," "zamba," or "morena." If you fall in love with a white man, his family will likely oppose the union, although they will not mind if you are just friends. You will not see many positive representations of people who look like you in the media and in advertisements, except for a few token representations. The extent to which individual blacks will face exclusion will depend on the level of intimacy of the relationship, the visibility of their African ancestry, and the particular context.

Achieving the understanding of blackness in Peru set forth in this book required an extensive dialogue between Latin American studies and African diaspora studies. My understanding of blackness in Peru is enhanced by tropes from both of these fields, although neither provides a complete picture. Both fields provide important guideposts for understanding the experiences of black Peruvians, the dialogue between them reveals the extent to which each field poses distinct questions.

Diaspora studies places Africa and slavery at the center of analysis, leading me to question why Africa and slavery are not important in the collective memory of Ingenieros. This questioning gave me key insights into how the agricultural history of Piura has shaped collective understandings of blackness in Ingenio. Latin American studies upholds mestizaje and blanqueamiento as the key tropes for understanding race in the region, leading me to ask why these processes work differently for blacks than for Indians.

This analysis shed light on how blacks and Indians have been incorporated in different ways in nation-making processes across Latin America.

Drawing from the literature in diaspora studies, I was able to unearth the ways that diasporic discourses are present among people from Ingenio. This analysis allowed me to think about the ways that blackness is defined and the possibilities for imagining the diaspora in new ways. Drawing from studies of race in Latin America, I was able to think about how whitening works for Afro-Peruvians and how skin color affects these processes. Both of these fields led me to see the importance of skin color, both for inclusion in global blackness and for inclusion in national whiteness.

Looking at these fields side by side, it becomes evident that the questions they pose are polar opposites. Diaspora studies looks at the possibilities for blackness whereas Latin American studies considers the possibilities for whiteness. Latin American studies has as its central focus gaining an understanding of the particularity of Latin America. Diaspora studies has as its goal uncovering the commonalities of blacks across the diaspora. Considering the limitations of both of these fields helps us to think about the uniqueness of black Peruvians as well as what they share with other people of African descent around the world. This dialogue thus sheds light on the fundamental differences between these two fields, and on how one's scholarly approach influences the questions one asks and the answers one finds. At the same time, meanings of blackness are changing in Peru. One force in their evolution is Afro-Peruvian social movements.

In August 2007, I went to a workshop on the human rights of Afro-Peruvians in El Carmen, a well-known Afro-Peruvian town in Chincha. The overnight workshop was organized by CEDET and funded in part by INDEPA. Its purpose was to educate Afro-Peruvians about human rights and to document human rights abuses in their communities. On the second day of the workshop, one of the organizers, Fiona, walked around with a pen and a pad of paper. She told me that she was writing down the names of attendees who were not Afro-Peruvian, so as to exclude them from future events, as she did not want indigenous or white people to speak for blacks. She pointed to a girl with copper skin and sleek black hair, and told me that she had nothing Afro about her. She then pointed to a fair-skinned girl with freckles and curly long hair, saying that this woman was Afro; she could tell. Fiona did not use the word *black*, but rather *Afro-Peruvian* or *Afro*, thereby focusing on the importance of (visible) African ancestry.

By including and excluding people from events on the basis of their appearance, Fiona is engaging in a process of redefining racial boundaries in Peru. In addition, this workshop is creating new terminologies insofar as *Afro-Peruvian* is not a popularly used term. The labels *Afro-Peruvian* or *Afro-descendant* are infrequently used in Peru, and even less so in the isolated village of Ingenio. This situation may change, however, and the change in terminology may also change the meaning of blackness in Peru, and who is and is not considered black.

If the label *Afro-descendant* were to become common, racial understandings would change. The woman whom Fiona identified as not being "Afro" had expressed her solidarity with the others present by saying, "We morenos face discrimination." She expanded the moreno category to include herself, but did not invoke "Afro," perhaps because she did not consider herself to be Afro-descendant. On the other hand, the woman Fiona had identified as "Afro" could be described as blanquita in other situations on the basis of her fair skin. If Fiona's understanding of who is and is not Afro becomes prevalent in Peru, we could see less distinction between Peru and the United States than we now do.

Fiona and others at the Afro-Peruvian NGO also differ from most people in Ingenio in one important way: for blacks in Ingenio, blackness is rarely politicized. In Ingenio, people may see themselves as black, but other identities are usually more important. In my conversations with men in Ingenio, they tended to talk about themselves as campesinos, peasants who work the land. Men would often explain to me with great care how rice is planted, harvested, processed, and sold. Discussions frequently revolved around the best going price for rice, when crops should be harvested, and whether or not to use machines for harvesting. When men would complain about their situation, it was often about the lack of water for two harvests, the failure of the government to ensure a good price for rice, and the lack of funds to improve technology. Thus, when INDEPA, the government's multicultural arm, organized a workshop near Ingenio in order to solicit proposals that met the needs of Afro-Peruvians, two noteworthy things happened. First, most of the demands centered around agricultural needs, which are not race-specific. People demanded water for irrigation and information about potential free-trade agreements. Second, the people who spoke on behalf of the communities were not always people who would be identified as black. Thus, although the workshop was designed to ascertain the needs of the Afro-Peruvian community, the Afro-Peruvians in Ingenio did not present their needs as race-specific.

Ingenieros' lack of interest in blackness and in Africa turned out to be a dilemma for me in my research. My project was on blackness, yet blackness was not a salient issue for people in Ingenio. Through researching and talking about blackness with them, I gave it importance. I am not alone in this endeavor. From the World Bank initiatives that promote the well-being of Afro–Latin Americans to Peruvian government initiatives, and to NGOs, artists, and intellectuals, there are a wide variety of people interested in the blackness of people in Ingenio.

Thinking of the African diaspora as both a process and a condition allows me to begin to resolve this dilemma. The people of Ingenio share with other diasporic blacks the condition of being black. The fact that they carry visible markers of African ancestry means that they are labeled as black. This label carries connotations associated with being a diasporic black—a history of slavery, oppression, and cultural production. At the same time, thinking of the diaspora as a process allows for some flexibility in our understanding. As a process, it is fluid, and blackness is a label that is actively applied by others. People in Ingenio have varying levels of engagement with diasporic discourses, and these levels are subject to change in response to multicultural reforms and engagement with global media.

The fact that people in Ingenio self-identify as black is surprising in light of work on blackness in Latin America indicating that most people reject or deny the label *black*. The fact that people in Ingenio define blackness primarily as a color is surprising in the context of the assumption in diaspora studies that people who self-identify as black find deeper meaning in blackness.

I have argued that the way blackness is defined in Ingenio is a reflection of local realities and global discourses. Blackness is the norm in Ingenio, so there is no sense of shame surrounding blackness. Slavery is not salient in local history because it is overshadowed by the more recent history of tenant farming. Africa has lost its importance due to the passage of time combined with the lack of transmission of ancestral knowledge over generations. Global and regional discourses of blackness are often of limited importance in this isolated town, which is exactly what one would expect under these circumstances.

In writing this book, I used historical documents to gain insight into the history of Afro-descendants in Peru. I read novels and essays that opened a window into the elite imaginary. I carried out ethnography and interviews to discern how blackness was lived, experienced, and talked about. Finally, I drew from cultural production to think about how blackness is represented in Peru. This interdisciplinary exercise was designed to provide a nuanced understanding of the complexity of blackness in Peru. The understanding I have come to is that blackness in Peru is primarily a matter of skin color.

Much work remains to be done, however. It remains unclear to what extent my findings from Ingenio are applicable to other Afro-Peruvian towns. More ethnographic research on Afro-Peruvian communities is needed. In addition, the lack of historical scholarship on slavery and the post-slavery experience in northern Peru means that some of my conclusions are necessarily tentative. More historical research on blacks in northern Peru is needed. Within literary studies, few scholars have paid attention to the role of blacks in Peruvian cultural production, either in the contemporary period or in the past. More research is needed in this area as well. This book, then, is a first step toward developing an understanding of the multiplicity of meanings of blackness in Peru, and I look forward to continuing this conversation.

Glossary

Alcatraz: An Afro-Peruvian dance form.

Blanco/a: A white person; also a descriptor of any object that is white.

Blanqueamiento: Whitening.

Bozal: A slave who came directly from Africa to the New World.

Cajón: A boxlike percussion instrument typical of Afro-Peruvian music.

Campesinos: Peasants.

Caporal: The overseer at a plantation.

Chicha: A fermented beverage made with corn.

Chichería: A place where chicha is brewed and sold.

Cholo/a: An indigenous person. In Ingenio, *cholo* refers to indigenous people from the coast. In Lima, it is used to refer to indigenous people from the highlands who have acculturated to Lima society.

Colonos: Workers on northern Peruvian haciendas.

Corregimiento: A local administrative unit in the colonial era.

Criollo/a: Describes a Spaniard or African born in Peru during the colonial era. In modern Peru it is also a general term used to refer to people from the coast. In Ingenio, it is used to refer to people who are from Ingenio.

Cuadra: A unit of measure equal to about two hectares.

Cumanana: A form of call-and-response poetry of Afro-Peruvian origin. Can be sung or recited.

Cumananero: A person who recites or sings cumananas.

Décima: A form of poetry of Afro-Peruvian origin.

Djimbe: A kind of conga drum.

Enganche: Literally "hooking." A form of labor contracting where a contractor finds laborers who commit to working for a specific period, usually with an initial incentive—"the hook."

Festejo: An Afro-Peruvian dance and musical form derived from slave songs.

Hacienda: An estate or large landholding, often including a plantation.

Hacendado: The owner of an hacienda.

Indio/a: A common term for a person of indigenous ancestry; an Indian.

Indigenismo: An intellectual movement that valorizes indigenous contributions to society and culture.

Indigenistas: People who promulgate indigenismo.

Ingenieros: People from Ingenio; generically, *ingeniero* means "engineer."

Ladinos: Colonial term for acculturated slaves who spoke Spanish and had not been born in Africa.

Libertos: Children of slaves who were supposed to gain their freedom at age twenty for females and twenty-four for males.

Marinera: A coastal dance form in Peru.

Mestizaje: Racial and cultural mixture, an emblem of Latin American race relations.

Mestizo/a: A person who has a mix of white and indigenous ancestry.

Mita: A system of forced labor in Peru.

Mitayos: Laborers in the mita.

Mondongo: A tripe stew.

Moreno/a: An Afro-descended person with brown skin, typically lighter in color than negro.

Morropano/a: A person or thing from Morropón.

Moto-taxi: A motorcycle with attached seats, used for public transportation over short distances.

Mulata/mulato: A woman/man of mixed African and European ancestry.

Mulataje: Mixture between blacks and whites, the process of creating mulattos.

Mulatez: A literary movement that celebrated mixture between blacks and whites.

Música negra (or negroide): A descriptor for Afro-Peruvian music.

Negro: A black person; also the color black applied to any object.

Norteño/a: A person from northern Peru; northern Peruvian.

Pardos: A colonial term used in Peru to refer to people of mixed African and European ancestry.

Peruanos/as: People from Peru.

Poto: A gourd used for drinking chicha.

Reducciones: Resettlement sites for indigenous people.

San juanito: A typical indigenous musical and dance form.

Serrano/a: A person from the Andes Mountains.

Toma de tierras: "Taking of lands," the colloquial term for land reform.

Tondero: A barefoot dance similar to *marinera*, accompanied by the cajón.

Trigueño: Literally, wheat colored. Used to refer to a near-white skin color.

Zambo/a: In traditional colonial usage, a person of mixed black and Indian ancestry; in local usage in Ingenio, a person with curly hair, indicative of African descent.

A Note on Terminology and Translation

In this book, I have used the words I find to be most appropriate, in light of the usages I heard in Peru, instead of using what others might see as more politically correct terms, as I do not find it useful to change words in the hopes of making the conversation less messy. Talking about racial differences is complicated, and I have tried to be as straightforward as possible. At several junctures in the text, I explain my word usage. Here, I explain some more general decisions that apply throughout the text.

The most relevant word choice has to do with *Afro-Peruvian* versus *black*. I use *Afro-Peruvian* or *African-descended Peruvian* to describe some people of African descent, to describe the social movements that designate themselves as such, and to describe some cultural forms in Peru. I do not use *Afro-Peruvian* to describe people in Ingenio, as they do not use this term to describe themselves. When I describe people of African descent in Ingenio, I use the terms they use—mostly *negro* or *moreno*. When I translate *negro* into English, I use "black." *African-descended Peruvian* and *black* are not interchangeable. In Peru, only those people with visible African ancestry would be identified as black. Thus, a person could have African ancestry but not be defined as black. I do not capitalize *black* just as I do not capitalize *white*.

I do capitalize *Indian,* as is conventional in English, although not in Spanish. I use *indio* in Spanish and *Indian* in English. I occasionally use *indigenous* to refer to people and cultural forms. When talking about mestizaje, however, it makes more sense to contrast indios with mestizos, as mestizos can retain some attachment to their indigenous origins, even as they distinguish themselves from indios. I do not use *Amerindian* as I find "Indian" to be a better translation of *indio.* Just as *African-descended Peruvian* and *black* are not interchangeable, neither are *indigenous* and *Indian,* as a person could be of indigenous ancestry yet be identified as a mestizo.

Notes

Introduction

1. This and all other translations in the book are my own unless otherwise noted.

2. Afro-Peruvians are concentrated in particular towns along the coast because of the history of slavery. Slave plantations were situated in towns near valleys with enough water to sustain large-scale agricultural production.

3. The visited sites are Acarí, San Luis de Cañete, El Guayabo, San José, Carmen, Ingenio de Nazca, Yapatera, Ingenio de Buenos Aires, La Pilca, La Maravilla, La Banda, Buenos Aires, Morropón, San José de los Molinos, Zaña, Aucallama, Coyungo, Pisco, Las Lomas, and eight neighborhoods in Lima. See the CEDET website for their geo-ethnic map: www.cedet.net/. The map is also available at www.cimarrones-peru.org/mapa.htm (accessed June 24, 2010).

Chapter 1. Black, but Not African

1. The unique racial geography of Piura was explained to me by the late Octavio Céspedes, a local grassroots intellectual from Yapatera. This racial geography differs from the general pattern for Peru laid out by Marisol de la Cadena (2000)—where the coast is white and mestizo, the mountains are indigenous, and the Amazon basin is native. The differences between these three groups are located in the present as well as in history. The coastal inhabitants are associated with Spanish colonists. Indigenous people from the Andes speak Quechua or Aymara and are understood

to be the descendants of Incas. In contrast, the Amazonian natives speak a variety of other languages and are not associated with the heralded Inca culture.

2. I confirmed this in a visit to Silahuá in 2006. Many of the residents had their surnames on their doors, and the names were often Quechua. In addition, the people of Silahuá were, on average, darker and more likely to have straight black hair than villagers in other villages I visited in Alto Piura, such as Naranjo and Chalaco.

3. "Les registres de l'almojarifazgo: une source pour l'étude du trafic maritime dans le Pacifique Ibérique au 17ème et 18ème siècles," www.univ-paris-diderot.fr/hsal/archives/almoj/index.html (accessed April 7, 2009).

4. Jakob Schlüpmann has posted a complete list of the manifests for the port of Paita from 1704 to 1773 online at "Le trafic maritime du port de Paita au 18ème siècle: D'après les cahiers de l'almojarifasgo," http://aleph99.org/chal/navdb/navpaita.php3 (accessed June 9, 2010).

5. One *cuadra* is equal to about two hectares.

6. Another source is Nicholas Cushner's fascinating book, *Lords of the Land* (1980). It, however, addresses Jesuit haciendas, which were much larger and more economically stable than the smaller haciendas in northern Piura.

7. Puis, a partir de 1670 environ, il racheta les terres autour du rio de La Gallega, et forma peu a peu ce qui devint l'hacienda Morropon. (Around 1670, [Sojo] purchased the lands around Río La Gallega, and, little by little, formed what would become the Hacienda Morropón). Soto's 1691 will included the "Hacienda Buenos Ayres" (information from the Archivo Departamental de Piura, escribano Domingo Valencia, leg. 130, f. 92vta, 1691; reprinted in Schlüpmann 1991: 472).

8. Alfonso was described by other villagers as negro or moreno. He had dark skin and coarse hair, and in the United States would be perceived as black. He belonged to one of the darkest families in Ingenio. It is very likely that his grandmother was of African descent. The notable fact here is that, for Alfonso, the most important feature of her lineage is that she was from Morropón.

Chapter 3. Race and Color Labels in Peru

1. The distinction between race and color here is that a person who claims to have "black skin" does not necessarily consider herself to be part of the "black race." Nevertheless, a discussion of blackness always will have a subtext of race. In Peru, her friend could respond, jokingly, to the statement "I get black when I am in the sun all day" with "Yes, and then you look like an African." In the United States, an African American may take offense when a white person claims to "get black" as a result of sun exposure.

2. In Peru, *cholo* refers to a person of indigenous descent who does not live the peasant lifestyle associated with indigeneity in Peru. *Mestizo* refers to a person of

indigenous descent who shows signs of either cultural or biological mixture with people of European descent. *Mestizo* is a more polite term than *cholo*.

3. Chincha is a place south of Lima that is associated with Afro-Peruvians. Vicente is from Ingenio, not Chincha. His expression of solidarity with people from Chincha is evidence that he sees himself as part of the black race.

4. Recall that in Ingenio, *mulato* does not refer to the biracial descendant of a white and a black person but to a very dark black person.

5. There are other meanings of whiteness, such as access to privilege and resources, but the specific question addressed here is whether or not access to material goods renders a person whiter. Using that definition would thus be circular. For this reason, I focus on other meanings of whiteness, and argue that being racially or ethnically unmarked is functionally equivalent to whiteness.

Chapter 4. Diasporic Discourses and Local Blackness Compared

Epigraph note: Although *color* has a masculine gender in traditional Spanish, in Ingenio, people use the feminine instead.

1. In chapter 1, I explain why the people from the sierra are primarily white. In chapter 5, I discuss the significance of a poor white population called serranos in Ingenio and how their presence influences local color and race discourses.

2. The literal translation of "negra de mierda" as "black piece of shit" makes this phrase seem a bit more derogatory than it is in Spanish.

3. One could argue that Doris may in fact have access to these discourses, but chose not to invoke them or not to invoke them in my presence. This argument is conceivable but, to make this case, one would have to come up with a reasonable explanation for why Doris and Perla chose not to invoke those discourses while others did.

Chapter 5. Black Is Beautiful or White Is Right?

1. As of early 2010, cell phone service and even wireless Internet connections had come to Ingenio. Globalization, then, is proceeding apace but still primarily in the realm of access to new technologies.

2. Octavio Céspedes was a leader of the Afro-Peruvian community in Yapatera and conducted extensive research on blacks in northern Peru right up until his untimely death in September 2006.

3. *Criollos* originally referred to Spaniards and Africans born in the Americas. In Peru, it has evolved to refer to people who are from the coast. In Ingenio, it is used to refer to people who primarily identify with coastal culture, in specific opposition to serranos. A more extensive discussion of "criollo" appears in chapter 6.

Chapter 6. The Politics of Difference in Peru

1. www.indepa.gob.pe/index.php?id=70,0,0,1,0,0 (accessed May 1, 2007).

2. Notably, both Fujimori and Toledo, the last two presidents of Peru, donned ponchos and other indigenous garb at certain political or cultural rallies in the highlands. And, Eliane Karp, Toledo's wife, can be seen wearing traditional Peruvian fabrics. It is however safe to say that these are symbolic displays and, in the Peruvian ethnic hierarchy, neither the Japanese Fujimori, the Peruvian Toledo, nor the Belgian Karp became indigenous through these symbolic acts.

Bibliography

Aguirre, Carlos. 1993. *Agentes de su propia libertad: los esclavos de Lima y la desintegración de la esclavitud, 1820–1854*. Lima: Fondo Editorial del Pontificia Universidad Católica del Perú.

———. 2000. "La población de origen africano en el Perú: de la esclavitud a la libertad." In *Lo africano en la cultura criolla*, edited by Carlos Aguirre 63–75. Lima: Fondo Editorial del Congreso del Perú.

———. 2005. *Breve historia de la esclavitud en el Perú. Una herida que no deja de sangrar*. Lima: Fondo Editorial del Congreso del Perú.

Aldana, Susana. 1989. *Empresas coloniales: las tinas de jabón en Piura*. Piura, Peru: CIPCA.

Andrews, George Reid. 1980. *The Afro-Argentines of Buenos Aires, 1800–1900*. Madison: University of Wisconsin Press.

———. 1991. *Blacks and Whites in São Paulo, Brazil, 1888–1988*. Madison: University of Wisconsin Press.

Appadurai, Arjun. 1996. *Modernity at Large: Cultural Dimensions of Globalization*. Minneapolis: University of Minnesota Press.

Arce Espinoza, Elmer. 1983. *La reforma agraria en Piura: 1967–1977*. Lima: Centro de Estudios para el Desarrollo y la Participación.

Arnedo, Miguel. 2001. "Arte blanco con motivos negros: Fernando Ortiz's Concept of Cuban National Culture and Identity." *Bulletin of Latin American Research* 20(1): 88–101.

Arrizón, Alicia. 2002. "Race-ing Performativity through Transculturation, Taste, and the Mulata Body." *Theatre Research International* 27(2): 136–52.

Baca, Susana, Francisco Basili, and Ricardo Pereira. 1992. *Del fuego y del agua: el aporte del negro a la formación de la música popular peruana*. Lima: Pregón Editora.

Bailey, Stanley R. 2002. "The Race Construct and Public Opinion: Understanding Brazilian Beliefs about Racial Inequality and Their Determinants." *American Journal of Sociology* 108(2): 406–39.

———. 2009. *Legacies of Race: Identities, Attitudes, and Politics in Brazil.* Stanford, Calif.: Stanford University Press.

Bennett, Herman. 2000. "The Subject in the Plot: National Boundaries and the 'History' of the Black Atlantic." In "Rethinking the African Diaspora." Special issue, *African Studies Review* 43: 101–24.

Besnier, Niko. 2002. "Transgenderism, Locality, and the Miss Galaxy Beauty Pageant in Tonga." *American Ethnologist* 29(3): 534–66.

Blanchard, Peter. 1992. *Slavery and Abolition in Early Republican Peru.* Wilmington, Del.: SR Books.

Bonilla-Silva, Eduardo. 2004. "From Bi-Racial to Tri-Racial: Towards a New System of Racial Stratification in the USA." *Ethnic and Racial Studies* 27(6): 931–50.

Bourgois, Philippe. 1986. "The Black Diaspora in Costa Rica." *New West Indian Guide/Nieuwe West-Indische Gids* 60(3–4): 149–66.

Bourricaud, François. 1975. "Indian, Mestizo, and Cholo as Symbols in the Peruvian System of Stratification." In *Ethnicity: Theory and Experience,* edited by Nathan Glazer and Daniel P. Moynihan, 350–90. Trans. Barbara Bray. Cambridge, Mass.: Harvard University Press.

Bowser, Frederick P. 1974. *The African Slave in Colonial Peru, 1524–1650.* Stanford, Calif.: Stanford University Press.

Brennan, Denise. 2004. *What's Love Got to Do with It? Transnational Desires and Sex Tourism in the Dominican Republic.* Durham, N.C.: Duke University Press.

Briggs, Charles L. 2005. "Communicability, Racial Discourse, and Disease." *Annual Review of Anthropology* 34: 269–91.

Bronfman, Alejandra. 2003. *Measures of Equality: Social Science, Citizenship, and Race in Cuba, 1902–1940.* Chapel Hill: University of North Carolina Press.

Brown, Jacqueline Nassy. 1998. "Black Liverpool, Black America and the Gendering of Diasporic Space." *Cultural Anthropology* 13(3): 291–325.

Brubaker, Rogers, and Frederick Cooper. 2000. "Beyond Identity." *Theory and Society* 29(1): 1–47.

Carazas, Milagros. 2006. "Etnicidad, racismo e imagen del sujeto afroperuano: Palma, Mariátegui y Sánchez." Paper presented at the second international CEDET seminar "Los Medios de Comunicación Social, Hacia una Inclusión Étnica." Lima, November.

Castillo Román, José Leonidas. 1977. "Los rezagos esclavistas en Piura en el siglo XIX, 1800–1854." Licenciatura thesis. Department of History, Universidad Nacional Mayor de San Marcos, Programa Académico de Ciencia Histórico-Social. Lima.

Castro Pozo, Hildebrando. 1947. *El yanaconaje en las haciendas piuranas*. Lima: Compañía de Impresiones y Publicidad.

Centro de Investigación y Promoción del Campesino (CIPCA). 1986. *Buenos Aires, Morropón: historia de sus caserios*. Piura: CIPCA.

Collins, Patricia Hill. 2004. *Black Sexual Politics*. New York: Routledge.

Cuche, Denys. 1975. *Poder blanco y resistencia negra en el Perú: un estudio de la condición social del negro en el Perú después de la abolición de la esclavitud*. Lima: Instituto Nacional de Cultura.

———. 1981. *Pérou nègre: les descendants d'esclaves africains au Pérou—des grands domaines esclavagistes aux plantations modernes*. Paris: Éditions L'Harmattan.

Cushner, Nicholas P. 1980. *Lords of the Land: Sugar, Wine, and Jesuit Estates of Coastal Peru, 1600–1767*. Albany: State University of New York Press.

Daniel, Reginald. 2006. *Race and Multiraciality in Brazil and the United States: Converging Paths?* University Park: Penn State Press.

Davies, T. M. 1973. "Indian Integration in Peru 1820–1948: An Overview." *The Americas* 30(2): 184–208.

De la Cadena, Marisol. 1998. "Silent Racism and Intellectual Superiority in Peru." *Bulletin of Latin American Research* 17: 143–64.

———. 2000. *Indigenous Mestizos: The Politics of Race and Culture in Cuzco, 1919–1999*. Durham, N.C.: Duke University Press.

———. 2005. "Are Mestizos Hybrids? The Conceptual Politics of Andean Identities." *Journal of Latin American Studies* 37: 259–84.

De la Fuente, Alejandro. 2001. *A Nation for All: Race, Inequality, and Politics in Twentieth-Century Cuba*. Chapel Hill and London: University of North Carolina Press.

Degler, Carl. 1971. *Neither Black nor White: Slavery and Race Relations in Brazil and the United States*. Madison: University of Wisconsin Press.

Del Busto Duthurburu, José Antonio. 2001. *Breve historia de los negros del Perú*. Lima: Fondo Editorial del Congreso del Perú.

Del Busto Duthurburu, José Antonio, Jorge Rosales Aguirre, and Yanina Correa Gutiérrez. 2004. *Historia de Piura*. Piura, Peru: Instituto de Investigaciones Humanísticas, Departamento de Humanidades, Universidad de Piura, Peru.

Diez Hurtado, Alejandro. 1998. "Comunes y haciendas: procesos de comunalización en la Sierra de Piura (siglos XVII al XX)." Cuzco, Peru: CIPCA.

Duany, Jorge. 1998. "Reconstructing Racial Identity." *Latin American Perspectives* 25: 147–73.

Dyer, Richard. 1997. *White*. London and New York: Routledge.

Eakin, Marshall C. 1985. "Race and Identity: Silvio Romero, Science, and Social Thought in Late 19th-Century Brazil." *Luso-Brazilian Review* 22(2): 151–74.

Espinoza Tamayo, Alfredo. [1916] 1979. *Psicología y sociología del pueblo ecuatoriano*. Quito: Banco Central del Ecuador.

Estupiñán, Máximo. 2006. "Medios de comunicación y estereotipos raciales: las celdas que aprisionan la mentalidad humana." Paper presented at the second international CEDET seminar "Los Medios de Comunicación Social, Hacia una Inclusión Étnica." Lima, November. .

Euraque, Darío. 2003. "The Threat of Blackness to the Mestizo Nation: Race and Ethnicity in the Honduran Banana Economy, 1920s and 1930s." In *Banana Wars: Power, Production, and History in the Americas*, edited by Steve Striffler and Mark Moberg, 229–49. Durham, N.C.: Duke University Press.

———. 2004. *Conversaciones históricas con el mestizaje y su identidad nacional en Honduras*. Honduras: Centroeditorial.

Eyerman, Ron. 2004. "The Past in the Present: The Cultural Transmission of Memory." *Acta Sociologica* 47(2): 159–69.

Eze, Emmanuel Chukwudi. 1997. *Race and the Enlightenment: A Reader*. Malden, Mass.: Wiley-Blackwell.

Feagin, Joe. 2000. *Racist America: Roots, Current Realities, and Future Reparations*. New York: Routledge.

Feldman, Heidi. 2006. *Black Rhythms of Peru: Reviving African Musical Heritage in the Black Pacific*. Middletown, Conn.: Wesleyan University Press.

Foote, Nicola. 2004. "Race, Gender, and Nation in Ecuador: A Comparative Study of Black and Indigenous Groups, 1895–1944." Ph.D. diss., Department of History, University College, London.

———. 2006. "Race, State, and Nation in Early Twentieth-Century Ecuador." *Nations and Nationalism* 12(2): 261–78.

Ford, Richard. 2004. *Racial Culture: A Critique*. Stanford, Calif.: Stanford University Press.

Foucault, Michel. 1990. *The History of Sexuality*. Vol. 1, *An Introduction*. Trans. Robert Hurley. New York: Vintage Books.

Frankenberg, Ruth. 1997. "Introduction: Local Whitenesses, Localizing Whiteness." In *Displacing Whiteness: Essays in Social and Cultural Criticism*, edited by Ruth Frankenberg, 1–34. Durham, N.C.: Duke University Press.

Fraser, Nancy, and Axel Honneth. 2003. *Redistribution or Recognition? A Political-Philosophical Exchange*. New York: Verso.

Gallagher, Charles. 2000. "White Like Me?" In *Racing Research, Researching Race: Methodological Dilemmas in Critical Race Studies*, edited by France Winddance Twine and Jonathan W. Warren, 67–99. New York: New York University Press.

Gamson, William, David Croteau, William Hoynes, and Theodore Sasson. 1992. "Media Images and the Social Construction of Reality." *Annual Review of Sociology* 18: 373–93.

García, María Elena. 2004. "Rethinking Bilingual Education in Peru: Intercultural Politics, State Policy, and Indigenous Rights." *International Journal of Bilingual Education and Bilingualism* 7(5): 348–67.

―――. 2005. *Making Indigenous Citizens: Identities, Education, and Multicultural Development in Peru.* Stanford, Calif.: Stanford University Press.

García Canclini, Néstor. 1999. *La globalización imaginada.* Barcelona: Paidos.

García-Barrio, Constance. 1981. "Blacks in Ecuadorian Literature." In *Cultural Transformations and Ethnicity in Modern Ecuador,* edited by Norman Whitten Jr., 535–62. Urbana: University of Illinois Press.

Gilroy, Paul. 1993. *The Black Atlantic: Modernity and Double Consciousness.* Cambridge, Mass.: Harvard University Press.

Golash-Boza, Tanya Maria. 2011. "Had They Been Polite and Civilized, None of This Would Have Happened: Racial Discourses in Multicultural Lima." *Latin American and Caribbean Ethnic Studies* 6:1.

Goldstein, Donna. 2003. *Laughter Out of Place.* Berkeley: University of California Press.

Gonzales, Michael. 1985. *Plantation Agriculture and Social Control in Northern Peru.* Austin: University of Texas Press.

González Prada, Manuel. [1904] 1986. "Nuestros indios." In *Horas de lucha.* Electronic ed. Available online at http://evergreen.loyola.edu/tward/www/gp/libros/horas/horas19.html (accessed 30 June 2010).

Gordon, Edmund. 1998. *Disparate Diasporas: Identity and Politics in an African-Nicaraguan Community.* Austin: University of Texas Press.

Gould, Jeffrey L. 1998. *To Die in This Way: Nicaraguan Indians and the Myth of Mestizaje, 1880–1965.* Durham, N.C.: Duke University Press.

Gow, Peter. 1991. *Of Mixed Blood: Kinship and History in Peruvian Amazonia.* London: Oxford University Press.

Goyal, Yogita. 2006. "The Gender of Diaspora in Toni Morrison's Tar Baby." *Modern Fiction Studies* 52(2): 393–414.

Graham, Richard. 1990. *The Idea of Race in Latin America, 1870–1940.* Austin: University of Texas Press.

Greene, Shane. 2006. "Negotiating Multicultural Citizenship and Ethnic Politics in 21st-Century Latin America." In *Latin America after Neoliberalism,* edited by Eric Hershberg and Fred Rosen, 276–97. New York: New Press.

―――. 2007. Entre lo indio, lo negro, y lo incaico: The Spatial Hierarchies of Difference behind Peru's Multicultural Curtain." *Journal of Latin American and Caribbean Anthropology* 12(2): 441–74.

Gregory, Steven. 2006. *The Devil behind the Mirror: Globalization and Politics in the Dominican Republic* Berkeley: University of California Press.

Guerrero, Andrés. 1997. "The Construction of a Ventriloquist's Image: Liberal Discourse and the 'Miserable Indian Race' in Late 19th-Century Ecuador." *Journal of Latin American Studies* 29: 555–90.

Harris, Marvin. 1964. *Patterns of Race in the Americas.* Westport, Conn.: Greenwood Press.

Helg, Aline. 1990. "Race in Argentina and Cuba, 1880–1930: Theories, Policies, and Popular Reaction." In *The Idea of Race in Latin America, 1870–1940*, edited by Richard Graham, 37–70. Austin: University of Texas Press.

Helguero, Federico. 1928. *Guia departamentales.* Vol. 1, *Departamento de Piura.* Lima: Imprenta Torres Aguirre.

Helguero, Joaquín. 1802. *Informe económico de Piura.* Transcribed by Nadia Carnero. Peru: CIPCA, UNMSN.

Helms, J. E. 1990. *Black and White Racial Identity: Theory, Research and Practice.* Westport, Conn.: Greenwood Press.

Hinson, Glenn. 2000. *Fire in My Bones: Transcendence and the Holy Spirit in African American Gospel.* Contemporary Ethnography series. Philadelphia: University of Pennsylvania Press.

Hobson, Janell. 2005. *Venus in the Dark: Blackness and Beauty in Popular Culture.* New York: Routledge.

Hocquenghem, Anne Marie. 2004. "Una edad del bronce en los Andes centrales: contribución a la elaboración de una historia ambiental." *Bulletin d'Institute Français d'Études Andines* 33(2): 271–329.

Hoetink, H. 1967. *Caribbean Race Relations.* London: Oxford University Press.

Hooker, Juliet. 2005. "Indigenous Inclusion/Black Exclusion: Race, Ethnicity and Multicultural Citizenship in Latin America. *Journal of Latin American Studies* 37: 285–310.

hooks, bell. 1989. *Talking Back: Thinking Feminist, Thinking Black.* Boston, Mass.: South End Press.

Huertas Vallejo, Lorenzo. 2001. *Los negros y el mestizaje en Piura y Huamanga.* Lima: CEDET.

Hunefeldt, Christine. 1994. *Paying the Price of Freedom: Family and Labor among Lima's Slaves, 1800–1854.* Berkeley: University of California Press.

Hunter, Margaret L. 2002. "If You're Light You're Alright: Light Skin Color as Social Capital for Women of Color." *Gender & Society* 16(2): 175–93.

Irwin-Zarecka, Iwona. 1994. *Frames of Remembrance: The Dynamics of Collective Memory.* New Brunswick, N.J.: Transaction.

Jackson, Jeffrey T. 2005. *The Globalizers: Development Workers in Action.* Baltimore, Md.: Johns Hopkins University Press.

Jackson, Peter. 2004 "Local Consumption Cultures in a Globalizing World." *Transactions of the Institute of British Geographers* 29(2): 165–78.

Jenkins, Richard 1994. "Rethinking Ethnicity: Identity, Categorization, and Power." *Ethnic and Racial Studies* 17: 197–223.

———. 2000. "Categorization: Identity, Social Processes, and Epistemology." *Current Sociology* 48(3): 7–75.

Jenson, Jane. 2001. "Building Citizenship: Governance and Service Provision in Canada." In *Building Citizenship: Governance and Service Provision in Canada,*

1–22. CPRN Discussion Paper No. F/17. Ottawa: Canadian Policy Research Networks.

Knight, Alan. 1990. "Racism, Revolution, and Indigenismo: Mexico, 1910–1940." In *The Idea of Race in Latin America, 1870–1940*, edited by Richard Graham, 71–113. Austin: University of Texas Press.

La Pastina, Antonio, Cacilda M. Rego, and Joseph D. Straubhaar. 2003. "The Centrality of Telenovelas in Latin America's Everyday Life: Past Tendencies, Current Knowledge, and Future Research." *Global Media Journal* 2(2): 1–10.

Landale, Nancy S., and R. S. Oropesa. 2002. "White, Black, or Puerto Rican? Racial Self-Identification among Mainland and Island Puerto Ricans." *Social Forces* 81(1): 231–54.

Larson, Brooke. 2004. *Trials of Nation Making: Liberalism, Race, and Ethnicity in the Andes, 1810–1910*. Stony Brook: State University of New York Press.

Lassiter, Eric. 2005. *The Chicago Guide to Collaborative Ethnography*. Chicago: University of Chicago Press.

Leguía y Martínez, German. 1914. *Diccionario geográfico, histórico, estadístico, etc., del Departamento de Piura*, vol. 1. Lima. Tipografía El Lucero.

León Quirós, Javier. 2003. "The Aestheticization of Tradition: Professional Afroperuvian Musicians, Cultural Reclamation, and Artistic Interpretation." Ph.D. diss., Department of Ethnomusicology, University of Texas, Austin.

Lewis, Laura. 2000. "Blacks, Black Indians, Afromexicans: The Dynamics of Race, Nation and Identity in a Mexican Moreno Community (Guerrero). *American Ethnologist* 27(4): 898–926.

López Albújar, Enrique. 2005 [1928]. *Matalaché*. Piura, Peru: El Tiempo.

Losonczy, A. M. 1999. "'Memorias e identidad: los negro-colombianos del Choco." In *De montes, rios y ciudades: territorios e identidades de gente negra en Colombia*, edited by J. Camacho and E. Restrepo, 13–24. Bogota: Ecofondo-Natura-Instituto Colombiano de Antropología.

Luciano, José, and Humberto Rodríguez. 1995. "Peru." In *No Longer Invisible: Afro–Latin Americans Today*, edited by Minority Rights Group, 271–86. London: Minority Rights Publications.

Marchant, Elizabeth. 2000. "Naturalism, Race, and Nationalism in Aluisio Azevedo's *O Mulato*." *Hispania* 83(3): 445–53.

Martinez-Echazábal, Lourdes. 1998. "Mestizaje and the Discourse of National/Cultural Identity in Latin America, 1845–1959." *Latin American Perspectives* 25(3): 21–42.

Mato, Daniel. 2005. "The Transnationalization of the Telenovela Industry: Territorial References, and the Production of Markets and Representations of Transnational Identities." *Television and New Media* 6(4): 423–44.

McPherson, Lionel, and Tommie Shelby. 2004. "Blackness and Blood: Interpreting African American Identity." *Philosophy and Public Affairs* 32(2): 171–92.

Mendoza, Zoila. 1998. "Defining Folklore: Mestizo and Indigenous Identities on the Move." *Bulletin of Latin American Research* 17(2): 165–83.

Miles, Robert, and Rodolfo Torres. 1999. "Does 'Race' Matter?" In *Race, Identity, and Citizenship: A Reader*, edited by Rodolfo D. Torres, Luis F. Mirón, and Jonathan Xavier Inda, 19–38. Malden, Mass.: Blackwell.

Miller, Marilyn Grace. 2004. *Rise and Fall of the Cosmic Race: The Cult of Mestizaje in Latin America*. Austin: University of Texas Press.

Montiel, Edgar. 1995. "Negros en Perú: de la conquista a la identidad nacional." In *Presencia africana en Sudamérica*, edited by Luz M. Martínez Montiel, 213–75. Mexico City: Consejo Nacional para la Cultura y las Artes.

Mörner, Magnus. 1967. *Race Mixture in the History of Latin America*. Boston: Little, Brown.

Nagel, Joane. 1994. "Constructing Ethnicity: Creating and Recreating Ethnic Identity and Culture." *Social Problems* 41(1): 152–76.

———. 2003. *Race, Ethnicity, and Sexuality: Intimate Intersections, Forbidden Frontiers*. New York: Oxford University Press.

Oboler, Suzanne. 2005. "The Foreignness of Racism: Pride and Prejudice among Peru's Limeños in the 1990s." In *Neither Enemies nor Friends*, edited by Suzanne Oboler and Anani Dzidzienyo, 76–100. New York: Palgrave Macmillan.

Oliart, Patricia. 2008. "Indigenous Women's Organizations and the Political Discourses of Indigenous Rights and Gender Equity in Peru." *Latin American and Caribbean Ethnic Studies* 3(3): 291–308.

Orlove, Benjamin. 1998. "Down to Earth: Race and Substance in the Andes." *Bulletin of Latin American Research* 17(2): 207–22.

Ortiz, Alejandro. 2001. "El término raza como homonimia." In *La pareja y el mito. Estudios sobre las concepciones de la persona y de la pareja en los Andes*, edited by Alejandro Ortiz, 394–400. Lima: Fondo Editorial de la Pontificia Universidad Católica del Perú.

O'Toole, Rachel. 2006. "'In a War against the Spanish': Andean Protection and African Resistance on the Northern Peruvian Coast." *The Americas* 63(1): 19–52.

Pakulski, J. 1997. "Cultural Citizenship." *Citizenship Studies* 1(1): 73–86.

Panfichi, Aldo. 2000. "Africanía, barrios populares y cultura criolla a inicios del siglo XX." In *Lo africano en la cultura criolla*, edited by Carlos Aguirre, 137–56. Lima: Fondo Editorial del Congreso del Perú.

Patterson, Tiffany Ruby, and Robin D. G. Kelley. 2000. "Unfinished Migrations: Reflections on the African Diaspora and the Making of the Modern World." *African Studies Review* 43(1): 11–45.

Patton, Tracey Owens. 2006. "Hey Girl, Am I More Than My Hair?: African American Women and Their Struggles with Beauty, Body Image, and Hair" *NWSA Journal* 18(2): 24–51.

Paz Soldán, Carlos Enrique. 1919. "El saneamiento rural de la costa Peruana." *La Reforma Médica* 5: 75–86S.

Pineda, Baron. 2006. *Shipwrecked Identities: Navigating Race on Nicaragua's Mosquito Coast.* Piscataway, N.J.: Rutgers University Press.

Porter, Judith R., and Robert E. Washington. 1979. "Black Identity and Self-Esteem: A Review of Studies of Black Self-Concept, 1968–1978." *Annual Review of Sociology* 5: 53–74.

Portocarrero, Gonzalo 1993. *Racismo y mestizaje.* Lima: SUR.

Ramírez, Susan E. 1986. *Provincial Patriarchs: Land Tenure and the Economics of Power in Colonial Peru.* Albuquerque: University of New Mexico Press.

Ramírez Reyna, Jorge. 2003. "Acción afirmativa en el contexto afrodescendiente: Los casos de Brasil, Colombia y Perú." Available online at www.iidh.ed.cr/comunidades/diversidades/docs/div_docpublicaciones/accion_afirmativa.pdf (accessed February 11, 2010).

Ramos, Alonso. 2002. "La reina despojada." Available online at www.pucp.edu.pe/fac/comunic/perdigital/trab2002-1/alonso/Rosa%20Elvira.htm (accessed February 10, 2009).

Rénique, Gerardo. 2003. "Region and Nation: Sonora's Anti-Chinese Racism and Mexico's Postrevolutionary Nationalism, 1920s–1930s." In *Race and Nation in Modern Latin America,* edited by Nancy P. Appelbaum, Anne S. Macpherson, and Karin Alejandra Rosenblatt, 211–36. Chapel Hill: University of North Carolina Press.

Revesz, Bruno, Susana Aldana Rivera, Laura Hurtado Galván, and Jorge Piura Requena. 1997. *Piura: región y sociedad: derrotero bibliográfico para el desarrollo.* Piura: CIPCA.

Reyes Flores, Alejandro. 2001. "Libertos en el Perú, 1750–1854." *Historia y Cultura: Revista del Museo Nacional de Arqueología, Antropología e Historia del Perú* 24: 41–54.

Richardson, Diane. 1998. "Sexuality and Citizenship." *Sociology* 32(1): 83–100.

Robarge, Edward. 2004. "Race and the Formation of Identity in the Dominican Republic." Ph.D. diss., Department of History, University of Kansas, Lawrence.

Rodríguez, Clara E. 2000. *Changing Race: Latinos, the Census, and the History of Ethnicity in the United States.* New York: New York University Press.

Romero, Fernando and Mercer Cook. 1942. "Jose Manuel Valdés, Great Peruvian Mulatto." *Phylon* 3(3): 296–319.

Romero, Raúl. 1994. "Black Music and Identity in Peru: Reconstruction and Revival of Afro-Peruvian Musical Traditions." In *Music and Black Ethnicity: The Caribbean and South America,* edited by Gerard Béhague, 317–30. Coral Gables, Fla.: North-South Center Press.

Rosaldo, Renato. 1994. "Cultural Citizenship and Educational Democracy." *Cultural Anthropology* 9(3): 402–11.

Safa, Helen. 1998. "Introduction." *Latin American Perspectives* 25(3): 3–20.

Sansone, Livio. 2003. *Blackness without Ethnicity: Constructing Race in Brazil.* New York: Palgrave Macmillan.

Schirmer, Ute. 1977. "Reforma agraria y cooperativismo en el Perú: cambios estructurales y contradicciones de la nueva política agraria del gobierno militar del Perú." *Revista Mexicana de Sociología* 39(3): 799–856.

Schlüpmann, Jakob. 1988. "Piura du XVIème au XIXème siècle. Evolution d'une structure agraire et formation d'une société régionale au nord du Pérou." DEA thesis, Géographie, Histoire, Sciences de la Société, Université Paris VII Denis Diderot

———. 1991. "Structure agraire et formation d'un ordre social au nord du Pérou: Piura à l'époque coloniale." *Bulletin d'Institute Français d'Études Andines* 20(2): 461–88.

———. 1993. "Commerce et navigation dans l'Amérique Espagnole coloniale: le port de Paita et le Pacifique au XVIIIème siècle." *Bulletin d'Institute Français d'Études Andines* 22(2): 521–49.

———. 1994. "La structure agraire et le développement d'une société régionale au nord du Pérou. Piura, 1588–1854." Ph.D. diss., Géographie, Histoire, Sciences de la Société, Université Paris VII Denis Diderot. Available online at www.aleph99. org/chal/pub/js94-1.pdf (accessed February 10, 2010).

Schwartzman, Luisa. 2007. "Does Money Whiten?" *American Sociological Review* 72(2): 940–63.

Scott, James. 1987. *Weapons of the Weak: Everyday Forms of Peasant Resistance.* New Haven, Conn.: Yale University Press.

Segal, Ronald. 1995. *The Black Diaspora: Five Centuries of the Black Experience outside Africa.* New York: Farrar, Straus, Giroux.

Shelby, Tommie. 2002. "Foundations of Black Solidarity: Collective Identity or Common Oppression?" *Ethics* 112: 231–66.

Sheriff, Robin. 2001. *Dreaming Equality: Color, Race, and Racism in Urban Brazil.* Piscataway, N.J.: Rutgers University Press.

———. 2003. "Embracing Race: Deconstructing Mestiçagem in Rio de Janeiro." *Journal of Latin American Anthropology* 8(1): 86–115.

Sinardet, Emmanuelle. 1998. "A la costa de Luís A. Martínez: ¿La defensa de un proyecto liberal para Ecuador?" *Bulletin d'Institute Français d'Études Andines* 27(2): 285–307.

Skidmore, Thomas. 1990. "Racial Ideas and Social Policy in Brazil, 1870–1940." In *The Idea of Race in Latin America, 1870–1940*, edited by Richard Graham, 7–36. Austin: University of Texas Press.

———. 1993. "Bi-Racial USA versus Multi-Racial Brazil: Is the Contrast Still Valid?" *Journal of Latin American Studies* 25(2): 373–86.

Smedley, Audrey. 2007. *The Idea of Race in North America*. Boulder, Colo.: Westview Press.

Smith, Carol A. 1991. "The Symbolics of Blood: Mestizaje in the Americas." *Identities* 3(4): 495–521.

Steger, Manfred. 2004. *Globalization: A Very Short Introduction*. London: Oxford University Press.

Stepan, Nancy. 1991. *The Hour of Eugenics: Race, Gender, and Nation in Latin America*. Ithaca, N.Y.: Cornell University Press.

Stokes, Susan. 1987 "Etnicidad y clase social: los afro-peruanos de Lima, 1900–1930." In *Lima obrera, 1900–1930*, vol. 2, edited by Steven Stein, 171–252 Lima: Ediciones El Virrey.

Sue, Christina, and Tanya Golash-Boza. 2009. "Blackness in Mestizo America: The Cases of Mexico and Peru." *Latino Research Review* 7(1–2): 30–58.

Taylor, Charles. 1994. "The Politics of Recognition." In *Multiculturalism*, edited by Amy Gutman, 149–64. Princeton, N.J.: Princeton University Press.

Telles, Edward. 2004. *Race in Another America: The Significance of Skin Color in Brazil*. Princeton, N.J.: Princeton University Press.

Thomas, Deborah. 2004. *Modern Blackness: Nationalism, Globalization, and the Politics of Culture in Jamaica*. Durham, N.C.: Duke University Press.

Thomas, John III. 2008. "Theorizing Afro-Latino Social Movements: The Peruvian Case." Master's thesis, Department of Political Science, University of Chicago.

Tilley, Virginia. 2005a. "Mestizaje and the Ethnicization of Race in Latin America." In *Race and Nation: Ethnic Systems in the Modern World*, edited by Paul Spickard, 1–32. New York: Routledge.

———. 2005b. *Seeing Indians: A Study of Race, Nation, and Power in El Salvador*. Albuquerque: University of New Mexico Press.

Torres-Saillant, Silvio. 1998. "The Tribulations of Blackness: Stages in Dominican Racial Identity." *Latin American Perspectives* 25(3): 126–46.

Twine, France Widdance. 1998. *Racism in a Racial Democracy: The Maintenance of White Supremacy in Brazil*. New Brunswick, N.J.: Rutgers University Press.

Urrieta, Luis. 2003. "Las identidades también lloran, Identities Also Cry: Exploring the Human Side of Indigenous Latina/o Identities." *Educational Studies: A Journal of the American Educational Studies Association* 34(2): 147–212.

Van den Berghe, Pierre. 1974. "The Use of Ethnic Terms in the Peruvian Social Science Literature." In *Class and Ethnicity in Peru*, edited by Pierre van den Berghe, 12–22. Leiden, the Netherlands: E. J. Brill.

Varallanos, José. 1962. *El cholo y el Perú*. Buenos Aires: Imprenta López.

Vásquez Rodríguez, Rosa Elena. 1982. *La vida musical de la población negra de Chincha: la danza de negritos*. La Habana: Casa de las Américas.

Vasconcelos, José. [1925] 1997. *The Cosmic Race/La raza cósmica*. Baltimore, Md.: Johns Hopkins University Press.

Velázquez Castro, Marcel. 2005. *Las mascaras de la representación: el sujeto esclavista y las rutas del racismo en el Perú (1775–1895)*. Lima: Fondo Editorial de la Universidad Nacional de San Marcos.

Vinson, Ben. 2006. "Introduction: African (Black) Diaspora History, Latin American History." *The Americas* 63: 1–18.

Wade, Peter. 1993. *Blackness and Race Mixture: The Dynamics of Racial Identity in Colombia*. Baltimore, Md.: Johns Hopkins University Press.

———. 1995. "The Cultural Politics of Blackness in Colombia." *American Ethnologist* 22(2): 341–59.

———. 1997. *Race and Ethnicity in Latin America*. Chicago: Pluto Press.

———. 2004. "Images of Latin American Mestizaje and the Politics of Comparison." *Bulletin of Latin American Research* 23(3): 355–66.

———. 2005. "Rethinking Mestizaje: Ideology and Lived Experience." *Journal of Latin American Studies* 37: 239–57.

Wallerstein, Immanuel. 2003. "Citizens All? Citizens Some!: The Making of the Citizen." *Comparative Studies in Society and History* 45: 650–79.

Weismantel, Mary. 2001. *Cholas and Pishtacos: Stories of Race and Sex in the Andes*. Chicago: University of Chicago Press.

Weismantel, Mary, and Stephen Eisenman. 1998. "Race in the Andes: Global Movements and Popular Ontologies." *Bulletin of Latin American Research* 17: 121–42.

Whitten, Norman, and Arlene Torres. 1998. "To Forge the Future in the Fires of the Past: An Interpretive Essay on Racism, Domination, Resistance and Liberation." In *Blackness in Latin America and the Caribbean*, vol. 1, edited by Norman Whitten and Arlene Torres, 3–33. Bloomington: Indiana University Press.

Wilson, Fiona. 2007. "Transcending Race? Schoolteachers and Political Militancy in Andean Peru, 1970–2000." *Journal of Latin American Studies* 39: 719–46.

Winn, Peter. 2006. *Americas: The Changing Face of Latin America and the Caribbean*. 3rd ed. Berkeley: University of California Press.

Wright, Michelle. 2004. *Becoming Black: Creating Identity in the African Diaspora*. Durham, N.C.: Duke University Press.

Wright, Winthrop. 1990. *Café con leche: Race, Class, and National Image in Venezuela*. Austin: University of Texas Press.

Yashar, Deborah. 2005. *Contesting Citizenship in Latin America: The Rise of Indigenous Movements and the Postliberal Challenge*. Cambridge: Cambridge University Press.

Zeleza, Paul. 2005. "Rewriting the African Diaspora: Beyond the Black Atlantic." *African Affairs* 104(414): 35–68.

Zerubavel, Eviatar. 2003. *Time Maps: Collective Memory and the Social Shape of the Past*. Chicago: University of Chicago Press.

Zimmerman, Eduardo. 1992. "Racial Ideas and Social Reform: Argentina, 1890–1916." *Hispanic American Historical Review* 72(1): 23–46.

Index

Tanya Maria Golash-Boza is assistant professor of sociology and American studies at the University of Kansas. She is the author of *Immigration Nation?: Raids, Detentions, and Deportations in Post-9/11 America* (Paradigm Publishers, 2010) and has published articles in such journals as *Social Forces, Social Problems, Ethnic and Racial Studies*, and *International Migration Review*.